RADIATOR ENCLOSURE
⅛" PLYWOOD

3'-6"

1'-8"

PLYWOOD

= S K

S E A T

⅜" PLYWOOD

F L A

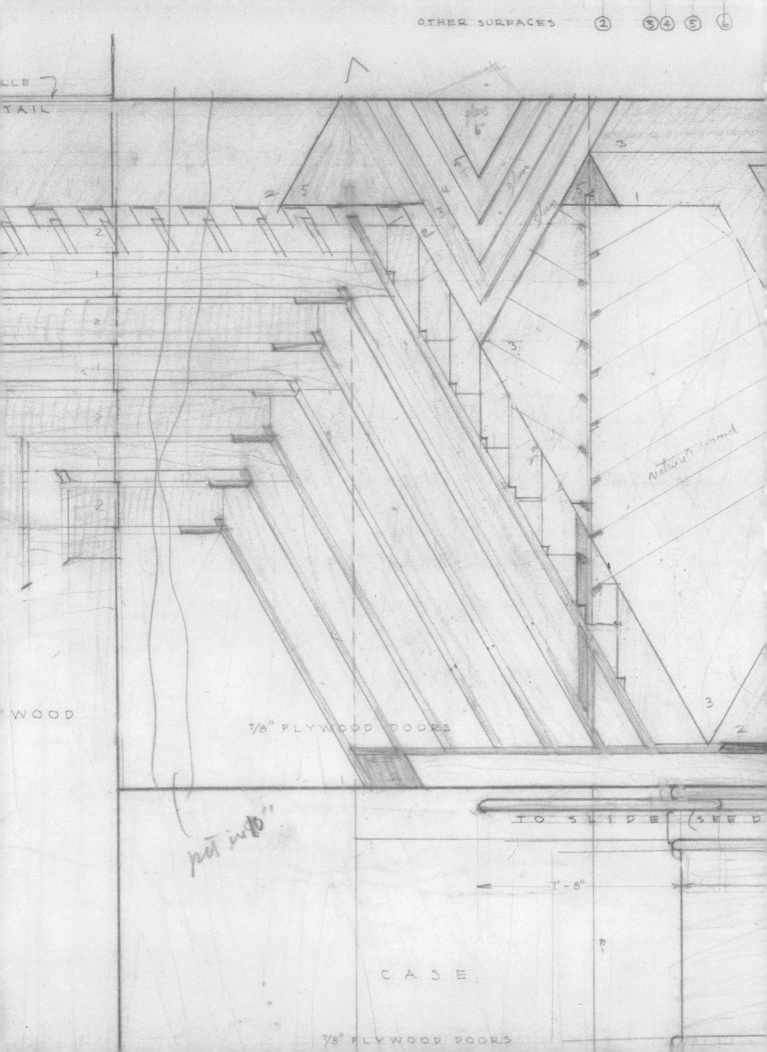

7/8" PLYWOOD DOORS

put in 9"

TO SLIDE (SEE D

1'-8"

C A S E

7/8" PLYWOOD DOORS

MERCHANT PRINCE
AND MASTER BUILDER

MERCHANT PRINCE
AND MASTER BUILDER

EDGAR J. KAUFMANN AND FRANK LLOYD WRIGHT

Richard L. Cleary

Introduction by *Dennis McFadden*

THE HEINZ ARCHITECTURAL CENTER
CARNEGIE MUSEUM OF ART
PITTSBURGH, PENNSYLVANIA

IN ASSOCIATION WITH
UNIVERSITY OF WASHINGTON PRESS
SEATTLE AND LONDON

1999

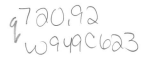
Published on the occasion of the exhibition *Merchant Prince and Master Builder: Edgar J. Kaufmann and Frank Lloyd Wright,* organized by and held at the Heinz Architectural Center from April 10 to October 3, 1999, in cooperation with the Frank Lloyd Wright Foundation, Scottsdale, Arizona.

Major funding for the exhibition and this publication was provided by the Henry Luce Foundation. Additional support has been provided by Kaufmann's, A Division of the May Department Stores Company, and The Alexander C. and Tillie S. Speyer Foundation. The programs of the Heinz Architectural Center are made possible by the generous support of the Drue Heinz Trust.

Library of Congress Cataloging-in-Publication Data
Cleary, Richard Louis.
    Merchant prince and master builder : Edgar J. Kaufmann and Frank Lloyd Wright / Richard L. Cleary; introduction by Dennis McFadden.
        p.   cm.
    Published in connection with the exhibition of the same name held at the Heinz Architectural Center, Carnegie Museum of Art, Apr. 10–Oct. 3, 1999.
    Includes bibliographical references and index.
    ISBN 0-88039-036-0 (alk. paper)
    1. Wright, Frank Lloyd, 1867–1959—Exhibitions. 2. Kaufmann, Edgar J., 1885–1955—Art patronage— Exhibitions. 3. Architecture—United States—Exhibitions. 4. Architecture, Modern—20th century—United States—Exhibitions. I. Wright, Frank Lloyd, 1867–1959. II. Heinz Architectural Center. III. Title.
NA737.W7A4 1999   98-48686
720'.92'273—dc21
                                    CIP

Published in 1999 by the Heinz Architectural Center, Carnegie Museum of Art, 4400 Forbes Avenue, Pittsburgh, Pennsylvania 15213

Produced by the Carnegie Museum of Art Publications Department: Gillian Belnap, Head of Publications; Elissa Curcio, Publications Associate

Editorial supervision: Gillian Belnap
Editor: Jennifer Harris, Seattle
Designer: Daniel Hale
Produced by Marquand Books, Inc., Seattle

Type composed in Trump Mediaeval and Balance
The paper is Multiart Matt.

Frontispiece: *left:* Frank Lloyd Wright, ca. 1935 (detail; fig. 11); *right:* Edgar J. Kaufmann, 1940s (detail; fig. 30)
Page 10: Fallingwater, 1937 (Bill Hedrich, Hedrich-Blessing, Chicago Historical Society)
Page 16: Edgar J. Kaufmann's private office, ca. 1936 (detail; cat. 33)
Page 36: Fallingwater, 1935 (detail; cat. 1)
Page 52: Point Park Civic Center Project, 1947 (detail; cat. 43)

The drawings of Frank Lloyd Wright reproduced herein (except cats. 27, 28, and 40) are © The Frank Lloyd Wright Foundation, Scottsdale, Arizona. All rights reserved.

Distributed by
University of Washington Press
P.O. Box 50096
Seattle, Washington 98145

PRINTED AND BOUND IN HONG KONG

Contents

Foreword

This exhibition and book describe an extraordinary and sustained instance of architectural patronage in the mid-twentieth century. From 1934 until his death in 1955, the Pittsburgh department store magnate Edgar J. Kaufmann was a patron and friend of Frank Lloyd Wright. This relationship was bolstered by Kaufmann's wife, Liliane, and their son, Edgar Kaufmann jr. Their famous country house, Fallingwater, a guest house, and the interior of Edgar Kaufmann's private office, designed in the 1930s, are the most tangible products of this association, but architect and patron dreamed of building more—much more—together. Among the unrealized projects were additional buildings around Fallingwater, a house in Palm Springs, California, and, in Pittsburgh, a civic center, a parking garage, and an apartment building. These proposals were informed by a shared belief in the power of architecture to enrich the quality of life.

Merchant Prince and Master Builder is the first exhibition devoted to the Kaufmanns' patronage of Wright and brings together drawings for all their commissions. While Fallingwater serves as the centerpiece of the exhibition and catalogue, our goals are more ambitious than exploring the architecture of this remarkable structure. Rather, we hope to provide the context necessary for a fuller appreciation and understanding of the house and the significant role the Kaufmann family played in its realization, as well as the family's importance in Wright's career from 1934, when work began on Fallingwater, to his death in 1959. Moreover, although the designs for many of the Kaufmann projects, such as the Pittsburgh Point and the Rhododendron Chapel, have been exhibited, they have been presented as discrete themes in Wright's oeuvre rather than as a set of works commissioned by a single patron. Here they can be seen as continually evolving and formally interconnected.

We are indebted to Richard Cleary for his leadership in organizing the exhibition and in producing this book. Together with his previously published studies of the projects for Pittsburgh, Mr. Cleary has significantly broadened our view of Frank Lloyd Wright's architectural practice, and we are grateful for his scholarship. We owe additional thanks to the Frank Lloyd Wright Foundation for its enthusiastic cooperation in the realization of *Merchant Prince and Master Builder.* Dennis McFadden, curator of the Heinz Architectural Center, has overseen the assembly and installation of the exhibition and guided the production of its catalogue; much of the success of this project is due to his thoughtful ministrations. McFadden has also contributed an insightful discussion of how our understanding of an architectural icon is enriched by the distinct but complementary experiences of visiting the building and studying its documentary history in the context of a museum gallery.

The Carnegie Museum of Art is grateful for the timely and substantial assistance of the Henry Luce Foundation in producing both publication and exhibition. We also appreciate the generous support of Kaufmann's and The Alexander C. and Tillie S. Speyer Foundation. The Drue Heinz Trust supports the activities and operation of the Heinz Architectural Center with fiduciary and intellectual generosity; we salute its leader, Drue Heinz.

Richard Armstrong
The Henry J. Heinz II Director
Carnegie Museum of Art

6

A Message from the Frank Lloyd Wright Foundation

Frank Lloyd Wright frequently advised young architects, "It is not always wise to make a client out of your friend, but you can always make a friend out of your client." In the case of Edgar J. Kaufmann, the friendship that developed between architect and client began at their first meeting. Even though several Wright-designed projects commissioned by Kaufmann were never built, the genuine affection Wright and Kaufmann felt for each other never diminished, and their friendship extended further into both men's families. Understandably, there were some turbulent moments over architectural work and construction methods, but despite these differences of opinion, Wright maintained that it was Kaufmann's integrity and vision that served as an inspiration to him. Out of this relationship sprang one of the most exciting and inspiring private residences ever conceived, Fallingwater, Kaufmann's country house on Bear Run in western Pennsylvania.

A guest house connected to Fallingwater was also built, and Wright designed an office interior for Kaufmann that was installed in Kaufmann's department store in Pittsburgh and is now on view at the Victoria & Albert Museum in London. Additional, but unbuilt, projects were commissioned by the Kaufmann family, including a gate lodge, chapel, and farm cottage near the Fallingwater site. In addition to Wright's unbuilt designs for the Kaufmann property in Pennsylvania and in Palm Springs, California, Kaufmann commissioned other designs of great significance: two civic centers, two apartment buildings, and a self-service parking garage.

This exhibition brings together for the first time the astonishing breadth and depth of these commissions as outstanding examples of vision and variety in the annals of architecture. The present selection was culled from files containing close to 690 drawings in the Frank Lloyd Wright Archives through the careful study of Richard Cleary and Dennis McFadden, starting with their first visit to the Frank Lloyd Wright Foundation in the summer of 1995. On later visits to the Frank Lloyd Wright Archives, Cleary completed a more intensive and at the same time more feasible selection, and also conducted an investigation into the enormous quantity of Wright-Kaufmann correspondence. Along with a collection of beautiful and informative original drawings, Cleary's essay provides a detailed insight into the alliance between Kaufmann and Wright.

The Frank Lloyd Wright Foundation, many of whose members were also closely associated with the Kaufmann family—Edgar Kaufmann, his wife Liliane, and their son, Edgar jr.—is especially grateful to the Heinz Architectural Center at the Carnegie Museum of Art for bringing these works together to form a personal and artistic tribute to both architect and client. The Frank Lloyd Wright Foundation is likewise grateful to the Heinz Center for its support in contributing to the conservation of many drawings in the exhibition.

Bruce Brooks Pfeiffer
Director, The Frank Lloyd Wright Archives
The Frank Lloyd Wright Foundation
Scottsdale, Arizona

7

Acknowledgments

Merchant Prince and Master Builder: Edgar J. Kaufmann and Frank Lloyd Wright has benefited from the interest and support of many people. Credit for suggesting the exhibition lies with my colleague and friend Richard J. Betts at the School of Architecture, University of Illinois, Urbana-Champaign. It was Dick who proposed that Richard Cleary's research on the relationship of the Kaufmann family to Frank Lloyd Wright would make a fascinating exhibition. Christopher Monkhouse, founding curator of the Heinz Architectural Center, and Phillip M. Johnston, the former Henry J. Heinz II Director of the Carnegie Museum of Art, were both enthusiastic supporters of the idea. Richard Armstrong, who succeeded Phillip Johnston, committed museum resources to the exhibition's successful realization, while Michael Fahlund, the museum's assistant director, skillfully guided the administration of the project from beginning to end. I am grateful to them both for their enthusiastic encouragement, advice, and support.

Bruce Brooks Pfeiffer, director of the Frank Lloyd Wright Archives, served as curatorial consultant for the project. Margo Stipe, Oscar Muñoz, and Indira Berndtson, also of the Frank Lloyd Wright Archives, provided invaluable assistance in our research and in the selection of the drawings, including many that have never been exhibited before. T. K. McClintock, Boston, did a masterful job of conserving the drawings and advising on their care.

Colleagues at other institutions have been generous in assisting with essential research and the arrangement of loans for the exhibition. In this regard, I am indebted to David Benjamin, Sarah Beyer, Gwynedd Cannan, Vicky Clark, Jack Holzhueter, Barbara Mirecki, Janet Parks, Clinton Piper, Peter Reed, Thomas Schmidt, John Vinci, Lynda Waggoner, Christopher Wilk, and Mary Woolever.

Many members of the Carnegie Museum of Art's staff have played crucial roles in the project. I am especially grateful to Gillian Belnap, who managed the publication, and with the assistance of Elissa Curcio, also supervised the editorial and production processes. Thanks also go to the those who aided in the development and implementation of the exhibition: Linda Batis, Meg Bernard, Rhonda Goldblatt, Patty Jaconetta, William Judson, Dan Lagiovane, Louise Lippincott, Charlene Shang Miller, Robin Moorcroft, Tracy Myers, Sarah Nichols, Chris Rauhoff, William Real, Allison Revello, Marilyn Russell, Jennifer Semper, Rebecca Sciullo, Tey Steitler, Lucy Stewart, Monika Tomko, and Heather Wahl. I also extend my gratitude to the museum's workshop staff for expert handling and installation.

Merchant Prince and Master Builder could not have been realized without Richard Cleary, who generously shared his pioneering research on the Kaufmann-Wright connection. His findings and the clarity with which he has presented them form the backbone of the exhibition. In addition, he has been a stimulating and congenial colleague with whom to share the excitement of bringing architectural ideas to the galleries of the Heinz Architectural Center. A final word of thanks goes to Judith S. Hull and Dorrie Hull McFadden, who have lived with this project over the last few years; they have contributed to it in countless ways.

Dennis McFadden
Curator, The Heinz Architectural Center
Carnegie Museum of Art

I have been the recipient of assistance and kindnesses from many institutions and individuals. I thank Richard Armstrong, director of the Carnegie Museum of Art, and Michael Fahlund, assistant director, for their wholehearted support of the exhibition. Dennis McFadden, curator of the Heinz Architectural Center, patiently guided and shaped the exhibition from initial idea to realization. Bruce Brooks Pfeiffer, director of the Frank Lloyd Wright Archives; his colleagues Margo Stipe, Oscar Muñoz, and Indira Berndtson; and gentle Geronimo graciously accommodated my visits to Taliesin West. Lynda Waggoner and the staff of Fallingwater, including Sarah Beyer, Clinton Piper, and Michele Risdal-Barnes, shared their unique knowledge of the magnificent house and landscape in their care.

I also acknowledge the assistance of Janet Parks, curator of drawings, Avery Architectural and Fine Arts Library; Carole S. Mazzotta, manager of media services, Kaufmann's; David Benjamin, photo and moving picture archivist, and Jack Holzhueter, editor, State Historical Society of Wisconsin; Martin Aurand, curator, Carnegie Mellon University Architecture Archives; and Susan Conley, registrar, Colorado Springs Fine Arts Center.

The University of Texas at Austin and its School of Architecture have contributed to the catalogue and exhibition in many ways. A university Summer Research Assignment funded work on the list of drawings. My colleagues Anthony Alofsin and Christopher Long offered thoughtful comments on the essay. Staff members who provided special assistance include Seth Bossung, Mike Farmer, Cynthia Merritt, Charlotte Pickett, and John Vehko. The models of Fallingwater and the Pittsburgh Point shown in the exhibition were planned and constructed by the following students, who made time for this project while meeting the exhausting demands of the School of Architecture program: John Allee, Dawn Allen, Adam Alsobrook, Christopher Brown, Catherine Gates, Matthew Haberling, Steve Handelman, Hope Hudson, Jessica Juarez, Ashley McClaran, Shawn Peter, Lisa Roman, Eric Standridge, Rommel Sulit, and William Watson.

I thank Joan K. Mendelsohn, Mary Michaely, Darthea Speyer, and Edgar Tafel for sharing their firsthand knowledge of the Kaufmanns. Lu Donnelly, Sean Garrigan, Judith Hull, Matilda McQuade, Paul Rosenblatt, Arnold Skolnick, Albert Tannler, and Franklin Toker also contributed insights, challenges, and nuggets of information.

My work as an author was facilitated by the attentive professionalism of Gillian Belnap, Elissa Curcio, and Jennifer Semper, Carnegie Museum of Art; Jennifer Harris, editor; and Marie Weiler, Marquand Books.

Richard L. Cleary
Associate Professor
School of Architecture
University of Texas at Austin

9

Introduction

Dennis McFadden

The subjects of architectural exhibitions, the physical buildings, are nearly always absent from the gallery setting. In their stead, architectural exhibitions rely primarily on visual representations. The favored media for these representations take two forms: those that were created in advance of the realization of a structure—the drawings and models used by the architect in designing a building—and, in the case of designs that have been built, depictions made by others after construction—primarily photographs. The former category must be seen as communicating the architect's aspirations, which in only rare cases can be completely realized in the actual structure; the latter, as documenting an interpretation of the structure. The building itself exists between the two somewhere outside the museum's walls.

Merchant Prince and Master Builder: Edgar J. Kaufmann and Frank Lloyd Wright is an exhibition that explores the importance of the architect-client relationship in the conception of an extraordinary group of buildings. In the absence of the buildings themselves, this exhibition makes extensive use of Frank Lloyd Wright's own drawings and drawings produced by his assistants. It is, therefore, an exhibition in which the architect's aspirations play a central role. However, by bringing together for the first time all twelve of the projects Wright designed for the Edgar J. Kaufmann family of Pittsburgh, *Merchant Prince and Master Builder* is also an exhibition about the clients' aspirations. The exhibition thus provides new insights into Wright's architecture and adds a crucial dimension to our understanding of Fallingwater, the most important of the buildings Wright designed for the Kaufmanns.

Fallingwater is among the best-known buildings of the twentieth century. Not only is it included in nearly every published survey of American or modern architecture, but also approximately 130,000 people from around the world now visit the house annually in its wooded setting in rural western Pennsylvania. Fallingwater's place as an icon of modern architecture and its popularity as a tourist destination can be attributed to certain things. For one, the house has been acknowledged as a work of creative genius ever since it was built.

Fallingwater was published in magazines and newspapers even before construction was completed in the fall of 1937. In the months following, it attracted additional press. *Time* magazine featured the architect and a drawing of the house on the cover of its 17 January 1938 issue. Inside, Wright was proclaimed "the greatest architect of the 20th Century" and Fallingwater, a photograph of which was prominently featured, described as his "most beautiful job."[1] With a circulation of nearly 800,000, the *Time* coverage brought Wright and this extraordinary house to the attention of a broad audience.

Also in January 1938, *Architectural Forum*, a professional magazine published by Time Incorporated, produced a special issue in collaboration with Wright and designed by the architect. An advertisement in *Life* magazine described the issue as "the most important architectural document ever published in America."[2] In it, Wright's new and previously unpublished work was shown along with several earlier projects. Eleven pages were devoted to Fallingwater, including a brief text by Wright, a set of plans and elevations, and nine photographs by Bill Hedrich (b. 1912), one of the preeminent architectural photographers of the day. One of Hedrich's photographs, printed in the magazine as a foldout, had also appeared in the *Time* article and in the *Life* advertisement for *Architectural Forum.* It is one of the best-known architectural photographs ever made.

In composing this photograph, Hedrich chose a vantage point below the house, alongside Bear Run, the stream on which Fallingwater was built. He aimed his camera lens up toward the house, creating a dramatic perspective view of the structure's cantilevered balconies projecting from the stone and glass core and imbuing the house with a palpable monumentality. The photograph was taken in autumn, and the house is framed by the stark skeletons of bare trees, some of whose branches cast shadows on the parapets of the balconies. A long exposure transformed the waterfall into a flowing veil of light, creating a foil for the balanced planes that seemingly float in space above.

This photograph immediately became the signature image of Fallingwater. The view it captured has been used routinely in art and architectural history lectures as well as in home slide shows about architectural pilgrimages and summer vacations. It is not uncommon for visitors to Fallingwater to seek out the spot from which the photograph was made, either to reaffirm their mental image of the house or to attempt to capture the building on film or in a sketchbook. Hedrich's photograph has also provided an archetypical image for cartoons about the modern house. Today, sixty years after it was taken, an abstraction of the view shown in Hedrich's photograph is used as the logo on Fallingwater's stationery and another version appears on the cover of a training manual for a computer-assisted design program.

Since its discovery in the 1830s, photography has been the principal visual medium through which knowledge of architecture has been disseminated; indeed, we often learn as much about architecture through photographic images of buildings as through the actual experience of them. Certain images have shaped our awareness, understanding, and expectations of an elite group of buildings. Because of their potency, it is important to consider the multiple messages embedded in photographs such as Hedrich's image of Fallingwater, including the messages in the original image itself and those that have accrued to it over time by virtue of its repeated use in critical contexts.

Three of these messages are especially relevant to this exhibition. First, Hedrich's photograph presents the house as a completely realized masterwork. Whereas the absence of any form work or stray tools in the photograph signals that construction of the house has been completed, the visual structure of the image implies that the aesthetic potential of the house is also complete. The building is presented as a carefully orchestrated play of horizontal and vertical planes, solids, and voids at the precise moment of equipoise, when nothing can be either added to or subtracted from the composition without causing the entire assemblage to tip out of balance. Second, Hedrich's photograph portrays the house as an isolated man-made object within an extraordinarily beautiful and undisturbed natural setting. And third, in keeping with a long-standing tradition in architectural photography still followed today, the photograph presents Fallingwater without its inhabitants.

The visual representation of Fallingwater as a fully consummated work has implications for our understanding of the history of the project and for our appreciation of the Kaufmanns' significance in Wright's career. As is the case with other Wright designs, the evolution of Fallingwater is storied. Edgar Tafel, who was studying with Wright at the time Fallingwater was designed, begins his book *Apprentice to Genius* with a description of a scene in the drafting room at Taliesin, Wright's Wisconsin home and office. The telephone rings; it is Edgar Kaufmann calling from the airport in Milwaukee to say he is on his way and expects to see the drawings for his house when he arrives. Tafel recounts that Wright responded, "Come along, E.J. We're ready for you," even though nothing had been drawn for the house. According to Tafel, Wright then sat down and, in a single burst of creative energy, prepared the preliminary drawings for Fallingwater before Kaufmann arrived a couple hours later.[3]

In contrast to this near-mythic tale of architectural genesis, Donald Hoffmann's account of the events leading to the design of the house indicates that Wright had previously thought about the project for some time, twice visited the site, and studied a topographic plan.[4] Although it is undeniable that Fallingwater's cantilevered slabs and the interior organization were established in Wright's initial sketches, annotations on subsequent drawings and Richard Cleary's informed discussion of the drawings and the course of the Fallingwater commission reveal that the project evolved in several important ways between September 1935, when the scene Tafel described took place, and December 1937, when the house was substantially complete.

In his description of Fallingwater in the 1938 *Architectural Forum*, Wright described the house as an example of "the inspiration of a site, the cooperation of an intelligent, appreciative client and the use of entirely masonry materials."[5] Wright's choice of the word "cooperation" to characterize his relationship with the Kaufmanns suggests that in the architect's eyes the clients' role was that of facilitator in the creative process. In fact, the Kaufmann family is a crucial part of the story of Fallingwater. More than just passive tenants of this extraordinary house, they were the ideal collaborators for Wright at this particular moment in his career.

If the clients influenced the creation of Fallingwater in substantive ways, their subsequent requests for alterations and additions—and Wright's willingness to explore these requests and, in the case of the guest house and the kitchen addition, actually design and build them—imply that the architect in no way considered the building an object whose integrity could not sustain alteration. In contrast to the message implicit in Hedrich's photograph that Fallingwater was that rare and immutable architectural creation, the floor plans reproduced in *Architectural Forum* indicate that the location for the bridge to the guest house had already been discussed. The inclusion of this bridge in these first published plans indicates that Fallingwater was conceived from the outset not as a single object in a pristine setting but rather as the centerpiece of a managed landscape. Taken together with the various proposals for other structures on the Bear Run property, brought together for the first time in this exhibition, Fallingwater was less of a completely realized ideal than part of an ongoing work in progress to which Wright and the Kaufmanns would return again and again until the architect's death in 1959.

With the Bear Run projects, the Kaufmanns entrusted Wright with the setting for their private lives. However, it is clear from the subsequent commissions that from the beginning the Kaufmanns found in the architect someone whose vision they wanted to incorporate into other facets of their life. Concurrently with Fallingwater, Wright designed an office for Edgar Kaufmann on the tenth floor of Kaufmann's department store in downtown Pittsburgh. In this commission, Kaufmann asked Wright to define an important, yet personal, setting for his professional life. He would later enlist the architect to design a combined retail and parking structure for the store, although this 1949 project was never realized.

The third area of his life in which Kaufmann turned to Wright to give form to his dreams was in Kaufmann's work as a civic leader. Kaufmann's early

13

interest in and support of the architect's Broadacre City project is easy to understand in light of Richard Cleary's account of the Pittsburgh Point projects, which are among the architect's most visionary. Wright's ability to define strikingly new and optimistic directions for American urban development would have held enormous appeal for a civic leader who was comfortable taking aesthetic and business risks and a retailer who was committed to the city but keenly aware of problems posed by Pittsburgh's then-dingy downtown.

The Kaufmann family's patronage of Frank Lloyd Wright is well documented by the twelve projects for which drawings have been included in this exhibition and catalogue. In his text, Richard Cleary identifies two other proposals: a planetarium and a new building for the Carnegie Institute's department of fine arts, neither of which resulted in actual designs. Only three projects were realized: Fallingwater, the guest house and servants' quarters, and Edgar Kaufmann's business office, now installed at the Victoria & Albert Museum in London. We are fortunate indeed that all three have survived and can be visited today. But were our knowledge of the Kaufmanns as clients and Wright as their architect limited to these three works, our understanding of their remarkably fruitful relationship would remain incomplete. Similarly, if our appreciation of these projects rested solely on what we experience from the realized spaces themselves, extraordinary though they may be, we would not understand how deeply they reflect the aspirations of those who contributed to their creation.

The experience of architecture and a visit to an exhibition about architecture are distinct but potentially complementary experiences. Today's visitor to Fallingwater, for example, encounters an extraordinary work of architecture in a beautiful setting. Beyond this, the visitor senses both the presence and absence of those who lived in the house. Photographs of the family and allusions to them by guides—often anecdotal accounts of how the Kaufmanns used a room or a piece of furniture—imbue the house with their aura. But the family is always portrayed in reference to the house, the tangible artifact. Although Fallingwater was an extremely important part of the Kaufmanns' life, their engagement with design preceded the house and extended far beyond

it. Materials illustrating the family's commitment to design at Kaufmann's department store and, in the case of Kaufmann jr., at the Museum of Modern Art confirm this and serve as the introduction to the exhibition to establish a context for considering the entire course of the Kaufmanns' patronage of Frank Lloyd Wright.

The forty-nine drawings presented in the exhibition were either drawn by Wright himself or prepared under his direction. They can be read as documents, interpreted as evidence, and in some cases appreciated as objects of aesthetic merit. For the three realized projects, the drawings record what was built, illustrating aspects of the spatial organization and structural design of these buildings. The visitor's on-site experience of these spaces today is carefully controlled and monitored, in the interest of preservation. At Fallingwater and the guest house, the visitor follows a carefully defined path; the business office is viewed from without. There are no opportunities to freely wander through and around these built spaces. Yet it is precisely by such wandering, moving back and forth between rooms, from one floor to the next, that one comes to understand the spatial qualities and relationships within an architectural design and perceive its structural logic. Although the drawings in this exhibition cannot take the place of that highly personal learning experience, they can diagrammatically convey some of the information typically gained in this way. Their presentation in a museum context allows the visitor to study them at length, to draw comparisons between them, and to understand the completed buildings and also the temporal evolution of their design.

For the architect, the finished building is the culmination of a process that is recorded in drawings, notes, models, and increasingly, in bits of data stored electronically. By interpreting the drawings in this exhibition, it is possible to discern the evolutionary paths that were followed in the development of the buildings Wright designed for the Kaufmanns. In the case of Fallingwater, this process is of great interest not only because it shows how the design of this masterwork evolved in the architect's mind but also, as previously discussed, because it demonstrates the clients' role in the realization of the house. Furthermore, several of the drawings illustrate the crucial part Wright's on-site representatives played in the resolution of problems that emerged during the course of construction.

Viewed as the record of a sequence of projects, the drawings enable us to trace the clients' thinking and the architect's artistic growth. This is especially exciting with a designer such as Wright who throughout his career never stopped exploring ideas. As Richard Cleary points out, the 1950–51 Boulder House design is related to Wright's studies of curvilinear forms, while the gate house project of a few years later relates to his concept of the Usonian Automatic. In the case of the Kaufmanns, the sequence of projects shows the family's commitment to architecture expanding to encompass all aspects of their lives. It is tempting to infer from these parallel evolutions that the Kaufmanns and Wright inspired each other through the course of their remarkable relationship. In answering the challenges the Kaufmanns presented, Wright expanded his clients' vision of what they might achieve through architecture.

The most satisfying aspect of an exhibition of architectural drawings is that it brings us into contact with the architect and client at work. Architects draw to explore, and their drawings reveal their struggles to solve practical problems, give form to their dreams, and then reconcile their dreams with the realities of what can be built. They also draw to communicate. At one level, this communication is between the architect and those who will transform pencil lines into steel and concrete. At another, it is a communication between architect and client.

Although they may reveal the aspirations of architect and client as the two seek to imbue form with beauty, architectural drawings, like photographs, can never substitute for the building itself. Those who have never visited Fallingwater should not look to *Merchant Prince and Master Builder* as a substitute for a visit to that remarkable structure. At the same time, the building, even at its most ravishing, cannot disclose the collaboration between the client and the architect as they strove to produce it. We hope with this exhibition and catalogue to reveal the crucial role played by the Kaufmanns in Wright's career and in so doing to provide a context for one of the greatest buildings of the twentieth century.

NOTES

1. "Usonian Architect," *Time* (17 January 1938): 29–32.

2. *Life* (17 January 1938): inside front cover.

3. Edgar Tafel, *Apprentice to Genius: Years with Frank Lloyd Wright* (1979; reprint, New York: Dover, 1985) 1–7.

4. Donald Hoffmann, *Frank Lloyd Wright's Fallingwater: The House and Its History* (New York: Dover, 1993), 12–17.

5. *Architectural Forum* 68 (January 1938): 36.

15

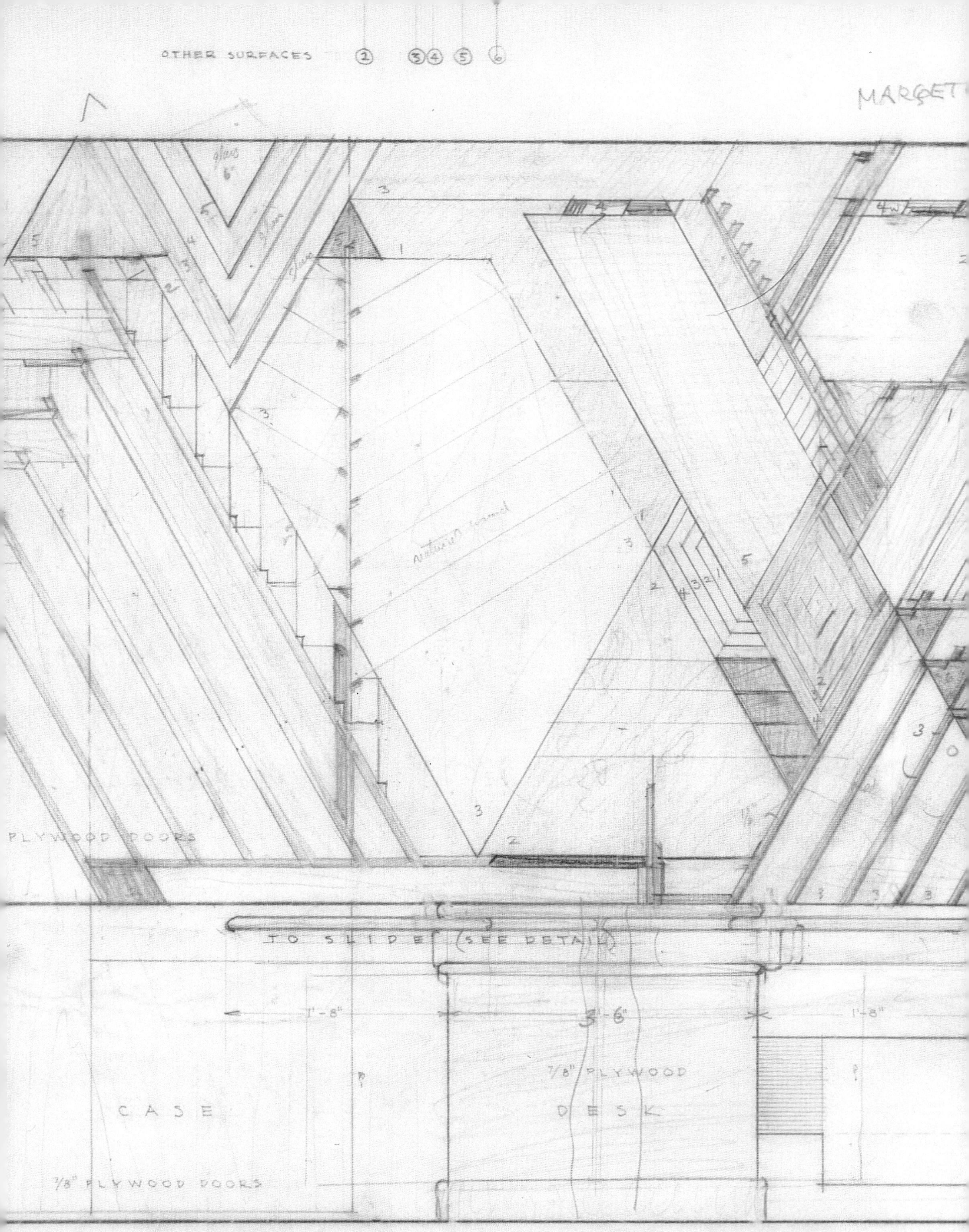

OTHER SURFACES ② ③④ ⑤ ⑥
MARQUET
natural wood
PLYWOOD DOORS
TO SLIDE (SEE DETAIL)
1'-8"
3'-6"
1'-8"
7/8" PLYWOOD
CASE
DESK
7/8" PLYWOOD DOORS

1 *The Kaufmanns, Wright, and Good Design*

EDGAR JONAS KAUFMANN'S death on 15 April 1955 was headline news in Pittsburgh. The city mourned the loss of its "merchant prince." Fallingwater, the celebrated weekend house that Kaufmann had built in 1936–38 on Bear Run in the Allegheny Mountains southeast of Pittsburgh, was just one of many accomplishments for which he was recognized as an innovative retailer, civic leader, philanthropist, and patron of the arts. Frank Lloyd Wright, Kaufmann's architect, mourned him as a patron and friend of more than twenty years (fig. 1). Then eighty-seven, Wright had recently visited the sixty-nine-

Fig. 1. Edgar J. Kaufmann and Frank Lloyd Wright at Taliesin West, late 1940s. Fallingwater Archive, Avery Architectural and Fine Arts Library, Columbia University in the City of New York.

17

year-old Kaufmann in Palm Springs, California, and his note of condolence to Kaufmann's son invited the younger Kaufmann for an extended stay in the recuperative atmosphere of Wright's own home, Taliesin West, in Scottsdale, Arizona.[1]

Wright's reputation as a solo figure fighting for "truth against the world"—his ancestral motto—is such an ingrained part of his mythology that his relationships with people outside the tightly knit community of his immediate family and the inner circle of the Taliesin Fellowship are often overlooked. Wright did enjoy many lasting friendships, however, and Edgar Kaufmann, his wife Liliane, and Edgar jr. (he preferred the lowercase form "jr.") were among a number of remarkable patrons who possessed vision as well as cash and who brought more than a job to the studio. Other members of this group of men and women included the mail-order retailer Darwin D. Martin, responsible for the Larkin Building (1903–6) and residences in the area of Buffalo, New York; Aline Barnsdall, heiress to an oil fortune and an active patron of avant-garde theater, who built the Hollyhock House (1916–21) in Los Angeles; and Herbert "Hib" Johnson, head of Johnson Wax, who built the company's corporate headquarters (1936–39) and a private residence (1937–39) in Racine, Wisconsin.[2]

At first consideration, the Kaufmanns' turn to Wright might appear surprising. Fallingwater is a far cry from La Tourelle, the Norman-style house the family built in 1922 in Fox Chapel, a suburb of Pittsburgh. The decade that separates the two houses, however, was a time when a new spirit, labeled "modern" but loosely defined, infused architecture and design in the United States. As innovative retailers with strong ties to New York and Europe, the Kaufmanns were unusually well situated to observe and participate in this development, and they wholeheartedly embraced it in their personal and professional lives. Wright's vision for architecture and design complemented their own convictions, and although they were extraordinarily generous in their financial support of his work, they were not passive vessels for his genius. The roughly one dozen projects that the family commissioned from Wright from 1934 to his death in 1959—of which only three, Fallingwater, the guest house, and Edgar Kaufmann's

private office in the department store, were realized—were informed by their convictions.

In this chapter, we will begin to trace the Kaufmanns' interaction with Wright in light of the family's professional activities in Kaufmann's department store and their advocacy of the emerging concept of "good design." Chapter 2 will consider the commissions for their country houses and related buildings at Bear Run and Palm Springs. The final chapter will address Edgar Kaufmann's civic idealism and the projects he commissioned in downtown Pittsburgh.

Edgar Kaufmann was born in 1885.[3] He was the eldest son of Morris and Betty Kaufmann and had three siblings, Oliver, Martha, and Stella. Morris was one of four Jewish brothers who had emigrated from Germany to southwestern Pennsylvania, prospered as retailers, and in 1871 founded Kaufmann's department store in Pittsburgh. There appears to have been no doubt that Edgar would take his place in the family business. Following his secondary education at Shady Side Academy in Pittsburgh, he reportedly spent a brief time at the Sheffield Scientific School of Yale University and then began a

Fig. 2. Liliane Kaufmann, mid-1930s. Photo: Bachrach. Courtesy of the Western Pennsylvania Conservancy.

Merchant Prince and Master Builder

two-year apprenticeship in retailing at fine department stores in Chicago (Marshall Field's), Paris (Les Galeries Lafayette), and Hamburg (Karstadt) and, at the other end of the spectrum, at a general store in Connellsville, Pennsylvania.

In 1909, he joined his father at the family store in Pittsburgh and married his first cousin, Lillian Sarah Kaufmann (1889–1952; fig. 2), the daughter of his paternal uncle Isaac. Lillian, who changed her first name to Liliane, had had a sheltered childhood in the neighborhood of prosperous Jewish families in Pittsburgh's Manchester district, which was home to the extended Kaufmann family. She was not reticent, however, and made full use of her sharp mind, gift for foreign languages, and innate sense of style.[4]

Edgar and Liliane Kaufmann formed a striking couple. He was handsome and fit and possessed a captivating gaze and a rakish saber scar acquired during a fencing bout in Heidelberg. A profile in *Fortune* magazine noted his exceptionally well-modulated voice, the power and beauty of his hands, and the elegance of his gestures. Liliane was tall, blonde, and moved with grace. Both were strong-willed and, by turns, could be generous and demanding. They enjoyed the company of others, and Liliane was a superb hostess who could deftly orchestrate food, setting, and conversation. As Jews, they encountered boundaries that limited the scope of their ambitions in Pittsburgh society, but this liability was offset by the creativity of the people within the circles in which they moved. These social circles included other prosperous Jews in the city, among them Tillie S. Speyer, a sculptor who, with her husband Alexander, was an assiduous collector of painting and furniture, and Celia and Robert Frank, who in 1937 built a house designed by Walter Gropius and Marcel Breuer.[5] The Kaufmanns' homes reflected their cosmopolitan outlook and frequent travels. They collected paintings and objets d'art, and their taste, as we shall see, embraced folk crafts and contemporary design. These interests were shared by their only child, Edgar jr. (1910–1989).

Despite the couple's resources of beauty, charm, and wealth, the Kaufmanns' marriage was not the idyll one might imagine. Edgar's extramarital affairs, neither discreet nor infrequent, were a particularly visible aspect of their difficulties. Apart from their personal feelings, their marriage was instrumental in consolidating the ownership of the department store. It brought Liliane's shares into closer proximity to Edgar's branch of the family and thus furthered the long, often rancorous, but ultimately successful campaign directed by his father, Morris, who lived until 1917, to acquire the shares of the three other founders. By 1913, Edgar, at twenty-eight, was effectively running the store, and his brother-in-law, Samuel Mundheim, was titular president.

An immediate challenge to Edgar Kaufmann's leadership was the announcement by the disenfranchised heirs of his uncle Jacob and a set of distant cousins, the Baers, that they would build a rival store named Kaufmann & Baer's just down the street from Kaufmann's. Edgar quickly commissioned Pittsburgh architect Benno Janssen (1874–1964) to replace the oldest section of his store, built in 1885, with a much larger twelve-story block. Completed before the competition could open its doors, the new Kaufmann's, its exterior adorned with terra-cotta tiles embellished with Renaissance motifs, stole much of its rival's thunder.[6]

Kaufmann made the most of Pittsburgh's robust economy during World War I and reportedly tripled the store's net sales from $10 million in 1913 to $30 million in 1920.[7] This growth was made possible by the store's broad appeal to Pittsburghers of varied economic classes and ethnic backgrounds. Competitive prices and wide selection were the primary attractions. A popular anecdote recounted how even the famously rotund William Howard Taft was able to find trousers in his size at Kaufmann's when the need unexpectedly arose during a trip to the city.[8]

If the store was to continue to grow in the 1920s, however, it needed to do more than attract additional customers. It had to convince them to buy more as well. Retailers and manufacturers across the United States addressed these tasks, and Kaufmann's was among the innovators responding with marketing strategies intended to stimulate desire for new products, create tempting opportunities for impulse purchases, and above all make the sale.

Fig. 3. International Exposition of Industrial Arts, *Kaufmann's, November 1926. Inspired by the* Exposition Internationale des Arts Décoratifs et Industriels Modernes *held in Paris in 1925, this promotion presented the store's regular merchandise, such as the vacuum cleaner on the table at center, with sale items and historic artifacts from around the world. Products from Ireland are shown at left. Courtesy of Kaufmann's.*

Although intuition remained a vital attribute of the successful retailer, education became increasingly important for managers and sales personnel alike.[9] The demand for more systematically defined knowledge led to the creation of research institutions, such as the Harvard Bureau of Business Research founded in 1911, to analyze marketing, merchandising, and distribution practices, and to the development of training programs housed in colleges and universities.[10] In 1915, for example, the Prince School of Salesmanship opened at Simmons College in Boston, and Anne Morgan, the activist daughter of banker J. P. Morgan, and Percy Strauss, the vice president of Macy's department store, took the first steps toward the creation of the School of Retailing at New York University.[11]

Edgar Kaufmann followed these developments closely and wasted no time in establishing a similar venture in Pittsburgh.[12] In April 1918, a year before New York University's program was fully under way, he led a consortium of local department store merchants and representatives from the Carnegie Institute of Technology (now Carnegie Mellon University), the University of Pittsburgh, and the city's board of education in founding the Research Bureau for Retail Training. Based at the University of Pittsburgh starting in October 1918, the Research Bureau was devoted to improving the quality of retail service through employee training and innovation. Kaufmann chaired the program's executive committee from 1929–53, and in 1943 he received an honorary doctor of science from the University of Pittsburgh in recognition of his contributions. Following the example of the city's leading manufacturers, he also supported research projects, funding investigations regarding the quality of consumer products conducted at the Mellon Institute in Pittsburgh.

Quality, understood in terms of durability, was an established selling point. Alongside it, Kaufmann and other retailers promoted the concept of good design as a no less important criterion for product selection. The principled design of mass-produced consumer products was a topic discussed throughout the industrialized world in the late nineteenth and early twentieth centuries in ethical, political, economic, technological, and aesthetic contexts. For some businessmen, the concept was primarily a marketing tool. Others, like the Kaufmanns, took it to heart in their professional and personal lives.

In the 1910s and early 1920s, the influence of the Arts and Crafts movement had waned, and popular taste in the decorative arts in the United States favored historicist design inspired by European, colonial American, and Federalist styles.[13] Work by recognized designers occupied a minute portion of the mass-produced market, and there was little critical attention to how manufacturers designed their product lines. The quality of what was available varied widely.

Around the time of World War I, a number of

museum curators, primarily in the New York area, began to argue that the quality of furnishings and other household products in the United States was in a decline that if left unchecked would lead to aesthetic and economic losses against competition from European manufacturers. These curators promoted the concept of good design by encouraging U.S. manufacturers and designers to utilize their collections as resources for understanding fundamental principles of composition and developing new products. Among the leaders of this effort was Richard F. Bach (1887–1968), who joined the Metropolitan Museum of Art as the associate in industrial arts in 1918 and assumed responsibility for the museum's newly instituted annual exhibitions of American design.[14] Initially, Bach emphasized good design as a quality largely independent of any particular style, but by the early 1920s he began to link it to a quest for a style demonstratively expressive of the character of contemporary society. This theme gained currency following the opening of the *Exposition Internationale des Arts Décoratifs et Industriels Modernes* in Paris in 1925.

The exposition confronted visitors with a dazzling concentration of products selected as exemplars of modernity. Many museum curators and retailers who made the trip from the United States returned convinced that they had seen the future and made much of America's absence at the exhibition. They chastised Herbert Hoover, then secretary of commerce, for declining the French invitation to participate on the basis that the United States had nothing modern to exhibit. In short order, the Metropolitan Museum of Art presented a traveling exhibition of objects shown in Paris, and the managements of Saks Fifth Avenue and Lord & Taylor in New York undertook redesigns of sales floors inspired by the show.

In Pittsburgh, Kaufmann's staged its own *International Exposition of Industrial Arts* in November 1926.[15] Displayed throughout the store were artifacts representing "thirty great periods of design" from around the world (fig. 3). These objects included reproduction ancient bronzes from the collection of the Carnegie Institute in Pittsburgh, a copy of the first bible printed in the United States, Beethoven's piano, Russian enamels and icons, Sung paintings, Gobelin tapestries, and items from the

Fig. 4. Cover of Storagram, *June–July 1929. Drawn by Ferdinand Sesti. This image of a modern, steel-winged Daedalus, drawn by a member of the interior decorating department, introduced the in-house magazine's celebration of the store's fifty-eighth anniversary. In his preface, Edgar J. Kaufmann wrote, "This issue is dedicated to the spirit of the modern movement in all phases of life, to bring forcefully before the fellow-workers of this institution the significance of the movement." Courtesy of Kaufmann's.*

Paris exposition. The didactic purpose of the show was to illustrate the evolution of design over time and demonstrate how the best modern forms are an outgrowth of what has gone before. On a more commercial level, in addition to drawing the curious into the store, the show proclaimed the worldwide range and sophistication of Kaufmann's buyers.

In the years following the Paris exposition, many observers believed that a fundamental change was occurring in product design. Trade journals, such as the weekly *Dry Goods Economist* read by department store buyers and managers, covered the phenomenon as something more than a passing style. In August 1928, the journal declared, "Good Design Is Good Business: Not Utility Alone, but Design Befitting the Motif of the Age, Will Determine Products' Selling Success."[16] An editorial published a month

21

1. The Kaufmanns, Wright, and Good Design

Fig. 5. Skyscraper Furniture, ca. 1928. Paul T. Frankl, designer. Frontispiece, Paul T. Frankl, New Dimensions: The Decorative Arts of Today in Words & Pictures *(New York: Payson & Clarke, 1928).*

later heralded modernity in even stronger terms under the headline "Ignorance & the Right to Modern Art." "Modernism," Isabel Hamilton wrote, "far from being lack of design, IS design—design stripped of conventional restraint in the form of 'gew gaws' and presented as an entity." Hamilton asserted that modernism was here to stay and declared that the public "has a right" to modern art and modern goods.[17] Kaufmann's was fully apace with these developments. An innovative series of special programs from the 1920s into the early 1950s identified the store with technological and scientific progress. In 1928, for example, a year after Charles Lindbergh's solo flight across the Atlantic Ocean, Kaufmann's staged an aircraft exhibit that attracted 50,000 visitors in one week, and in 1935, inspired perhaps by the recent *Century of Progress* exposition in Chicago (1933–34), the store inaugurated an annual *Peaks of Progress* festival that included exhibitions, lectures, and essay contests.[18]

In 1929, Edgar Kaufmann dedicated the anni-

versary issue of the store's in-house magazine, *Storagram,* to "the spirit of the modern movement in all phases of life."[19] The cover portrayed a man with wings of steel (no doubt forged in Pittsburgh) flying toward the future, and the text featured brief essays by civic leaders on the future of the theater, newspapers, and commercial art (fig. 4). Earlier that year, the store's executives attended lectures on the meaning and importance of modernism to business presented by Richard Bach and Paul T. Frankl (1886–1958). The department store venue was familiar to both men. Bach's views of modernism appeared frequently in the *Dry Goods Economist,* and he lectured and organized staff training programs on art and design at stores around the country.[20] Frankl was a prominent designer of furniture and interiors and a leader of the American Union of Decorative Artists and Craftsmen (AUDAC), which he had helped to found in 1928 to foster cooperation among artists, designers, artisans, manufacturers, and retailers and to champion a distinctly American modern design aesthetic (fig. 5).[21]

Frankl likely drew his remarks at Kaufmann's from his recently published book, *New Dimensions: The Decorative Arts of Today in Words & Pictures* (1928), in which he applied the term "modern" to "the creations in art that come nearest to expressing the ideal of beauty of their own time" and described the task of contemporary design as tempering the complexity of industrialized civilization through an aesthetic of simplicity.[22] This tempering was to be realized through an alliance of art and business. "Good forms," he wrote, "sell much better and cost no more. The work of the artist has become profitable both in industry and in business."[23] Consequently, Frankl noted, businesses were increasingly turning to artists to coordinate design across all aspects of corporate activity, from advertising to product development.

Frankl saw the artist and the businessman as having much in common in contemporary society: "They must both have a clear and keen understanding of modern humanity and human psychology. Enterprise, for both, depends upon this."[24] In a passage that may have been especially appealing to Edgar Kaufmann, Frankl compared department store planning to city planning:

Fig. 6. Project for remodeling the first floor of Kaufmann's, ca. 1928. Joseph Urban, architect. Perspective view of sales counters. Courtesy of Rare Book and Manuscript Library, Columbia University in the City of New York.

The modern department store presents a problem that is not in some ways unlike the problem of a modern city. A store-planning department not unlike a city-planning department should be installed. While the merchandising manager of a large department store has been specially trained in merchandising methods as well as economic conditions, the manager of the planning department must assume full responsibility for all present and future developments, both from the utilitarian and the artistic viewpoints. He must also understand the traffic problems with which every large department store is confronted, and, at the same time, he must also be in close touch with new ideas developing in Europe as well as ideas in his own country.[25]

Years later, but fittingly in this spirit, Kaufmann's ran an advertising campaign on the theme "a city of shopping."[26]

If one of the store's executives had asked Frankl for his views on the Paris exposition of 1925, his response, assuming consistency with his published position, would have been that the show was less

important for the specific forms it had introduced than as a demonstration of how harmony might be achieved in architecture and interior decoration. The present challenge, he believed, was for the United States to realize that goal on its own terms. If asked to name someone who was answering the challenge, Frankl would have cited Frank Lloyd Wright.

Frankl dedicated his book to Wright. In his preface, he published a letter from the architect welcoming him to "the cause of Style as against 'Styles.'" The first plate is a photograph of La Miniatura, the house Wright designed in 1923 for Alice Millard in Pasadena, California. Frankl viewed Wright as both a father figure—indeed, he placed his own son under Wright's care—and as an ongoing creative presence. Later, in *Form and Re-Form: A Practical Handbook of Modern Interiors* (1930), Frankl presented Wright as the first of the "protagonists" bringing about a new age in design: "The ideas of this American pioneer exerted a tremendous influence on continental architects. His influence fertilized the ideas of the *avant-garde* of the Continent. It has returned to us in new forms and new thoughts. To Wright, more perhaps than to any other man, we owe our appreciation of the inherent beauty of materials and media."[27]

Frankl was the link in Wright's membership in AUDAC, which absolved the architect of paying dues.[28] Wright reciprocated by presenting talks at two AUDAC meetings in 1929 and providing a short essay on "Principles of Design" and drawings of his St. Mark's Tower project in the association's book, *Modern American Design*, published in 1930.[29] These activities, and others such as the exhibition of the architect's "renderings, drawings, and types of ornament" presented by the Architectural League of New York in 1930, demonstrate that although Wright did not have major commissions under construction in the late 1920s and early 1930s, he had not dropped out of sight. On the contrary, Wright was known to a wide network of designers, Frankl among them, who offered many channels through which he may have become known to Edgar Kaufmann several years before Edgar jr. would join the Taliesin Fellowship.

When Frankl and Bach spoke in Pittsburgh, plans were well advanced for a major remodeling

1. The Kaufmanns, Wright, and Good Design

Fig. 7. First floor of Kaufmann's, 1930. Benno Janssen, architect. This view conveys a sense of the rich materials and innovative diagonal layout of the sales floor. At rear is Boardman Robinson's painting The English in China—The Seventeenth Century, *one of the ten murals by the artist depicting the history of commerce.* Pittsburgh Sun-Telegraph, "Kaufmann's Supplement," 11 May 1930. Courtesy of Kaufmann's.

that would transform Kaufmann's ground floor into a more sympathetic setting for the products of the modern age.[30] Edgar Kaufmann apparently had initiated this project in 1925 or 1926, during the flurry of store remodelings in New York that followed the opening of the Paris exposition. Sometime between then and 1928, he commissioned a scheme from Joseph Urban (1872–1933), the acclaimed designer of buildings, interiors, and stage settings (including the Ziegfeld Follies) who, since emigrating from Vienna in 1911, had been one of the leading voices for progressive design in the United States.[31] Urban proposed cladding the exterior of the store's ground floor with dark polished stone and opening the facade along Fifth Avenue to create an arcade lined with show windows and small shops. The main retail floor was to be reorganized around spotlighted sales areas, with sleek metal and glass display cases

centered in bays defined by the existing structural columns (fig. 6).

In addition to Urban, Kaufmann apparently consulted with another progressive New York designer, Eugene Schoen (1880–1957), but placed the responsibility for the remodeling in the hands of his longtime architect, Benno Janssen, who had enlarged the store in 1913 and designed the Kaufmanns' home in suburban Fox Chapel in 1922.[32] The result, completed in April 1930, was dramatic and set the store apart from all others in Pittsburgh (fig. 7). The walls, elevators, and interior columns had facings of black reflective marble and Carrera glass, a new product of the Pittsburgh Plate Glass Company. Lighting fixtures were contained within glass moldings that began at the top of each column and traced the beams supporting the ceiling. Underneath this grid stood blond mahogany display cases, which had their own hidden lighting sources.

Seeming to float on the walls high above the merchandise were ten large murals, each measuring approximately 7 feet high by 14 feet wide, titled the *History of Commerce.* These murals were painted by Boardman Robinson (1876–1952), whom Schoen had recommended to Kaufmann in 1927.[33] Both the act of awarding the commission and the works themselves are a significant early instance of what would become a sustained effort to revitalize mural painting in the United States, an art many at the time regarded as moribund. Robinson, who had made his reputation as a political cartoonist and illustrator, and his friend, the painter Thomas Hart Benton, had recently begun to investigate ways of expressing contemporary themes in monumental murals executed in paint or fresco. The Kaufmann commission provided Robinson with his first opportunity to put his ideas into practice and would be the first of a series of ambitious murals realized in the 1930s by artists such as Benton, José Clemente Orozco, and Diego Rivera.

It is not known how Kaufmann came upon the idea for the commission, but it may not be coincidental that Pittsburgh possessed a number of murals executed around the turn of the century on themes of importance to the city. The most spectacular of these was the cycle *The Crowning of Labor* (1905–8) by John White Alexander, decorating the new entrance hall at the Carnegie Institute. Nearby, at the

Fig. 8. Trade and Commerce in the United States—The Twentieth Century, *1929. Boardman Robinson. Automotive paint on canvas on board, 88½ × 162 in. Courtesy of Colorado Springs Fine Arts Center.*

Carnegie Institute of Technology, the interior of the College of Fine Arts Building featured murals by J. M. Hewlett and others from around 1912 representing the history of the arts, and downtown, in the Golden Triangle, the Bank of Pittsburgh (demolished in 1944) had a mural by Edwin Blashfield depicting *Pittsburgh Presenting Its Iron and Steel to the World* (ca. 1895).[34]

The *History of Commerce,* now in the collection of the Colorado Springs Fine Arts Center, added the merchant to the ranks of manufacturers and artists ensconced in the city's pantheon of prosperity.[35] The cycle begins with *The Persians and the Arabs—Before the Christian Era* and concludes with *Trade and Commerce in the United States—The Twentieth Century.*[36] Robinson conceived each painting, executed with automotive paint on canvas mounted on board, as a tableau with a primary group of figures arranged as if on a shallow stage in front of a backdrop representing a distant landscape (fig. 8). Although he abstracted the figures and landscape features to emphasize their underlying volumetric forms, he included carefully researched details, such as costume, that established time and place. The final scene portrays four muscular workers dressed in overalls building a modern industrial city not unlike Pittsburgh, with a high-rise commercial center amidst steel mills and factories and a concrete bridge recalling the George Westinghouse Bridge then under construction in nearby Turtle Creek. Robinson's murals and Janssen's interior finishes created an elegant environment for the store's customers, whose well-being was enhanced

by technical systems that were as sophisticated as the decoration was chic. Among these was the introduction of air conditioning, improved vertical circulation provided by three sets of escalators and sixteen passenger elevators, and state-of-the-art electrical wiring that included provisions for the emerging technology of television, which Edgar Kaufmann must have felt would soon be an integral part of retailing.[37]

The feature that most impressed the editors of retailing trade journals was the layout of the sales aisles. In contrast to the traditional orthogonal organization of central aisle and cross aisles, which often resulted in dead ends, Kaufmann's arrangement included diagonal aisles, which offered customers multiple possibilities for movement yet directed them toward the elevators and escalators and new temptations for purchase. "This new layout is the most radical that has been made in the retail field and one well worthy of study," concluded the report in the *Dry Goods Economist.*[38]

The opening festivities went far beyond a sale and balloons for children—it was more like the dedication of a civic monument. One component was a national essay contest on the theme of "Art in Industry" announced in *Fortune* magazine. The jury consisted of Edgar Kaufmann, Joseph Urban, and the equally flamboyant industrial designer Norman Bel Geddes. The winner was Catherine K. Bauer, who wrote on housing in Frankfurt, Germany.[39]

The unveiling of the murals on Sunday, 27 April 1930, was accompanied by an elaborate ceremony that included speeches by Robert Lamont, the U.S.

25

1. The Kaufmanns, Wright, and Good Design

secretary of commerce, who spoke on the theme of "Art and Commerce," and James J. Davis, the U.S. secretary of labor, who spoke on "Art and Labor." Edgar Kaufmann addressed the theme of "Art and the Merchant." His speech is one of his few recorded public statements and demonstrates his affinity with the ideas promoted by figures such as Richard Bach and Paul Frankl:

> The development of art should be the cultural goal of America. . . . No modern organization is in a better position to observe this artistic evolution than a large department store. Close contact with the varied demands of human beings has indicated to us the public's increasing appreciation of color and form. The dollar is no longer the sole issue. Many people have become willing to invest a considerable portion of that dollar in beauty, in spite of the fact that they consider they are thereby depriving themselves of an apportionate percentage of utility. . . . As a general appreciation of beauty grows, we are prompted and inspired to cherish more and more zealously the principles of art and the laws of harmony. We are encouraged in our efforts along this line

by the increasing popularity of the simple and beautiful in all types of merchandise and commodities.[40]

Liliane Kaufmann pursued this cause on her own terms. In 1933, she took control of the store's unprofitable eleventh floor and established the Vendôme shops, named to recall the elegant Place Vendôme in Paris—the address of the Ritz Hotel, where she stayed on her buying trips to the city, and of many boutiques in which she enjoyed shopping for fine jewelry and apparel. With the Vendôme shops, she sought to offer sophisticated customers a similarly interesting and tasteful selection of quality goods, including designer dresses, furnishings, bedding, and gifts. In setting the tone for the housewares and furniture departments, Liliane stressed quality, rather than stylistic homogeneity, and an aesthetic sensibility that encouraged a creative mix of modern forms and antiques, high-style design and folk crafts. This sensibility can sometimes reflect a casual attitude toward style, but in the case of the Kaufmanns, it was consistent with a conscious theory of design promulgated by friends and acquaintances moving in overlapping circles centered, respectively, in New York and Vienna.

Edgar and Liliane Kaufmann drew on their contacts in both cities to further their son's interest in art. Although Edgar jr. (see fig. 9) was the heir apparent to the presidency of the department store, his parents did not impose upon him formal studies in business or the apprenticeship that his father had served. In his memoir of Fallingwater, Kaufmann jr. recalled that Paul Frankl had passed along drawing tips during visits to the family's home in Pittsburgh and that it was the ceramist Valerie "Vally" Wieselthier who persuaded the family that he should pursue his studies at the Kunstgewerbeschule in Vienna, where she had received her own artistic training.[41] Edgar jr.'s stay in Vienna in 1929 was facilitated by the staff of Kaufmann's local buying office. So intertwined were the affairs of business and family that Edgar jr.'s nineteenth-birthday celebration in Vienna was a news item in the store's in-house magazine.[42]

After a year in Vienna, Kaufmann jr. moved to Florence to study with Viktor Hammer, a Viennese artist his mother had met in London who painted the portrait of Edgar Kaufmann that now hangs in

Fig. 9. Edgar Kaufmann jr. (at left), Frank Lloyd Wright, and Edgar J. Kaufmann at Taliesin West, late 1940s. Photo: © Pedro E. Guerrero.

Merchant Prince and Master Builder

Fallingwater. Kaufmann jr. remained in Europe until 1934, when he returned to the United States with plans to settle in New York and paint. That summer, however, his life took an unplanned turn. As he related the story, he read Frank Lloyd Wright's *An Autobiography* (1932) on the advice of a friend, and the book inspired him to join the Taliesin Fellowship, which Wright and his wife, Olgivanna, had recently founded as an institute for artistic growth. In September, Kaufmann jr. traveled to Wisconsin for an interview with Wright, and a month later he was officially inscribed as a member of the fellowship. In November, his parents came for a visit that, as we shall see, would set in motion their first commissions with Wright. Despite the immediate rapport his family forged with the Wrights, Kaufmann jr. remained with the fellowship for less than six months. In April 1935, he returned to Pittsburgh to take his long-deferred place in the family store, where he eventually became merchandise manager for the home department. Over the next seven years, he played a pivotal role in integrating the family's interests in progressive design, Wright, and business.

A particular concern for Kaufmann jr. and his parents was the welfare of their friends in Austria, many of whom were becoming targets of discrimination both as Jews and as practitioners of modernist art and design, regarded as suspect by the political right. The family assisted a number of artists and designers in immigrating to the United States.[43] The first of these, apparently, was the Hungarian-born artist László Gábor (b. 1895), whom Kaufmann jr. had met in Vienna. The family brought him to Pittsburgh in 1935 as the store's art director. His designs for show windows and in-store displays frequently challenged conventional practice and, occasionally, notions of propriety. Among the other designers whose immigration or early experiences in the United States included a Kaufmann connection were Bernard Rudofsky, remembered today primarily for his book *Architecture Without Architects* (1964), who worked briefly at Kaufmann's in 1936; Walter Sobotka, who obtained a position in 1941 teaching at the Research Bureau for Retail Training at the University of Pittsburgh, founded by Edgar Kaufmann; and Hans Vetter, who joined the architecture faculty of the Carnegie Institute of

Fig. 10. Bedroom furnishings, Steiner house, Vienna, ca. 1933. Designed by Josef Frank (1885–1967). These furnishings, sold in shops such as Haus & Garten in Vienna, illustrate the Wiener Wohnkultur aesthetic known to the Kaufmanns through their contacts in New York and Vienna. Frank drew freely on historical styles to create items that expressed the casual elegance and flexibility that he and his colleagues regarded as characteristic of modern living. The bed at left reflects American Shaker design, the three-legged stool has an Egyptian pedigree, and the chair at right issues from Windsor examples. With the fabric-covered cabinet and stand at left, Frank transformed a traditional type dating from the Renaissance into an ensemble that is lighter, simpler, and engagingly different. Innen Dekoration, vol. 44, 1933.

Technology in 1948, apparently through the intervention of Sobotka and Gábor. Gábor also helped Josef Frank and Oskar Wlach through the immigration process.[44] In 1951, Frank organized an exhibit at Kaufmann's of his furnishings designed for the Swedish firm Svenskt Tenn.[45]

Collectively, these men are identified with a design philosophy known as the *Wiener Wohnkultur*, which emphasized comfort, flexibility, and variety as objectives for modern design and accepted history as a viable resource for formal invention.[46] In the late 1920s and early 1930s, adherents to the

27

Fig. 11. Edgar Kaufmann jr. (at left), apprentice William Bernoudy, and Frank Lloyd Wright inspect a model for the Broadacre City display, ca. 1935. Courtesy of The Frank Lloyd Wright Foundation.

Fig. 12. Advertisement for the Broadacre City display and the Federal Housing Administration's New Homes for Old *exposition as part of Kaufmann's sixty-fourth anniversary sale.* Pittsburgh Post-Gazette, 16 June 1935. Courtesy of the Carnegie Library of Pittsburgh.

Wohnkultur aesthetic, such as Josef Frank, criticized functionalist designers such as Walter Gropius and Hannes Meyer for creating mere images of practicality rather than genuine solutions to clients' physical and psychological needs.[47] Frank, Wlach, and Sobotka had demonstrated how these needs could be met in their store in Vienna, Haus & Garten (1925–38), which offered a selection of modern furnishings from which clients could create their own ensembles (fig. 10). This spirit accorded well with the Kaufmanns' approach in their personal collecting and their strategy in merchandising.

Kaufmann jr. described his family as "drifting towards Wright" in the years before he joined the Taliesin Fellowship. "Drifting," however, can suggest a passiveness that does not reflect the family's progressive engagement with designers in the United States and Vienna who defined modernism primarily in terms of expressing the spirit of the age through open-ended vocabularies of form and materials. "Modernism means liberty of choice if it means anything," Paul Frankl wrote in *Form and Re-Form,* and as retailers and as private collectors, the Kaufmanns exercised that liberty fully in creating their own *Wohnkultur.*[48] When they finally met Wright in the fall of 1934, the Kaufmanns may have known little about his architecture, but they would have been aware of the regard in which he was held by progressive designers familiar to them, such as Frankl and Joseph Urban. Wright's positions on the state of architecture and design clearly resonated

Merchant Prince and Master Builder

Fig. 13. Edgar Kaufmann's private office on the tenth floor of Kaufmann's department store in Pittsburgh. The office is now in the Victoria & Albert Museum in London.

with what they had heard for years from their friends in New York and Vienna.

Edgar Tafel (b. 1912) has recalled that at the Sunday dinner Edgar and Liliane Kaufmann shared with the fellowship on their visit to Taliesin in November 1934, Wright spoke of Broadacre City, his vision for decentralization that would render traditional cities, such as Pittsburgh, obsolete and provide Americans with a more equitable distribution of property.[49] In describing this idyllic scene, Wright mentioned that a wooden model could dramatically illustrate the character of Broadacre but that alas funds to build it weren't in hand. Edgar Kaufmann picked up the cue and offered a contribution, making the first step from client to patron.

As the apprentices, among them Kaufmann jr., built the model of Broadacre at their winter quarters in Arizona, Wright and Kaufmann apparently decided that it would be effective to display the model to a broad audience by using department stores as venues (fig. 11). Kaufmann planned to coordinate this traveling exhibition through the Associated Merchandising Corporation, with which his store was affiliated, but the opportunity arose for the model to make its debut in New York at the *Industrial Arts Exposition* held at Rockefeller Center in April 1935.[50] Plans for the model to travel to Washington, D.C., for exhibition in the lobby of the Department of Commerce or the Department of Labor failed to materialize, so the next venue was on the eleventh floor of Kaufmann's in Pittsburgh, where it

was shown alongside another exhibit titled *New Homes for Old*, sponsored by the Federal Housing Administration, which displayed new building materials, furnishings, and information about estimating costs and arranging financing.[51]

The exhibits were attractions linked to the store's annual anniversary sale, and both the sale and the exhibits were well publicized (fig. 12). "Home Owners' Utopia! Future Housing Shown" proclaimed the title of an article in the *Pittsburgh Sun-Telegraph* that presented Broadacre City as a society with no unemployment and good government. Pittsburgh's mayor, William McNair, thought otherwise. "Pure socialism," he declared. "This town is built for a lot of social workers."[52] High praise and excoriation probably were equally effective in attracting Pittsburghers to the displays and, once they were in the store, to the tempting sale items.

The Broadacre model survives today and remains impressive.[53] It measures about 12 feet square and represents an area of about 4 square miles (at 1 inch = 75 feet) occupied by residences, farms, businesses, and public buildings linked together by modern highways. Every family was assured at minimum a one-acre lot with a house and sufficient land for a substantial garden. Some people would farm full-time, but others would drive their cars to work at their chosen professions. In addition to the Broadacre City model, the exhibit included models at larger scale illustrating typical buildings. Members

1. The Kaufmanns, Wright, and Good Design

of the Taliesin Fellowship stood by to answer the questions of Pittsburghers, some of whom may have found Broadacre as remote from their own experience in a city crippled by the Great Depression as the Land of Oz.[54]

While his fellow citizens considered the new urban landscape exhibited on the eleventh floor of his store, Edgar Kaufmann, working in the executive suite one floor below, dreamed of the private office he had commissioned from Wright—and wondered when the drawings would arrive. The two had conceived the project during the previous winter, and Kaufmann planned on building it in the fall. The long route to its completion two-and-one-half years later, however, would coincide with the design and construction of Fallingwater.

The Kaufmann office can be seen today in the Victoria & Albert Museum in London; its history has been thoroughly documented by Christopher Wilk, the museum's curator of furniture and woodwork (fig. 13).[55] In the store, it occupied the northwest corner of the tenth floor adjacent to a conference room lined with sixteenth-century German paneling. As Kaufmann had done in the conference room, Wright transformed the raw space with wood paneling, but whereas carved ornament and illusionistic views of German towns defined the character of the former, carefully matched grains of cypress veneer on all surfaces, including the ceiling, set the tone for the latter. Wright planned the room using a 4-foot-square module, and the major elements, such as the 8-foot ceiling height and the 2-foot-high cabinet doors, correspond to the full or half module. Exterior views were not a concern, and he screened the existing windows with louvers.

Edgar Kaufmann's desk and the plywood relief mural above it were the focal point of the room (see cats. 32–34). In sharp contrast to the neatly framed scenes in the conference room, Wright's mural seemingly has no boundaries, horizontally or in depth, and no center. Composed of up to seven layers of quarter-inch plywood and a triangular light fixture, the mural is an abstract composition of lines and shallow planes generated by a 30-60-90-degree triangle.

The office and furniture were constructed by a Nicaraguan-born cabinetmaker, Manuel J. Sandoval, who had recently resumed an independent practice in Chicago after working for several years with the Taliesin Fellowship.[56] The fabrics for the carpets and upholstery were woven by Loja Saarinen, wife of the architect Eliel Saarinen. Wright had met the couple in 1930 and had visited their home at the Cranbrook Academy of Art, near Detroit, where Loja headed the weaving workshop and Eliel served as director.[57] The Kaufmanns (father and son appear most frequently in the correspondence) followed the work closely and did not hesitate to intervene when they sensed problems. The elder Kaufmann took a particularly active interest in Saarinen's work and communicated with her regularly.[58]

The office was substantially complete in January 1938. Delighted with both it and Fallingwater, Kaufmann's enthusiasm for Wright was unabated. He immediately initiated the design for Fallingwater's guest house and, a few months later, conceived an idea for promoting Wright's architecture through the store. Following a visit with his son to the recently completed Herbert Jacobs house in Madison, Wisconsin, Kaufmann directed his vice president (and brother-in-law), Irwin Wolf, to approach Wright about marketing a version of the house as part of a promotional campaign planned for August. Wright offered to design an improved version for a fee of 10 percent and control over its reproductions. Wolf agreed to the terms but backed away from the deal, citing the uncertain conditions of the lingering Depression.[59]

Edgar Kaufmann jr., working in an office furnished all in white on the store's eighth floor, took over the idea. He contacted his friends at the Taliesin Fellowship about producing plans and specifications for a more modest house to be built with stock materials. In a letter to Eugene Masselink, Wright's secretary, Kaufmann jr. wrote:

> I take it for granted that the plan would be used as a product of the Taliesin Fellowship with our name [Kaufmann's department store] mentioned. Naturally, we would like to feature Mr. Wright in connection with the Fellowship, and would also like to know what final arrangements he would like to make for the use of the plans, both as we would erect the house in the store and as other people might want to duplicate it in the country here.

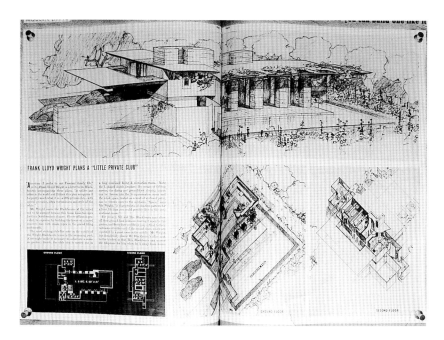

Fig. 14. Life *magazine house. Frank Lloyd Wright.* Life *5 (26 September 1938).*

We would also very much like to consider the possibility of this house being featured in a national magazine.[60]

The proposal sounds innocent enough, but Wright did not encourage his apprentices to take on independent work, and Masselink replied that the only acceptable terms were those previously agreed upon with Wolf.[61] On 25 August, Kaufmann jr. wrote Masselink that the store was still interested in commissioning a demonstration house, but this discussion was soon subsumed by an ambitious project undertaken by *Life* magazine and another Time Incorporated publication, *Architectural Forum.*[62]

Life planned a twenty-two-page article titled "Eight Houses for Modern Living," featuring an architectural duel in which four pairs of architects were assigned to families representing different middle-class income brackets (fig. 14). One member of each pair was a designated "traditionalist," the other a "modernist." The pairings were intended to demonstrate the range of design possibilities now available to home buyers.[63]

The editor of *Architectural Forum,* Howard Myers, had invited Wright's participation at the beginning of August. In a subsequent letter, he enclosed photographs of the client family, described the parameters of the competition, and noted that Wright's opponent would be Royal Barry Wills,

"that staunch defender of New England conservatism." He also included a check for $350.[64] Wright accepted the challenge, and the studio raced to meet the deadline three weeks away.

In the meantime, the staffs of the two magazines worked to organize another important component of the competition. Although the designs were based on specific sites, they were to be marketed nationally through department stores allied with local builders. Kaufmann's, affiliated with a Pittsburgh developer, Barone & Lind, headed *Life*'s list of participants, which also included John Wanamaker in New York, the May Company in Baltimore and Los Angeles, Carson Pirie Scott in Chicago, and the Emporium in San Francisco.

The exhibition of model homes by department stores was not in itself an innovation in 1938. Bamberger's in Newark, New Jersey, for example, had built model houses in 1923 and 1927, and Marshall Field's in Chicago had displayed Buckminster Fuller's revolutionary Dymaxion House in 1929.[65] *Life*'s campaign, however, was intended to streamline the way Americans built houses by offering one-stop shopping that would simplify the home-building process for the consumer and provide new opportunities for department stores to market furnishings and other durable goods. In principle, potential home-buyers would see a house they liked in the magazine and send away for a build-it-yourself

31

Fig. 15. Organic Design *installation at Kaufmann's, 1941. Organized by the Museum of Modern Art with the assistance of Edgar Kaufmann jr. Emrich Nicholson,* Contemporary Shops in the United States *(New York: Architectural Book Publishing, 1945), 148.*

cardboard model. Once they had identified their dream house, they would then head to a participating department store, which would connect them with a developer who would take charge of building the house. In the meantime, consumer and retailer would have ample opportunity to discuss how the house would be furnished.

The scheme invites comparison with the marketing of houses by the retailing giant Sears, Roebuck & Company. Although the company abandoned the business in 1940 in the wake of heavy losses during the Depression, its modern homes department had flourished from 1908 to 1932, offering houses that could be ordered by catalogue or from a regional sales office. In the areas served by the sales offices, customers merely had to select a design from the catalogue, show title to a lot, and sign a check for the down payment. Sears would assume the mortgage and supervise construction. Unlike the *Life* houses, which were custom-built, Sears sought to achieve economies of scale through the use of standardized, precut parts shipped by rail from a central warehouse.

The Sears houses were comfortable and economical, but like the store's other products, they were also anonymous and somewhat perfunctory. In contrast, *Life* promoted its houses as designer

homes accommodating distinctly modern tastes and upscale ambitions. The participating department stores, unlike Sears, were places where customers took refreshment in tearooms rather than at snack counters and sought style along with substance. By comarketing the *Life* houses, stores such as Kaufmann's could take advantage of the national publicity and association with renowned designers to enhance their local reputations as progressive institutions.[66]

Life devoted considerable effort to arranging for at least some of the houses to be under construction around the time of the campaign's debut on 26 September. The magazine assured Wright, for example, that it would pay his fees up to $800 if his "clients," the Blackbourns of Minneapolis, would build his house.[67] The family, imagining a home largely paid for by product endorsements, played their role with gusto and drove to Taliesin on two occasions to meet with Wright.[68] Meanwhile, Kaufmann's and its developer, A. J. Barone, tentatively agreed to build at least three of the *Life* houses, including Wright's design, on a speculative basis.[69]

A week after *Life* published "Eight Houses for Modern Living," the *Pittsburgh Sun-Telegraph* reported that work was under way on the first of the houses, designed by Royal Barry Wills, in Baldwin Manor, a suburban development just south of Pittsburgh.[70] It and the houses that were to follow were to be furnished by Kaufmann's, whose decorators were to be advised by a "consumers' congress" of club women, civic leaders, and housing experts. The completion of the Wills house was celebrated on a cold day in January 1939, which was warmed by the stellar radiance of actress Gertrude Lawrence, who recited a scene from Noel Coward's *Private Lives.*[71]

Although *Life* optimistically published accounts of sales and on-budget construction, the houses were not profitable. In Pittsburgh, the Wills house was sold at a loss for $14,500, nearly $8,000 less than cost of construction, which had been discounted in return for publicity.[72] In hopes of avoiding a similar problem in the construction of his house, Wright located a contractor, Harold Taylor of Scottsdale, Arizona, who agreed to build Wright's design for $10,000, but A. J. Barone remained uneasy. He and Edgar Kaufmann made inquiries about the cost of other Wright houses, and the answers convinced

Merchant Prince and Master Builder

Fig. 16. Sales counters at Kaufmann's, ca. 1945. Designed by László Gábor. Emrich Nicholson, Contemporary Shops in the United States (New York: Architectural Book Publishing, 1945), 152.

him that the project was not feasible in the current economic climate.[73] Barone withdrew. The Blackbourns in Minneapolis backed out for similar reasons.[74] Wright did find a client for his *Life* house, Bernard Schwartz of Two Rivers, Wisconsin, who successfully built it in 1939.

The *Life* campaign was a unique event that simultaneously engaged the Kaufmanns' interests in architecture, design, innovative marketing, and Wright. Subsequent promotions were more narrowly focused.[75] The family emphasized home furnishings and the notion of good design as a quality that might be found in traditional crafts, contemporary custom design, and modern mass-produced items. In 1940, Kaufmann jr. and his mother, Liliane, presented an exhibition of Mexican antiques and folk art. The following year, Kaufmann jr. brought the Museum of Modern Art's traveling exhibition *Organic Design* to the store (fig. 15). He had played a central role in organizing the exhibit, and the experience set him on a course that would take him from the store and a career in retailing to his life's work as a curator and scholar.

Kaufmann jr.'s association with the Museum of Modern Art had begun in 1937, when John McAndrew, its curator of architecture and industrial art, visited Fallingwater as the house was nearing completion. In January 1938, the museum exhibited photographs of the house. Later that year,

Kaufmann's became a site for the museum's newly instituted program of traveling exhibitions, the first of which was titled *Useful Objects Under $15*. Subsequent exhibitions covered aspects of art, architecture, and design. In January 1940, for example, the store presented *40 Prints by Modern Artists, War Etchings by Goya and Dix*, and *What Is Modern Architecture?*[76]

On 25 January 1940, Kaufmann jr. wrote the museum's director, Alfred Barr, proposing a collaborative project intended to encourage creativity and high quality in furniture design. He envisioned an annual competition in which the museum would invite three American designers to create furnishings for living, eating, and sleeping. Manufacturers would assist in the development of prototypes. The work was to be displayed at Kaufmann's and adjudged by a committee selected by the museum. Kaufmann's would purchase the winning pieces and donate them to the museum's permanent collection.[77]

Over the following months, the Museum of Modern Art modified Kaufmann jr.'s idea by broadening the scope of the competition to allow participation by more designers from the United States and, in a separate division, Latin America, and to center the project at the museum under Eliot F. Noyes, the director of industrial design. Although he is not acknowledged in the exhibition catalogue, Kaufmann jr. worked closely with Noyes in an unofficial capacity, touring designers' studios and serving on the jury. He, and likely his father, also played an important role in recruiting twelve department stores across the country, including his own, to support the exhibition and, most importantly, to offer contracts to manufacturers for the production of winning pieces.[78] At Kaufmann's, these products were sold in the Vendôme department.

The main exhibition, titled *Organic Design in Home Furnishings*, and a satellite exhibit at Kaufmann's opened simultaneously on 25 September 1941.[79] The star of the show was the line of molded-plywood chairs collaboratively designed by Eero Saarinen and Charles Eames. The light-colored wood and curved lines evident in these and many of the other pieces inspired László Gábor's redesign of display cabinets in several departments in the store (fig. 16).[80]

33

1. The Kaufmanns, Wright, and Good Design

Fig. 17. Sketch for Good Design *installation, 1955. Pencil on paper, 8½ × 11 in., A. James Speyer, designer. In 1954 and 1955, Edgar Kaufmann jr. commissioned longtime family friend A. James Speyer to create* Good Design *installations for the Merchandise Mart in Chicago and the Museum of Modern Art in New York. Courtesy of the Art Institute of Chicago.*

Kaufmann jr. served in the Army Air Force during World War II. When his enlistment ended in 1946, he didn't return to the family store. Instead, he moved to New York and succeeded Noyes as the head of the industrial design department at the Museum of Modern Art. He held this position until 1948, when his department was abruptly merged with the architecture department under the direction of Philip Johnson, with whom he was at odds both professionally and personally.[81] Although no longer a department head, Kaufmann jr. remained with the museum until 1955, pursuing the campaign he had begun before the war to promote contemporary furniture design among manufacturers, retailers, and consumers.[82] He organized the *International Competition for Low-Cost Furniture Design* in 1948, but his greatest accomplishment was the Good Design program of 1950–55, in which the museum joined forces with the Merchandise Mart in Chicago, the nation's largest wholesale market for home furnishings.

Under Kaufmann jr.'s direction, the phrase "good design" became, literally, a label akin to the Good Housekeeping Seal of Approval or the "UL" of Underwriters' Laboratories. Twice a year for five years, he led juries in the selection of between 175 and 400 products for exhibition in a special Good Design section at the January and June housewares shows at the Merchandise Mart (fig. 17). In Decem-

ber, a third exhibition drawn from these collections was shown at the Museum of Modern Art. When displayed for sale in stores, the products were marked with a Good Design tag, affirming their adherence to the exhibited designs. The program built on the idea of exemplary selection that underlay the Museum of Modern Art's previous exhibitions of furnishings and housewares and promotions at Kaufmann's department store, such as the "Quality Merchandise Program" of 1935 and the "Better Taste and Decent Merchandise" campaign of 1945. The latter, incidentally, was organized by Viennese émigré Walter Sobotka.

Good Design products included textiles, silverware, glassware, and furniture produced by hand or machine. The definition of what was good design was resolved subjectively by each jury in keeping with general precepts articulated by Kaufmann jr. In his influential booklet, *What Is Modern Design?* (1950), he wrote, "Good design in any period is simply: *the best its designers produce*" (italics in original), and explained that "the best" successfully merge form and function and demonstrate "an awareness of human values expressed in relation to industrial production for a democratic society." The test of this principle, he maintained, is to ask, "Does it [the product] enhance your life?"[83] The items that most typically met these criteria for Kaufmann jr. and his jurors looked innovative, celebrated their

34

materials, and eschewed ornament. The absence of a defined ideology or theoretical position was a point of contention for some critics, but it allowed for considerable flexibility in choosing work across traditional lines of nationality, process of manufacture, and even gender of designers. It also was in keeping with the inclusive spirit that governed the Kaufmann family's buying policies at the department store.

The Merchandise Mart and the Museum of Modern Art ended the Good Design program in 1955, and Kaufmann jr. left the museum in the same year. These professional changes coincided with a difficult time in his personal life. This was the year of his father's death, less than three years after his mother's suicide. He was involved in a painful dispute over the estate with the woman his father had married in 1954, Grace Stoops. The department store now belonged to the May Department Stores, and his long-standing and intimate links to the worlds of retailing, design, and art museums were fundamentally altered.

Kaufmann jr.'s subsequent career was devoted to writing on architecture and design, teaching at Columbia University, philanthropy through the Kaufmann Charitable Foundation and Trust, and advising museums, such as the Metropolitan Museum of Art, on the development of their design collections.[84] He donated Fallingwater and the family's land holdings at Bear Run to the Western Pennsylvania Conservancy in 1963 but attended to the furnishings of Fallingwater throughout his life. The house, as we shall see in Chapter 2, remains an eloquent and exemplary statement of his parents' *Wohnkultur* and his own aesthetic of good design.

35

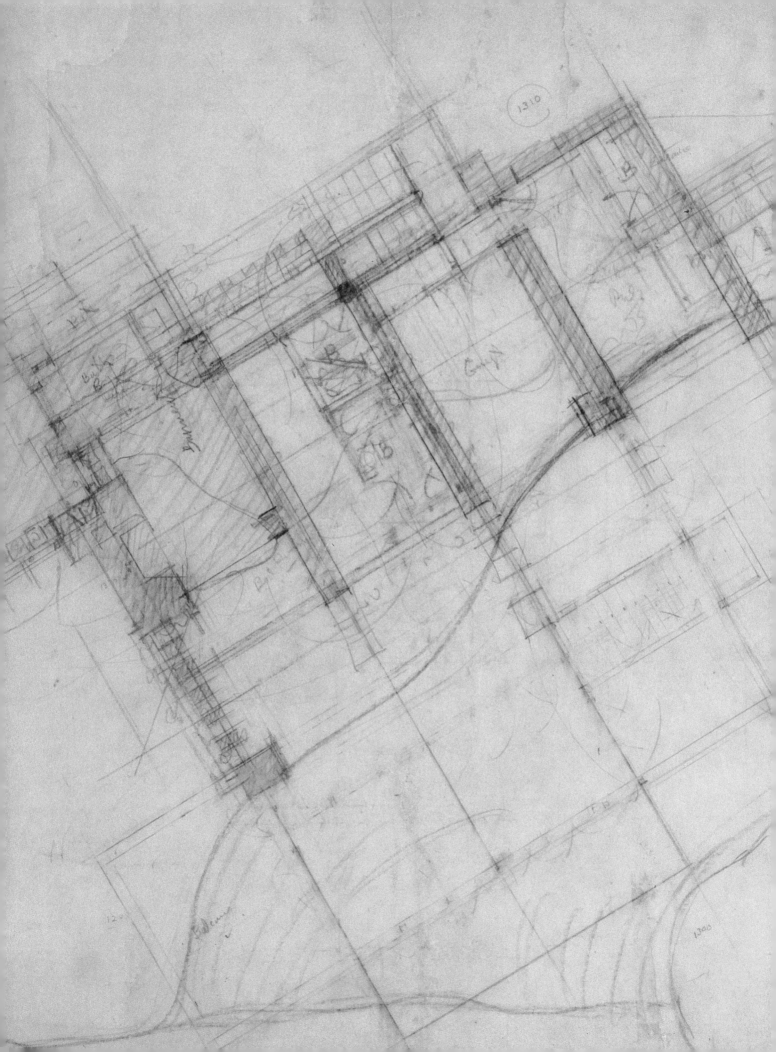

2 *The Kaufmanns' Country Houses at Bear Run and Palm Springs*

THE KAUFMANNS BUILT their first weekend house at Bear Run in 1921.[1] It was a simple, prefabricated cabin set on high ground above the unpaved road (Route 381) linking the villages of Mill Run and Ohiopyle, and it provided the family with its own living quarters at Kaufmann's Summer Camp, which Edgar Kaufmann had established on leased property for the department store's female employees in 1916. Few traces of the camp remain today, but in 1920 it consisted of fourteen buildings, including a clubhouse, a dance pavilion and bowling alley, six cottages, and a brook trout hatchery.[2] In 1926, Kaufmann arranged for the store employees' association to purchase the buildings and nearly 1,600 acres along Bear Run, but the camp remained popular for only a few years. It failed during the Depression, and in July 1933 the Kaufmanns took it over as their personal estate (fig. 18). Additional purchases would eventually increase their holdings to more than 1,900 acres.

Fig. 18. Edgar and Liliane Kaufmann at Fallingwater, 1940s. Fallingwater Archive, Avery Architectural and Fine Arts Library, Columbia University in the City of New York.

37

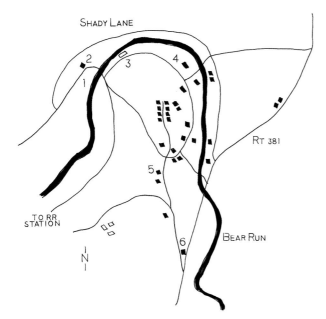

Fig. 19. Diagram of buildings and landscape features on the Kaufmann family's estate at Bear Run before construction of Fallingwater. 1: waterfall; 2: cottage on site of future guest house; 3: trout hatchery; 4: dance pavilion; 5: clubhouse; 6: the Kaufmanns' cottage. The unlabeled buildings include cottages and service buildings and a church and school on Route 381.

The familiar image of Fallingwater set above the falls on Bear Run eclipses our perception of the estate's varied topography. The land to the east of Route 381 gently rolls upward toward Laurel Hill and has supported farms since the late nineteenth century. Bear Run winds its way down this slope and, after crossing Route 381, enters a wide ravine bordered by sandstone ledges. A gravel drive, known as Shady Lane, runs along a ridge above the right bank, from the highway to the guest house and servants' quarters. Above the left bank, an area of high ground, now occupied by the visitors' parking lot, was the site of the camp's cottages, and to the south, the clubhouse stood in the vicinity of the present maintenance buildings (fig. 19). The ravine is widest in the area below and to the east of the present parking lot, and its flat bottom accommodated a number of service buildings and the dance hall. It narrows as Bear Run veers westward and descends rapidly from the waterfall to the Youghiogheny River.

The varied terrain supports abundant plant life. The dominant trees include red maple, oak, black cherry, tulip poplar, and black birch. In contrast to these deciduous species, the primary shrubs are evergreen, including mountain laurel and rhododendron. There is also a rich mat of ferns and mosses and a variety of wild roses, mountain roses, and native bulbs.[3] This colorful, varied landscape rewards continued observation throughout the seasons as well as first-time impressions.

Long before he assumed personal ownership of the property, Edgar Kaufmann took an interest in its long-term management. In 1920, he commissioned a Pittsburgh engineering firm to undertake a comprehensive survey of the property's man-made and natural features, addressing such issues as water quality and the diversity of wildlife.[4] This information provided him with data useful in subsequent financial negotiations and also served as a foundation for his future efforts to develop the property as a protected forest.

As Donald Hoffmann has pointed out, Bear Run was not a virgin landscape and had no particular value as a vacation place until 1890, when it was acquired by a Masonic organization from Pittsburgh.[5] Before then, it had been repeatedly logged, mined, and quarried. Exposed mine faces and new growth timber were reminders of this industrial usage. The Kaufmanns took active measures to develop the diversity of plant and animal life on the estate and to provide pleasing settings for their own activities. In 1933, for example, they responded to a chestnut tree blight by removing dead trees and replacing them with fast-growing Norway spruce. Extensive plantings of pine in the forest between Bear Run and Route 381 continued in the 1940s.

The family demolished many of the camp buildings and planted gardens in their place (fig. 20). Under Liliane Kaufmann's direction, a large vegetable garden was established on the high ground where the cottages had been, and flower gardens replaced the dance hall on the flat bottomland. The family also planted an orchard and built a swimming pool a short way upstream of the site of Fallingwater. In the immediate vicinity of the house, they experimented with different arrangements of native and exotic flowering plants. Tempting as it is today to view Bear Run as a wild site, the Kaufmanns regarded it more as a picturesque garden molded with aesthetic intent informed by their current interests.

Architecture was part of their vision. In addition to Fallingwater and the guest house, they com-

38

Merchant Prince and Master Builder

missioned Wright to design a gate lodge, a chapel, and a farmhouse, but none of these buildings was realized.

Despite the extensive written documentation and many firsthand accounts describing the construction of Fallingwater, the origins of the commission are obscure. No correspondence defining its scope has come to light, and it appears that the Kaufmanns and Wright settled the preliminaries through informal conversations. Edgar Kaufmann jr., who was in residence with the Taliesin Fellowship from October 1934 to April 1935, likely served as an intermediary between his parents and the architect.

Given Edgar Kaufmann's impulsive character, it isn't difficult to imagine the idea forming spontaneously as he and Liliane inspected Taliesin in November 1934, sixteen months after they had assumed ownership of Bear Run. Like the Wrights, the Kaufmanns appreciated vigorous engagement with nature. Edgar Kaufmann may never have taken to driving a road grader, as Wright was doing at age sixty-nine, but he shared, as we shall see, an interest in farming, albeit from a gentlemanly perspective. At Bear Run, he and Liliane enjoyed hiking in the forest and swimming in the cold mountain stream, and Liliane excelled at fly-fishing. The Kaufmanns, like so many other visitors to Taliesin, may well have been enchanted by the world Wright had created and sought something in a similar spirit for themselves.

Wright was taken to Bear Run on his trip to Pittsburgh in December, and in May 1935 Kaufmann wrote him of his willingness to proceed with drawings for the house and the Pittsburgh office interior.[6] Wright visited Bear Run again at the end of June, when he traveled to Pittsburgh to see the installation of the Broadacre City exhibition at Kaufmann's department store.

The story of the first drawings for Fallingwater is a set piece in epic recountings of Wright's career.[7] On Sunday, 22 September 1935, Kaufmann telephoned Wright from Milwaukee and reported that he was on his way to Taliesin, near Spring Green, about 120 miles to the west, to see the drawings for the house, which he assumed were well under way. Wright, it is said, calmly gathered his pencils and apprentices, sat down at a drafting table, and drew

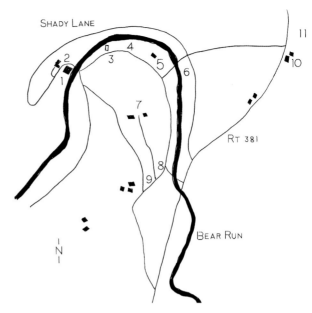

Fig. 20. Diagram of buildings and major landscape features realized or planned on the Kaufmann family's estate at Bear Run, 1936–57. 1: waterfall; 2: Fallingwater and guest house; 3: swimming pool; 4: fruit orchard; 5: flower garden; 6: possible site for chapel project; 7: vegetable garden (location of present parking lot and visitors' center); 8: site for gate lodge project of 1942; 9: site for gate lodge projects of 1956–57; 10: dairy barn and farmhouse; 11: possible site for farm cottage. The unlabeled buildings include service buildings, staff residences, and a church and school on Route 381.

the first plan, section, and elevations, completing them shortly before Kaufmann's arrival only a few hours later. After reviewing these drawings, architect and client retired to a leisurely lunch, while apprentices Edgar Tafel and Bob Mosher (1909–1992) hurriedly generated additional elevations.

Kaufmann was surprised to see the house perched above the waterfall rather than on the opposite bank oriented with a view of the falls, but acceded to Wright's admonition, "E. J., I want you to live with the waterfall, not just to look at it, but for it to become an integral part of your lives."[8] Kaufmann returned to Pittsburgh eager to begin construction. Kaufmann jr. conveyed this enthusiasm to Wright in a letter of 27 September:

Father spent quite some time at Bear Run showing just where the various rooms would be and Edgar [Tafel] sent a rough drawing of the wall masses so that we are all tremendously anxious to see just what the house really will look like.

39

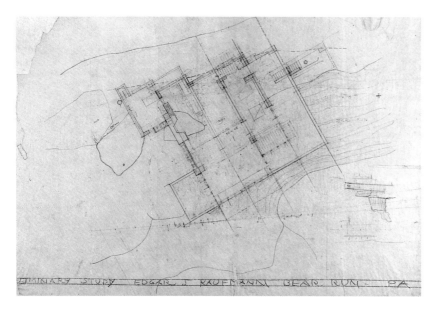

Fig. 21. Preliminary first floor plan, Fallingwater. Pencil and color pencil on tracing paper, 28 × 43 in. The drawing indicates the locations of the foundation piers supporting the cantilevered first floor and of the oak and tulip trees framing the house. At right is a small section of the house and waterfall. The Frank Lloyd Wright Foundation, 3602.048.

As far as I am concerned, it keeps floating around in a half formed way almost continually asking for a little more information on which to complete itself.[9]

He had a while to wait for that information—Wright's studio did not complete the first set of working drawings until January 1936. In the meantime, his father skirmished with Wright over the cost of the house. Responding to a cavalier statement that the minimum cost of the house and furnishings would be $35,000, Kaufmann wrote, "Your inserting the words 'minimum cost of $35,000 for the house including furnishings' is a nice way of telling me that you think it is going to cost more. We sort of agreed that you were going to try to make $35,000 the maximum. However, we will work this out together when the time comes."[10] Whether $35,000 was to be the minimum or the maximum cost—the final total would be over $70,000—the sum indicates that from the beginning the Kaufmanns envisioned a considerably grander house than their Readi-Cut cabin.

The Kaufmanns developed their property at Bear Run fully aware of the estates of other members of Pittsburgh society clustered around nearby Ligonier. Among these, for example, is Richard K. Mellon's private Rolling Rock Club, built in 1928 by Benno Janssen, the longtime architect of the Kaufmanns. It and many of the estates nearby have the look of English manor houses. Fallingwater rep-

resented a different type of residence: the weekend house designed to efficiently and directly engage stressed city-dwellers with the recuperative powers of nature. This was a theme then being promoted by contemporary architectural journals such as the *Architectural Record,* which in 1930 published an article by Knud Lönberg-Holm titled "The Weekend House" that urged architects to give priority in their designs to providing as much direct contact with nature as possible, developing dynamic spatial qualities ("not a box"), and creating a strong sense of unity.[11]

Wright provided the Kaufmanns with a textbook example of such a house, which certainly conformed to their vigorous enjoyment of Bear Run and their self-image as progressive, modern people. The striking form of Fallingwater may also have been a calculated gesture, as Franklin Toker has suggested, intended to secure the Kaufmanns a level of distinction that would override the social barriers they encountered as Jews.[12]

The drawings that Wright presented to Edgar Kaufmann on that September morning in 1935 established the essential form of the house that they built together (see cats. 1–13). The first floor is occupied by the living room, its terraces, and the modest kitchen. The second floor has two suites composed of bedroom, bathroom, and terrace designated for Edgar and Liliane Kaufmann; a guest room and bath; and a sleeping porch to the east. The third floor includes a bedroom and bathroom designated for Edgar

Kaufmann jr., a terrace, and a narrow gallery planned as the terminus of a bridge spanning the driveway toward the site of the future guest house. The entrance to the house and all internal circulation are located along the north wall. Rooms and terraces open toward the southeast.

In addition to providing basic information about size and location, Wright's schematic drawings shed light on his design process. One of their most notable features is the oblique orientation of the house on the paper (fig. 21). At first glance, this seems odd, given the building's orthogonal plan, but as Donald Hoffmann has shown, it is a result of the tracing paper being laid over a site plan that Wright's apprentices had prepared from the topographic map furnished by the Kaufmanns.[13] By maintaining this orientation rather than rotating the site plan to square it with the page, Wright and his assistants maintained a vivid sense of how the house relates to its site.

Wright located the house on a shelf of land on the right bank of Bear Run bounded by a bridge to the east, an access road (the present driveway) to the north, and a cluster of large boulders to the west. Using a 30-60-90-degree triangle set on his parallel rule, he oriented the house on this plot facing 30 degrees east of south, his preferred alignment for solar angles, and away from the falls. The rotation sets the stage for the diagonal path visitors follow in the living room as they are drawn by the sound of the falls and the anticipation of a view from the entrance at the northeast corner to the southwestern balcony.

The relationship of the house to its setting in the schematic drawings is reinforced by the representation of key landscape features, including the boulder forming the living room hearth, a cluster of large boulders just to the west of the kitchen, and two trees—a 28-inch-diameter oak among the boulders and an 18-inch-diameter tulip at the east side of the house site. The trees and boulders appear in plan and elevation and are integral to the composition of the house.

Wright's awareness of the oak and tulip trees as three-dimensional entities is demonstrated by indications of their canopies as well as their trunks in the plans. Their importance was greater in the initial conceptualization of the house than in the con-

struction, when errors in identifying their precise location on the site altered the relationship of the tulip to the house and led to the removal of the oak.

The schematic drawings also indicate devices that Wright used as guides in establishing the dimensions of key features of the plan and section. Although he generally employed grids in laying out plans, there is no evidence that he did so in the drawings for Fallingwater. Instead, as Hoffmann has shown, he organized the plan with respect to the bays defined by the four foundation piers (five piers, in the earliest plan), which Wright termed "bolsters," set on 12-foot centers. On the first floor, for example, the fireplace wall is supported by the first bolster, the dining room table is centered above the second, the piers separating the entry and music-listening areas from the main part of the living room are supported by the third bolster, and the eastern wall is carried by the fourth.

Wright adjusted the heights of the floors, ceilings, balcony parapets, and other horizontal elements with reference to a 17-inch unit. His reasons for the choice of this dimension aren't clear, but one drawing for the living room relates it to the dimensions of a person 68 inches (5 feet, 8 inches) tall, which perhaps incidentally was Wright's own height (fig. 22). The unit appears in the guidelines of some drawings, but it served more as a reference than as a prescriptive feature. In Wright's drawings and in the construction of the house, dimensions frequently depart from the unit. In cases such as the heights of the roof canopies, Wright seems to have adjusted the dimensions for visual effect, but other departures from the unit were due to accidents of construction, such as the irregular dimensions of the stones used in building the walls and piers. In contrast to the aspiration to technological precision that informed many strands of modernist architecture in the 1920s and 1930s, Fallingwater is a work in which apparent order was achieved through approximation.

Although the essential components of Fallingwater are present in the schematic drawings, several features underwent refinement as Wright and his assistants developed the design. One well-documented instance is the design of the entrance (fig. 21; cat. 2). Wright elevated the living room and its terraces on a plinth two steps above ground level. Initially, he located the steps so that visitors would

41

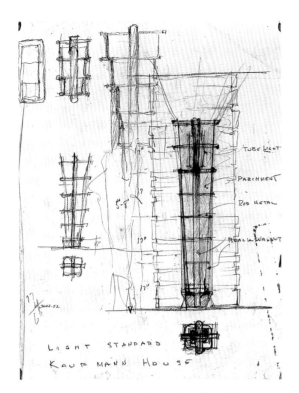

Fig. 22. Living room light fixture details, Fallingwater, ca. 1936–37. Pencil on tracing paper, 11 × 8½ in. The lamp is shown against a masonry pier. The 17-inch markings refer to the unit that Wright used to guide the vertical dimensions throughout the house. Lightly drawn to the left of the pier is a human figure 5 feet, 8 inches tall—Wright's own height. The Frank Lloyd Wright Foundation, 3602.052.

had their own representatives managing the construction of the house. Wright's principal agents were two apprentices from the Taliesin Fellowship: Bob Mosher, who began construction, and Edgar Tafel, who took over in October 1937. Mosher and Tafel were expected to interpret Wright's ideas to client and contractor and to report on the progress of the work. These were daunting tasks. With little previous building experience to guide them, both Mosher and Tafel found themselves working at a remote site with unusual materials and construction techniques. They frequently had to extemporize when drawings from Taliesin were late, and they constantly had to navigate among the strong-willed and mercurial personalities of Wright, Hall, and the Kaufmanns.

Edgar Kaufmann employed private engineering firms and staff from his department store to look after his interests. Among the latter were his building manager, Carl F. Thumm, whose surname would provide Wright with considerable amusement, and the head of his in-house design department, László Gábor. Kaufmann jr., who had returned to Pittsburgh from his stay with the Taliesin Fellowship, had responsibilities at the store that were flexible enough to allow him to be at the site regularly. Wright resented interference from Kaufmann's advisors and routinely chastised his client for lacking faith.

step up on the plinth and cross it to reach the entry door. He subsequently changed this arrangement so that visitors would enter the house first at grade level and then step up into the living room from the vestibule. A separate set of exterior steps lead up to the terrace. The new arrangement added a level of complexity to the transition from outside to inside —a common theme in Wright's work.

The move from planning to construction required the addition of a third party, a contractor, and after some false starts the Kaufmanns and Wright agreed on Walter J. Hall (1872–1952) from Port Allegheny, Pennsylvania. Hall had no particular expertise in working with reinforced concrete, but Wright liked his independent character, and the Kaufmanns may have thought that his experience working in a remote part of the state would be applicable to the conditions that he would encounter at Bear Run.

In addition to Hall, Wright and the Kaufmanns

Fig. 23. Masons working on the second floor, Fallingwater, 31 October 1936. Apprentice Edgar Tafel is at far left. Photo: Henry S. Churchill. Fallingwater Archive, Avery Architectural and Fine Arts Library, Columbia University in the City of New York.

Fig. 24. Steel framing (unusual in residential architecture) of the interior partitions, Fallingwater, 20 February 1937. Fallingwater Archive, Avery Architectural and Fine Arts Library, Columbia University in the City of New York.

Construction on the house began in June 1936 and was substantially complete by the end of 1937 (figs. 23, 24).[14] One of the most trying moments for all parties came when the first floor cantilever was poured at the end of August 1936. Kaufmann, understandably, was concerned about the stability of the great tray that was to project 18 feet from the foundation piers. Although Wright had talented in-house expertise—his son-in-law Wesley Peters and structural engineer Mendel Glickman—who translated his intuitive sense of structure into quantified specifications, Kaufmann sought a second opinion from structural engineers at the Metzger-Richardson Company in Pittsburgh (see cat. 9). They concluded that Wright's studio had underestimated the amount of steel reinforcing that was to be embedded within the concrete, and Kaufmann commissioned them to prepare new drawings, which were sent directly to Hall without review by Wright.

Exactly what happened next will not be certain until a thorough mapping of the steel reinforcement throughout the cantilever can be conducted, but two things are clear: Hall did increase the amount of steel in the structure, and the cantilever deflected more than anticipated, causing cracking and related problems that have been matters of concern throughout the history of the house. Wright became furious when Mosher reported what Kaufmann and Hall had done. In his view, they had panicked and caused the

deflection by increasing the weight of the cantilevers. Recent engineering studies of the house, however, suggest that even with the additional steel, the reinforcing is inadequate to carry the combined load of the first floor cantilever and the second floor, which bears on it through steel T-bars set in line with the front living room windows.[15]

As construction continued, the Kaufmanns didn't hesitate to request changes that they believed would enhance their enjoyment of the house. Among the most significant and well-documented examples was the addition of the plunge pool to the east of the living room terrace.[16] The Kaufmanns greatly enjoyed swimming and had been disappointed that Wright had not designed a pool for the house. When Mosher discovered that due to an error in the site plan a set of steps from the living room terrace to the bank of Bear Run would land instead in the stream, the opportunity arose to respond to the family's request and build a plunge pool. This decision, approved by Wright, led to another change: the construction of an exterior staircase allowing guests to move directly between the second floor guest room terrace and the pool without having to use the interior stairs and cross the living room.

The family paid close attention to the furnishings. Wright conceived the built-in seating and cabinetwork as an integral feature of the house. The black-walnut veneers offered a warm contrast to the sandstone and concrete surfaces, and the carefully matched graining (horizontal for cabinetwork, vertical for doors) reinforced the compositional lines of the masonry and steel window mullions. The Kaufmanns examined the drawings closely and made suggestions. Kaufmann jr., for instance, is credited with inventing the sliding cane shelving of the bedroom wardrobes and recommending the use of cork in the bathrooms. His father specified the dimensions of the bathroom fixtures and even asked Mosher to investigate having them carved from stone found on the site (see cat. 8).[17] Liliane Kaufmann paid close attention to the selection of fabrics.

Edgar Kaufmann's interest in stone bathtubs was an enthusiastic expression of the family's view of Fallingwater as a place of luxurious rusticity. Informality was another dimension of this aesthetic, and the family occasionally rejected Wright's proposals for furnishings that they felt would make

43

Fig. 25. Second floor, Edgar J. Kaufmann's room, Fallingwater. Furnishings as selected by Edgar Kaufmann jr. At left is a "Butterfly Chair," designed in 1938 by Jorge Ferrari-Hardoy, Antonio Bonet, and Juan Kurchan; at right is a wood armchair designed ca. 1936 by Josef Frank. Photo: Oberto Gili. Courtesy of House & Garden.

the house too formal. In this spirit, they approved Wright's designs for ottomans and side tables, which could be arranged in a variety of combinations, but declined the round-back chairs he recommended for the dining table. They also rejected his proposal for living room pole lamps (fig. 22; cats. 11–12). When the family began to occupy the house in the final weeks of 1937, they brought furniture from their cabin, including tree-stump side tables made from chestnut trees that had once stood on the property and well-worn easy chairs. New acquisitions included three-legged wooden chairs, which Liliane had purchased in Florence.[18]

As we saw in Chapter 1, the standard of taste that the Kaufmanns promoted in their store fostered a personalized eclecticism governed by the notion of quality. At Fallingwater, they applied this aesthetic in such a way that over the years Wright's furnishings became the unifying background for a colorful variety of folk items and fabrics, objets d'art, antiques, and modern pieces, including the remarkable series of chairs in the bedrooms by such designers as Jorge Ferrari-Hardoy, Finn Juhl, and Josef Frank. Wright was consulted about the potential locations of some items, but his word was not final.

The furnishings found in the house today reflect primarily the taste of Kaufmann jr., who defined the

collection conveyed to the Western Pennsylvania Conservancy in 1963 and monitored it until his death in 1989. He exercised greater scrutiny in the selection of objects than his parents had but maintained their spirit of diversity. A listing of the furnishings now displayed in his father's second floor bedroom illustrates the scope of his interests (fig. 25). The furnishings designed by Wright include the bed, the corner desk, a swivel lamp, and the shelving. The room has two chairs by other designers. One is a leather sling chair, known as the "Butterfly Chair," designed in 1938 by Jorge Ferrari-Hardoy, Antonio Bonet, and Juan Kurchan and manufactured by Knoll International. It is not known when the Kaufmanns acquired the chair, but Kaufmann jr. was certainly familiar with it by 1950, when he published it in his booklet *What Is Modern Interior Design?* The other piece is a wood armchair designed around 1936 by Josef Frank for the Swedish firm Svenskt Tenn. Frank organized an exhibition of Svenskt Tenn furnishings for Kaufmann's department store in 1951, and it is believed that the family acquired this chair following the exhibition. Among

Fig. 26. Fallingwater, 1939. Peter Blume. Oil on canvas, 10 × 14 in. The Kaufmanns collected and commissioned works by Peter Blume (1906–1992), and he was a guest at Fallingwater. This painting evokes the family's life at the house through an imaginative selection of characteristic details of the architecture and landscape. Shown at right are Edgar Kaufmann, his mother, and the family's dachshunds watching Liliane fly-fishing in Bear Run. As a surrealist touch, Blume repeated the scene in miniature underneath the upper terrace, between the masonry pier and the rhododendron. Unidentified collection. Frank Anderson Trapp, Peter Blume *(New York: Rizzoli, 1987), 72. Courtesy of Chameleon Books.*

*Fig. 27. Edgar Kaufmann, Liliane Kauf-
mann, and Edgar Kaufmann jr. (back to
camera) in the living room at Fallingwater.
This photo, likely taken shortly after the
completion of the house in 1938, shows
the tree-trunk tables and comfortable
armchairs the Kaufmanns brought from
their cabin. Courtesy of Kaufmann's.*

the two-dimensional pieces in the room is an undated oil painting from perhaps the late 1930s by
an Italian artist named Corrado Cagli, informed by
synthetic cubism and the abstraction of artists such
as Joan Miró. There is also a woodblock print by the
nineteenth-century Japanese master Andō Hiroshige,
which Wright gave to Kaufmann jr. in 1951. Among
the objets d'art displayed on the shelves are a Pima
Apache woven basket; a nineteenth-century stone-
ware jug made in Beaver County, Pennsylvania
(west of Pittsburgh); a vase designed in 1936 by the
Finnish architect and designer Alvar Aalto; and a
Tiffany candlestick.

As an ensemble, these elements convey an
image of the casual elegance of the Kaufmanns' life
at the house. Their many guests were treated to fine
china set without a tablecloth, good food and lively
conversation deftly coordinated by Liliane Kaufmann, and the unending sound of the falls accompanied from time to time by the clatter of the family's
dachshunds scampering across the polished flagstone floors (figs. 26, 27).

Soon after its completion, many critics hailed
Fallingwater as a masterpiece, and it entered the
consciousness of American high and popular culture
through a remarkable wave of publicity. In January
1938, photographs were exhibited at the Museum of
Modern Art and published in *Architectural Forum*
and two of the nation's most popular magazines,
Life and *Time*.[19] Flushed by this triumph, the Kauf-

manns forged ahead with a new project: the guest
house and servants' quarters. On 25 January 1938,
Kaufmann sent Wright a topographic map of the
hillside above Fallingwater along with a letter setting out requirements for a servants' wing and guest
rooms. The former was to include a garage for at
least four cars, four single bedrooms, a bathroom,
and a combination kitchen, laundry, and sitting
room. Accommodations for guests were to include
two single bedrooms, a double bedroom, and a bathroom.[20] Wright, preoccupied with the construction
of the Johnson Wax Administration Building and
Wingspread in Racine, Wisconsin, was slow to respond, despite Kaufmann's desire to begin construction as soon as possible. The Fallingwater guest
house and servants' quarters were built in 1939 by
Walter Hall, who had returned as contractor, but
delays from Wright's office persisted to such an ex-
tent that the buildings were nearly finished before
the working drawings were completed.

The layout of Fallingwater's third floor with its
dead-end gallery indicates that the Kaufmanns and
Wright had planned some kind of construction on
the hillside from the beginning. Given the absence
of parking at the house, it is likely that this was to
be the site of the garage and servants' quarters.
Although the program that Kaufmann outlined for
Wright was not complex, the site was challenging.
Shady Lane, a service road, defined the north edge
of the site. The hillside was steep and marked by

45

springs, boulders, and several large trees, including a 37-inch-diameter white oak. A two-story wooden cottage, which would be demolished, stood just below the road.

In contrast to the design of Fallingwater, which Wright set out with apparent ease, the planning of the servants' quarters and guest house required considerable study by Wright's apprentices, who presented revisions for his approval. The surviving drawings are laid out with the servants' wing aligned north-south and set slightly above the guest wing, which is aligned east-west along the contour lines. All also indicate the major trees on the site, notably the large white oak.

These drawings indicate three stages in the evolution of the design. What appears to be the earliest scheme, which would have been drawn in the spring of 1938, orients the garage eastward toward Shady Lane and establishes a grand entry sequence from the courtyard, descending steps around a hickory tree to a trellis-covered passage at the angle of the servants' quarters and guest house with lateral entrances to each, and then continuing down a canopy-covered walk to the bridge to the main house (see cat. 13). The plan of the servants' wing is similar in its essential features to what was built—garage and laundry room below; bedrooms, bath, and sitting room above—but the proposal for the guest house differs considerably from what we know today. A thick retaining wall forms the north edge of the house. Along it runs a corridor from which the sitting room, bedrooms, and bath open to the south. The south facade of the sitting room projects beyond the rest of the house, engaging the white oak and a terrace. On the east side of the house is a swimming pool that was to be fed by one of the natural springs.

The second scheme, which was presented to the Kaufmanns in May 1938, reoriented the garage to the west, as it is today, and eliminated the grand entrance (see cats. 14–15). This design suggests that guests were to be received at the main house. The organization of the guest house is similar to that in the first scheme except that the sitting room has been reduced in size and no longer projects toward the oak tree. Instead, this gesture is made by a curve in the covered walk.

The studio completed the schematic drawings for the definitive version at the end of January 1939

(see cat. 16). The changes reduced the number of bedrooms in the servants' quarters and greatly simplified the guest house so that it consisted of a large bedroom and rectangular sitting room separated by a bathroom. Elimination of the long corridor facilitated cross-ventilation through clerestory windows along the top of the retaining wall. The new version also placed the bridge farther down the slope so that it would enter the main house on the second floor. A tight, curving staircase at the end of the walkway accommodated the difference in height.

The comfortable scale and privacy of the guest house, its cross-ventilation, and above all its immediate proximity to the swimming pool were as attractive to the Kaufmanns as to their guests on hot summer days. Liliane Kaufmann especially would sometimes invite her friends to stay in the main house and retain the amenities of the guest house for herself.[21]

The servants' quarters suitably housed the Kaufmanns' personal staff and provided workspace for the laundry and other chores but did not solve some other problems encountered in running the house. The kitchen, for example, was small and lacked a space where servants could sit while on duty. On 2 November 1945, two months after the end of World War II, Kaufmann raised the matter in a letter to Wright and included a sketch proposing a room underneath his bedroom terrace. Wright agreed to the idea a few days later and promised to develop the scheme.[22] The work was undertaken the following summer.[23] The modest room is large enough for a table and chairs and is tucked between the masonry kitchen wall and the large boulder upon which Kaufmann's bedroom terrace rests. The enclosure is formed by two low masonry walls and a plate-glass window that wraps around the outside corner.

The Kaufmanns evidently found themselves entertaining on a more ambitious scale than they had first envisioned and considered the advantages a more formal dining room offered over the open area at the back of the living room. In 1947, Wright responded with a proposal that called for opening the exterior wall behind the existing dining table and the construction of a double-height, skylighted room that would occupy the driveway and utilize the face of the cliff as a rocky hanging garden (see cats. 17,

19–20). Part of the upper area of the room would have been occupied by the existing bridge to the guest house, which was to be transformed into an interior balcony. Underneath would be an area with built-in seating like that in the living room. The new dining table was to be a continuation of the old one but more than twice its size.

The extension into the driveway required a new arrangement of the principal vehicular access to Fallingwater, an issue that may have been in the minds of Wright and the Kaufmanns since the planning of the guest house. Wright proposed reversing the orientation of the garage to receive cars arriving from Shady Lane and widening the staircase between the servants' quarters and the guest house (see cat. 18). Visitors would descend the steps to the covered walkway and enter the main house through the second-story bridge. A steep service stairway offered a shortcut to the kitchen.

Although these revisions would not have altered the play of pier and cantilever that is the defining image of Fallingwater, they would have profoundly changed the way visitors would have moved through the house and, with the addition of the dining room, would have introduced an enclosed, vertically oriented space unlike any other room in the house. Nevertheless, Wright freely made the changes and went so far as to tell Kaufmann in a letter written on 1 August 1947 that "the idea of the Shady Lane entrance is working out economically and improves the whole place no end, I think."[24] This willingness to tinker with an acclaimed masterpiece was not an isolated instance in Wright's work and brings to mind the major changes he made in the entrance sequence of his own house, Taliesin, in 1925.

As the Kaufmanns' interests and needs evolved at Bear Run, they turned to Wright for other buildings. In 1940, they purchased the farm that bordered their property along Route 381. The new property included a barn, enlarged in 1943 and remodeled by the Western Pennsylvania Conservancy in 1968, and the existing frame farmhouse, built in 1871. Edgar Kaufmann had decided to develop a sizable dairy herd, which he would manage for a decade with more passion than wisdom. In 1948, Wright, who kept a dairy herd at Taliesin, wrote Kaufmann asking whether he could spare any Guernseys. Kaufmann replied that he had only Jerseys and added,

"Besides, my herd, due to my lack of knowledge how to handle this sort of project, has been, unfortunately, too inbred and I would not recommend them."[25]

In 1941, Kaufmann decided that he needed an additional farmhouse on the property and commissioned Wright to design it (see cats. 25–26). The proposed site has not been verified, but Wright's drawings suggest that it was to have been on the hillside in the vicinity of the older buildings. Wright responded to the slope by laying out the house on two levels: an L-shaped wing containing three bedrooms, kitchen, entry foyer, toolrooms, and springhouse, and below, a living/dining room lined with windows opening to a deep porch. A dramatic shed roof tied the two parts together.

In a letter to Kaufmann in April 1942, Wright estimated the cost of building both the farmhouse and a proposed gate lodge at $26,000 and remarked, "As building is now—under inflation (and will be for a long time) [it] is not very much."[26] For Kaufmann, however, that sum may have reminded him of the $20,000 that had been the initial estimate for what would become Fallingwater, and he declined to proceed with the project. The entry of the United States in World War II eight months later put the matter out of the question. After the war, Kaufmann commissioned a simple house from a local builder.

The gate lodge mentioned in Wright's letter was to have been located on Bear Run, upstream of Fallingwater (see cats. 21–22). The Kaufmanns may have commissioned it as an initial step in replacing the assemblage of buildings left over from the summer camp and perhaps as a consequence of the growing fame of Fallingwater, which by now may have required a more formal checkpoint to control visitors. Wright proposed a formidable barrier that would have spanned nearly the full width of the ravine with a high wall of coursed stone surmounted by the caretaker's house. Its windows and terrace were to be shaded by the broad eaves of a flat roof, and it would have been oriented to assure a clear prospect along the approach road. Like the farmhouse, this project likely was stalled by World War II.

Bear Run was not the Kaufmanns' only vacation spot. They traveled north to Canada during the hottest periods of the summer and southwest to California for respite from the cold damp of western

47

Pennsylvania's winters. In 1946, Edgar Kaufmann decided to build a house in Palm Springs, but instead of awarding the commission to Wright, he turned to Richard Neutra (1892–1970), the Viennese architect who had immigrated to the United States in 1923, worked briefly for Wright in 1924, and established himself in Los Angeles the following year. The circumstances by which Kaufmann and Neutra met

Fig. 28. Kaufmann house, Palm Springs, California, 1946. Richard Neutra, architect. Photo: Julius Shulman.

have not come to light, but the introduction may have occurred during one of Kaufmann's frequent visits to Los Angeles, facilitated perhaps by Paul Frankl, who had established his studio there in 1934. In any case, the planning of the house moved ahead rapidly, and Kaufmann and Neutra enjoyed each other's company. As construction began in the spring of 1946, Kaufmann enthusiastically reported on the progress to his son and added, "I find it very pleasant to be working with Mr. Neutra and he is calling me 'Mr. Henry Kaiser, the second' [the reference is to the American industrialist, then a household name as a great builder of wartime housing, matériel, and vast civic engineering works]." Neutra reciprocated this affection a year later in a letter to Kaufmann praising him as an understanding client.[27]

The house was bold and contrasted dramatically with Fallingwater (fig. 28). Whereas the design of the house on Bear Run echoed its setting, the desert house engaged its site through contrast and reflection. Neutra described it in the following terms:

an artifact, a construction transported in many shop-fabricated parts over long distance. Its lawns and shrubs are imports, just as are its aluminum and plate glass; but plate glass and aluminum, the water of the pool [also an import], all reflect the dynamic changes [in] the moods of the landscape. While not grown there or rooted there, the building nevertheless fuses with its setting, partakes in its events, emphasizes its character.[28]

When Wright learned of Kaufmann's infidelity, he did not take the news lightly. It was bad enough that Kaufmann had turned to another architect, but his selection of Neutra, with whom Wright had had a falling-out, was too much. In a letter to Kaufmann written on 17 June 1946, Wright angrily broke off their friendship. "Henceforth," he wrote, "you will never, as a Patron of the Arts, be in a position to help me with one hand and hurt me with the other, because I shall never trust my work to you again."[29] Kaufmann jr.'s tactful intercession, however, eventually mended the rift. Over the following months, the family provided legal assistance to the Frank Lloyd Wright Foundation, and Wright agreed to work on the addition to Fallingwater and Edgar Kaufmann's projects for downtown Pittsburgh (see Chapter 3).

During the winter of 1950–51, the Kaufmanns presented Wright with an opportunity to go head-to-head with Neutra by commissioning another house in Palm Springs. Their surviving correspondence on the subject is limited, but much of it is between Wright and Liliane Kaufmann. Boulder House, more than any of Wright's other commissions for the family, was for her (see cats. 30–31). "The house for the queen is designed," he wrote on 15 January 1951. "Boulder House it is. Feminine in essence; broad as the hills in feeling. I will get you out of the nasty nice cliché [the Neutra house] with a fine sweep."[30]

As its name suggests, Wright keyed the design of Boulder House to the boulder fields of Palm Springs. He also related the house to the rolling profiles of the surrounding mountains. In contrast to the orthogonal, sharp-edged lines of the Neutra house, Wright based Boulder House on curvilinear forms expressed in plan and elevation, and whereas the former emphasized manufactured materials— plate glass and aluminum—the latter featured coursed masonry walls and rounded copper roofs that could be imagined as being of the site. One feature especially intended to interest Liliane was a swimming pool that wrapped around the house and could be entered from a water gate inside her bedroom.

For Wright, the project offered an opportunity to explore a formal vocabulary that had become of interest to him a decade earlier with the project for the Lloyd Burlington house planned for the west Texas desert near El Paso and would develop in other commissions, but it also marked his way of trying to save the Kaufmanns' marriage, for Edgar and Liliane had separated. "Have cure for all your troubles," he wrote Kaufmann jr. on 1 February. A week later, on 9 February, he pursued the theme with Liliane:

I am sure you would all—Mother Father and Son—be delighted and brought together by what I've done for you all on the drawing boards.

It is not ordinary opus I have worked out but a prescription for genuine Kaufmann unity and happiness—real relief.

My heart goes out to you all with a great hope and meantime I am waiting for some favorable signs.[31]

Liliane did respond favorably and told Wright that she'd like to travel from Pittsburgh to Taliesin West to see the drawings. Meanwhile, Wright sought to secure her husband's interest. When Kaufmann, who was in residence at the Biltmore Hotel in Los Angeles, nibbled at the bait and asked whether the drawings could be sent, Wright sought to bring him to Taliesin: "Have ready to show you crowning work so will take no less than opportunity to present in person. Take your time."[32]

No dramatic reconciliation took place at Taliesin, but the Kaufmanns did take steps to build Boulder House. Between January and April, they purchased a lot and hired a local contractor who undertook some preliminary sitework, but the design for the house apparently was not developed beyond the schematic stage.

Wright was not misreading the Kaufmanns when he sought to link their personal affairs to architecture. They shared his belief in the power of architecture to touch people in profound ways. Acting on

that belief, Kaufmann jr. addressed the following inquiry to Wright on 2 September 1951:

Dear Mr. Wright: will you build a place of prayer at Bear Run? All three of us would like a focus of attention for the spiritual reality which we know underlies life and work and the joys we share here.

Nature is the great restorer, concentrated here to balance our city living. The dignity and beauty of your architecture gives us a way of life in and with nature, beyond our best dreams. Mother brings a choice of flowers and foods and comforts, Father brings broad scope of action and actualities, and I some ideas and music; all this combines into a rich life for which we are grateful and humbly so.

Yet black storm clouds clash around us, often within us, born of wrongs, blindness and sin that bind the world and with which we bind ourselves. We know that only by special efforts of will can we be restored from these stormy depths to peace and well-being, even here among many blessings. For this we would like a spot set aside.

Kaufmann jr. went on to say that he had been inspired to propose the project to his parents following a visit to Taliesin and the recently completed Unitarian Church in Shorewood Hills, a small municipality adjacent to Madison, Wisconsin. He added that this "oratory private in scale and carried out with perfection" should also be thought of as a feature that would be meaningful to future visitors to Fallingwater: "It would be well if then they saw that the artists and people of our times wanted the special music of spiritual renewal as well as all the other joys provided here."[33]

The idea sprang more from a personal spirituality than from any formal religious direction. Although the Kaufmanns were members of the Tree of Life Synagogue in Pittsburgh, they were not known to be particularly devout. The language of Kaufmann jr.'s letter to Wright, however, indicates a faith in revelation through introspection that relates closely to the architect's own views, which the younger Kaufmann had known of since his days as an apprentice at Taliesin.

Three weeks after the initial letter, Kaufmann jr. reported to Wright that he and his mother had examined possible sites for the chapel and that his father

49

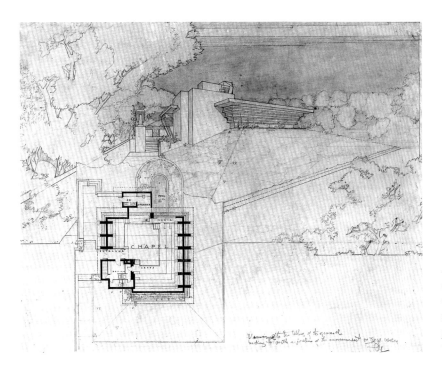

Fig. 29. Memorial to the Soil project, chapel for the Newmann family, Cooksville, Wisconsin, 1934. Perspective view and plan. Pencil on tracing paper, 22 × 25 in. The Frank Lloyd Wright Foundation, 3710.001.

was fully interested in the project.[34] Wright accepted the commission, and the studio produced schematic drawings dated 28 April 1952 (see cats. 27–29). He named the building the Rhododendron Chapel in reference to the lush growth of the plant along Bear Run. On one of the drawings he also included the subtitle, "'Private to the Beauty of Thought,' (Temple to Poetry for E J Kaufman)." In July, the Kaufmanns paid Wright's fee for the preliminary design, $4,000, which represented 10 percent of a projected budget of $40,000.[35] Liliane's suicide at Fallingwater six months later put an end to the project, although Wright did attempt to interest father and son in building it as a memorial to her.

The building is one of a series of small chapels that Wright designed throughout his long career, beginning in 1886 when he assisted in the construction of Unity Chapel, designed by Joseph Lyman Silsbee for the Lloyd Joneses in Wisconsin. Other examples include the project for a Unitarian Chapel (1887) in Sioux City, Iowa; the Pettit Memorial Chapel (1906) built in Belvedere, Illinois; and the Memorial to the Soil (1934) planned for the Newmann family near Cooksville, Wisconsin (fig. 29). All have simple programs consisting of a high-ceilinged room flanked by one or two smaller rooms.

The chapel Wright designed for the Kaufmanns has three parts: a broad, stepped terrace leading to the entrance; a rectangular room with seating for thirty; and a smaller, square reading room dominated by a large fireplace. The rooms are bounded on the sides by thick fieldstone walls that extend beyond the interior spaces and above by a broad, flat roof that becomes a steep, spire-topped gable of glass and copper panels over the main room. Deepset triangular windows illuminate the rooms from the side.

The site intended for the chapel has not been confirmed, but the information conveyed in the drawings regarding the slope of the terrain, the orientation of the entrance terrace, and the location of the rhododendron suggests that it may have been upstream of Fallingwater on the right bank of Bear Run, near the present location of the family crypt. Seen at a distance from the driveway leading to the house, its most striking features would have been the sharp horizontal of the copper-edged roof resting on the fieldstone walls and the crystalline panels of the steep gable.

The chapel was the last building Wright designed for Edgar and Liliane Kaufmann at Bear Run. In the months following his father's death in April 1955, Kaufmann jr., whose residency in New York precluded frequent visits to Bear Run, thought about how Fallingwater could be successfully transformed from a private retreat to more public usage.

50

In August, he asked Wright, then in his eighty-eighth year, to design a gate lodge complex on a site near the location of the present ticket booth that would include accommodations for visitors as well as staff. He proposed a fee schedule for Wright's work based on square-footage costs.[36] Wright accepted the commission but was of a different mind on the subject of fees:

> As to designing per square foot—that is the function of the "efficiency" architects running plan factories. Not in that class. However, as you know, I'll do my best to give you an economical design with the appropriate feeling for Fallingwater. If too expensive when estimated by reliable builders, will redesign or arrange under original fee. An honest architect is "an angel that can't do no more." Thanks for your good work on the *Testament* [published in 1957].[37]

Kaufmann jr. and Wright agreed to a not-to-exceed design fee of $4,500, and Kaufmann jr. sent a site plan and photographs to Taliesin. Swamped with other work, including the construction of a house (Kentuck Knob) for Mr. and Mrs. I. N. Hagan at Chalk Hill, just a few miles from Bear Run, Wright moved slowly on the commission. In December, he wrote Kaufmann jr., "Have started scheme so radical unwise to proceed without further cooperation from you if disinclined consider yourself free to proceed as you wish."[38]

Rejecting the approach informed by materials and formal elements of Fallingwater, which he had taken in the gate lodge project of 1942, Wright envisioned the new, "radical" scheme as a demonstration of the Usonian Automatic house, his most recent effort to systematize the building of moderate-cost residences. Usonian Automatics revived and simplified the textile block construction of thin concrete blocks reinforced by steel rods that Wright had developed in the 1920s. Beginning in the early 1950s, he promoted the system in lectures and publications, such as *The Natural House* (1954), as a way to lower the cost of labor by reducing the amount of work requiring highly skilled trade workers such as masons and plasterers. Indeed, much of the work, he argued, could be done by an owner with little more than the can-do spirit of G.I.'s returning from World War II and the Korean War.[39]

The enthusiastic tone of Wright's letter to Kaufmann jr. did not translate into action, and a year passed before a full set of drawings was ready for review. On 14 December 1956, Wright telegrammed Kaufmann jr.: "The champion Usonian is already to build according to a grouping you and I may devise. Where are you?"[40]

The drawing set dated 20 December 1956 called for three houses grouped closely together in an orthogonal arrangement around a garden court (see cats. 23–24). A large carport is to one side. The layout of the site and house represented in the plans is governed by a grid based on a 2-foot square. The houses are identical, except for the caretaker's residence, which has a workshop addition. Each house features a double-height living room bordered on two sides by the master bedroom, bathroom, and kitchen and, on a mezzanine, a second bedroom and an area that could be arranged for additional sleeping space or storage. The concrete block construction is revealed and articulated by glass inserts and a decorative cornice.

Kaufmann jr. decided to reduce the scope of the project and asked Wright to eliminate one of the guest houses. He added a 50-foot television tower, however.[41] The revised drawings, dated 10 April 1957, met with his approval, and Wright's studio completed working drawings the following September. The new scheme repositioned the buildings on the site so that they were set farther back from the approach road and so that the large corner living room windows had a southeastern exposure. Wright increased the distance between the guest house and the caretaker's residence but linked them with a pergola. The road to Fallingwater is marked by a pond, the television tower, and an iron gate. Kaufmann paid Wright's fee for the drawings but did not build the project. It was their final commission together.

2. The Kaufmanns' Country Houses at Bear Run and Palm Springs

3 *Kaufmann, Wright, and Pittsburgh*

"HELL WITH THE LID TAKEN OFF," is how the journalist James Parton described Pittsburgh in 1868.[1] Fifty-nine years later, H. L. Mencken assessed the city and its surroundings in even more disturbing terms:

> Here was the very heart of industrial America, the center of its most lucrative and characteristic activity, the boast and pride of the richest and grandest nation ever seen on earth—and here was a scene so dreadfully hideous, so intolerably bleak and forlorn that it reduced the whole aspiration of man to a macabre and depressing joke."[2]

Such observations were harsh but not without basis. Although Pittsburgh boasted a population of 669,817 residents in 1930 and possessed such positive features as splendidly housed cultural and religious institutions, large public parks, and impressive civic and commercial buildings in its downtown Golden Triangle, it continued to be plagued by horrific air quality, floods, and abysmal living conditions for many of its citizens. All of these problems were exacerbated during the years of the Great Depression. In 1934, one-third of the city's labor force was unemployed, and on St. Patrick's Day, 1936, a flood inundated most of the Golden Triangle, forcing 135,000 people from their homes.[3]

Frank Lloyd Wright, who rarely passed up an opportunity to point out the failings of American architecture and urbanism, found no lack of material to work with when he made a highly publicized visit to Pittsburgh in conjunction with the exhibition of his Broadacre City model at Kaufmann's department store in June 1935. "Pittsburgh," he wrote in an editorial published in the *Pittsburgh Sun-Telegraph*, "seems to have ignored all principle in getting itself born as a human asset." He went on to assert that by catering to the profit-driven demands of industry, the city's leaders had squandered the aesthetic potential of its hills and rivers and had failed to meet the most basic needs of its residents.[4] In an interview with the *Pittsburgh Post-Gazette*

Fig. 30. Edgar Kaufmann in his private office, 1940s. Courtesy of the Western Pennsylvania Conservancy.

sprinkled with similar comments, Wright suggested that "it would be cheaper to abandon it [Pittsburgh] and build another one. This is a disappearing city; nothing comes of it."[5] The phrase "disappearing city" came easily to him—it echoed the title of his book promoting the idea of Broadacre City, published in 1932.[6]

Pittsburgh journalists and officials responded to Wright's remarks in kind. "Frank Lloyd Wright," the *Post-Gazette* reported, "hailed as America's leading architect, lashed Pittsburgh with criticism of such a type that Pittsburghers may wonder whether his sharp words indicate culture or a bad case of indigestion."[7] If anyone suffered indigestion, however, it was probably Wright's sponsor, Edgar Kaufmann, who would have known that many prominent Pittsburghers would not react to the architect's pronouncements with a wink and a smile.

Kaufmann was among a growing number of businessmen and civic leaders who donated time and money to improving the city (fig. 30). Others included Andrew Mellon, who established the A. W. Mellon Educational and Charitable Trust in 1930, and the heirs of rival department store magnate Henry Buhl, who created the Buhl Foundation in 1927, which among its first ventures financed Chatham Village (1932–36), a model housing community in the city's Mount Washington neighborhood planned by Clarence Stein and Henry Wright (no relation to Frank Lloyd Wright).

The extended Kaufmann family participated in a variety of philanthropic activities. One of Edgar Kaufmann's four uncles, Henry Kaufmann (d. 1955), had founded the Irene Kaufmann Settlement in 1910, a social services center honoring his daughter, in the heart of the Hill District neighborhood heavily populated by Jewish immigrants.[8] Edgar's wife, Liliane, devoted herself to public health, and her work at Montefiore and Mercy Hospitals ranged from making policy in the board room to wrapping bandages in the emergency room.

Edgar Kaufmann's passion was physical planning. He was a board member of the privately funded Pittsburgh Regional Planning Association and a charter member of the influential Allegheny Conference on Community Development, founded in 1944, which spearheaded joint planning by the private and public sectors on issues such as flood control, air quality, and infrastructure.[9] In 1946, the governor of Pennsylvania appointed him to the newly formed Urban Redevelopment Authority, empowered to implement improvements.[10] Kaufmann's participation in these organizations was a matter of good business as well as personal interest because the future of his store depended on the vitality of the downtown business district. In the eyes of other committee members, his stature as a leading retailer made his endorsement a necessary step for any plans affecting the area.

During the Depression, Kaufmann was active in New Deal public works programs for Pittsburgh and Allegheny County, and these projects sparked some of his first known discussions with Wright. In the autumn of 1934, just as his son was joining the Taliesin Fellowship, Kaufmann invited Wright to serve as an architectural advisor to a county public works authority responsible for disbursing $24 million of federal funds earmarked for the construction of bridges, roads, a highway tunnel, and wharf improvements.[11] He urged Wright to visit Pittsburgh to become acquainted with the other members of the authority and the sites of the principal projects, and these matters were on the agenda for the architect's trip to the city in December, which was when Wright was taken for his first visit to Bear Run.[12] Wright, however, expressed reservations about working with Pittsburgh architects, and Kaufmann eventually dropped the matter.[13]

Merchant Prince and Master Builder

In addition to the public works projects, Kaufmann spoke to Wright about designing a planetarium on a lot adjacent to his department store, the site of the present parking garage. Their discussions continued into 1935 but apparently did not lead to any drawings.[14] Kaufmann's thoughts underlying the idea are not known. A planetarium would have been an unusual type of institution in downtown Pittsburgh—the city's other cultural attractions were in the Oakland district to the east—but its progressive, scientific character was in keeping with the store's promotional themes, and planetariums were a popular novelty in the mid-1930s. The Adler Planetarium in Chicago was built in 1930, and as Kaufmann and Wright discussed the subject, construction was under way on the Hayden Planetarium in New York. Wright had previously incorporated a planetarium in his unrealized designs of 1924–25 for the Gordon Strong Automobile Objective for Sugarloaf Mountain in Maryland.[15] Although Kaufmann did not pursue the project, Pittsburgh did receive a planetarium four years later, with money from the Buhl Foundation.[16]

Among the most pressing concerns of those planning Pittsburgh's future in the 1930s and 1940s was the redevelopment of the Point, where the Monongahela and Allegheny Rivers join to form the Ohio River (fig. 31). Wright no doubt had the fifty-nine acres adjacent to the central business district in mind when he accused the city's leaders of squan-

Fig. 31. The Pittsburgh Point, ca. 1940. The Allegheny and Monongahela Rivers at left and right, respectively, join to form the Ohio River. Courtesy of the Carnegie Library of Pittsburgh.

dering the natural surroundings. The site offered extraordinary views down the Ohio River and toward the Golden Triangle, but it was occupied by an unattractive and economically marginal jumble of old railroad yards, warehouses, an outdated exhibition building, and two ill-placed highway bridges crossing the rivers. Buried among the industrial buildings were traces of two eighteenth-century forts from the French and Indian Wars, the French Fort Duquesne and the English Fort Pitt, but only a small, derelict park at the tip of the Point com-

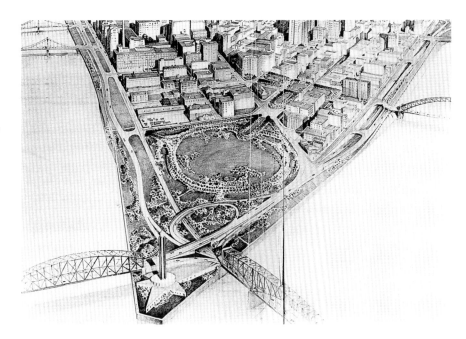

Fig. 32. Project for Point State Park, 1939. In a letter to Robert Moses, Wright wrote that he had a copy of the plan on his desk as he developed his own design for the Point. In both projects, a circular figure occupies the heart of the site. Wright's megastructure covers about the same area as the promenade proposed by Moses. Robert Moses, Arterial Plan for Pittsburgh (pamphlet printed for the Pittsburgh Regional Planning Association, 1939). Hunt Library, Carnegie Mellon University.

55

3. Kaufmann, Wright, and Pittsburgh

memorated the site's pivotal role in American colonial history. Although Pittsburgh faced many challenges that were more vital to the immediate health and welfare of its less-privileged residents, businessmen and politicians regarded the beautification of the Point as an essential step in preparing the city for the renewed growth expected in the future.

Several proposals for transforming the Point into a park were put forward in the 1930s.[17] In 1935, for example, the *Pittsburgh Sun-Telegraph* published a photograph and description of a project conceived by A. Marshall Bell, a former director of public safety, calling for a national monument, a museum, a meeting hall, green space, and parking facilities on 34 acres of the site.[18] In 1939, the Downtown Business Men's Association declared the creation of Point Park and improved traffic circulation in the central business district its highest priorities and endorsed a scheme that would include the relocation of the bridges and the construction of underground parking garages.[19] Later that year, the Pittsburgh Regional Planning Association published the arterial traffic plan it had commissioned from Robert Moses, who envisioned the site as a park featuring a circular promenade and a monument at the tip of the Point (fig. 32).[20] He planned to retain the bridges but reorganize the approach roads to improve the flow of traffic and to link the bridges with the Penn-Lincoln Parkway then being planned along the bank of the Monongahela River.

Federal, state, and local governmental agencies continued planning the redevelopment of the Point during the World War II years and clarified three goals: the creation of a park commemorating the site's history, improved traffic circulation through the construction of new roads and bridges, and designation of a portion of the site for new office buildings, intended to stimulate private investment in the Golden Triangle. In November 1945, the *Pittsburgh Post-Gazette* announced "Project Declared Within City's Immediate Grasp" and described how Richard K. Mellon, the president of the Pittsburgh Regional Planning Association, had turned over the plans, estimates, and technical reports it had commissioned over the years to Robert Doherty, the chairman of the Allegheny Conference, for implementation.[21] Doherty in turn assigned responsibility for this task to a twenty-eight-member Point Park Committee. Edgar Kaufmann was the committee's chairman.

A preliminary design for the Point had been prepared by a team composed of Charles Stotz (architect), Ralph Griswold (landscape architect), George Richardson (engineer), and Don McNeill (traffic engineer). It allocated 36.2 acres of the site for the park and reserved the remainder for high-rise commercial development, which became Gateway Center (built 1950–53). The program called for the reconstruction of Fort Duquesne, the restoration of the only remaining structure from Fort Pitt (the Block House), a museum, a fountain, a restaurant seating 350, a boat basin, parking for thousands of cars, and bridges connected to the Penn-Lincoln Parkway and surface roads. The projected cost was nearly $20 million, which included $4 million for land acquisition, $1.7 million for buildings and landscaping, and $14 million for the highway interchange and the bridges. An innovative combination of federal, state, and local sources was to pay for the project.

In light of the momentum this vision for the Point had gained over the years, it is surprising that Edgar Kaufmann chose this juncture to bring Wright into the picture. Given his decade-long friendship with the architect, he must have anticipated that Wright would challenge the prevailing wisdom and prolong the planning phase of the project. But that may have been exactly what he intended. As we shall see, Kaufmann advocated a more urban program for the Point than the park envisioned by the other leaders of the Allegheny Conference and the Urban Redevelopment Authority. He likely had some familiarity with Wright's 1938 proposal for a lakeside civic center in Madison, Wisconsin, and from building Fallingwater he certainly understood how Wright could manipulate architecture and landscape to create a work of art.

In 1946, Kaufmann arranged for Wright to meet with members of the Point Park Committee.[22] In what must have been a virtuoso performance, Wright began by describing how the Point could be developed as a civic center and then moved beyond it to explain how housing could be built on the steep hillside on the south bank of the Monongahela River and how an elevator-equipped tower downstream of the Point could rise from the riverbank to the summit of Mount Washington, which overlooks the Golden Triangle. Entranced by the presentation, and no doubt keeping their skepticism in check out of respect for Kaufmann and his pledge to personally underwrite the architect's fee of $25,000, the committee members approved further studies. They granted Wright a free hand to develop the civic center scheme but asked him to prepare a second, simpler treatment of the site as well.

Communication between Wright and Kaufmann ceased for a time in the summer and fall of 1946 following Wright's discovery that Kaufmann had commissioned Richard Neutra to build a house in Palm Springs (see Chapter 2), but Edgar Kaufmann jr. mediated their reconciliation, and by January 1947 Wright's studio had begun sustained work on the project for the Point. In February, Wright advised Kaufmann, "The magnum opus is thrown up to scale on the draughting board," and conceded, "It is good to be working with you once more before the inevitable drift to the beyond." He also asked for a check for $10,000.[23]

Kaufmann sent Wright information about the site and outlined an ambitious program for its development. He asked for 280,000 square feet of office space for federal, state, and community chest agencies; a 100,000-square-foot exhibition hall; a sports arena with a minimum of 16,000 seats; parking lots; and a performing arts center that was to include a 10,000-seat enclosable amphitheater and two smaller theaters of 1,000 and 300 seats.[24] All were prominent on the city's wish list, but the amphitheater was of particular importance to Kaufmann. His store was a major benefactor of the Pittsburgh Civic Light Opera, a popular summertime institution that performed under makeshift conditions in the University of Pittsburgh football stadium. Kaufmann dreamed of building a permanent home for the company along the lines of the St. Louis Municipal Opera's amphitheater, which had been renovated in 1939 to great acclaim for the beauty of its setting in Forest Park and the excellence of its technical facilities.

Wright was enthused by the project and crowed about being a city builder to Robert Moses, to whom he was related by marriage: "I want to thank you for the extraordinary (and futile) reports [the traffic plan of 1939] on the Pittsburgh you so kindly gave me

and that lies on my board as I write. How could you have left those goddam bridges where they are? No toothpicks could save them." Moses replied, "As to Pittsburgh—why argue? I bet you don't get tunnels." "Tunnels for Pittsburgh?" Wright exclaimed, "Yes and how! And if there is anything you haven't thought of for New York—see Pittsburgh."[25]

By mid-April 1947, Wright and his apprentices at Taliesin West had completed a set of drawings for the project, and on 6–7 May Kaufmann and two officials from the Allegheny Conference, Executive Director Park Martin and Executive Secretary Wallace Richards, traveled to Arizona to inspect the drawings. They saw that Wright had made good on his boast to Moses. His project, named the "Point Park Coney Island in Automobile Scale," transformed the Point into a civic center capable of holding one-third of the city's population (see cats. 35–39).

Wright planned to clear the site, demolish the existing bridges, and build new quays along the rivers. The focal point of the project was to have been a megastructure one-fifth of a mile in diameter and 175 feet high wrapped by a spiraling roadway. Attached to it were to have been multidecked cantilever bridges spanning the Allegheny and Monongahela Rivers, two smaller circular buildings with exterior ramps, and, extending westward toward the tip of the Point, a wing terminated by a 500-foot tower.

Immediately downstream of the bridges, Wright proposed two long, low office buildings set parallel to streets along the riverbanks. At the tip of the Point, he placed a circular building topped, like the megastructure, by a fountain. The open spaces were to contain a 15,000-seat "concert garden" and a zoo.

Like branches cantilevered from the trunk of a tree, the bridge structures tapered from their springing points as they crossed the rivers. Pedestrian, automobile, and truck traffic traveled on separate decks into the circular structure, where they would be channeled to the other bridge, the central business district, the spiral roadway, a loading zone for the principal auditorium, or parking lots.

Wright's design for the megastructure can be likened to a doughnut. The ring is the spiral ramp, which is cantilevered from finlike piers and supports a roadway on its outer edge and short-term parking areas and concession stands on its inside edge. The shops were to offer a variety of goods and services such as food, flowers, and books, resembling, in Wright's mind, "a county fair."

Within the ring are stacked lens-shaped structures anchored to massive pylons, which also serve as utility cores (see cat. 38). The structures vary in size and were to contain an opera house, three movie theaters, a convention hall, a planetarium, and at the top of the stack, a glass-domed sports arena. Combined, their capacity was to have been around 60,000 spectators. Wright linked these facilities to each other and to the outer ring by platforms and bridges offering interior views that would have been no less striking than those of the three rivers outside. The uppermost levels of the structure are given over to a winter garden and a "Sky Park" with landing facilities for helicopters and a garden planted with native trees and flowers.

Wright called the round flanking buildings "Fast Ramps." They were to provide an alternative to the long drive around the main ramp and elevators for pedestrians.

The wing linking the megastructure and the tower was to have been approximately ten stories tall. Its architectural character is defined by long, cantilevered balconies on each floor. The tower itself has a triangular plan echoing the shape of the Point and rises in two stages. The first stage was to contain approximately sixteen floors of offices, and the upper stage was to be equipped for displays of colored lights and music.

The low buildings parallel to the rivers were to have had two floors of offices and roof gardens raised above grade by slender piers. Along with the offices in the tower wing, they were to house the agencies specified in Kaufmann's program.

The circular building at the tip of the Point was to contain an aquarium displaying its specimens in large glass spheres, which could be viewed from encircling walkways above and below; an "insectorium"; a large restaurant; swimming and wading pools; and floating docks for pleasure craft (see cat. 39). Views through the building promised dramatic juxtapositions of the man-made aquatic environments with the natural scenery of the river valley.

The presentation to the Allegheny Conference officials was not a success. Wright's scheme far exceeded the scope they had envisioned, and questions of its economic and technical feasibility aside, it conflicted with the intentions of the Pennsylvania legislature to create a historical park on the site. Park Martin assumed the task of persuading Wright to prepare a simpler treatment and sent him a report with guidelines for commemorating the site's historical significance. Wright responded in no uncertain terms, criticizing the idea of reconstructing the old forts as maudlin. "But if among you," he concluded, "there is sufficient interest in a future for Pittsburgh not turned toward the grave (an empty sleeve of the G.A.R. [Grand Army of the Republic] past) but racing toward the recreation of a happy life for her citizens now and in future and I am so commanded, I will work."[26] Rhetorical flourishes aside, Wright raised an important issue regarding the use and meaning of Point Park that continues to have relevance today when tens of thousands of people crowd the area to attend an outdoor concert or fireworks display: Was the park to be a shrine marking an important episode of North American history or a place for recreation?

Kaufmann persuaded Martin to soften his position on the historical issues and Wright to return to the drawing board. On 19 July, Wright sent Martin a letter stating, "I'll play again—a simple melody but an organic harmony, I hope. Will work it out pretty soon."[27] About six months later, on 4 January 1948, representatives from the Allegheny Conference, Park Martin, Wallace Richards, and the engineer George Richardson, gathered at Taliesin West to inspect the new scheme.

It was no less striking than the first proposal (see cats. 40–43). A 1,000-foot tower, dubbed the "Bastion," anchored two cable-stayed bridges spanning the rivers. Although dramatically different in profile, the new scheme shared a number of features with its predecessor. Wright retained the first project's circular footprint and developed it as a platform elevating three "park bowls" and a promenade above parking and access roads. The "Fast Ramp" buildings of Scheme 1, reconfigured as office buildings, remained in their original positions, as did the circular building at the Point with its aquarium, restaurant, docks, and swimming pools. As before, the multidecked bridges were connected to a traffic interchange within the "Bastion," which would direct cars and trucks from bridge to bridge or into the city.

The surviving design studies for the "Bastion" scheme indicate that Wright had initially conceived the tower as a tall office building, named the Ohio Tower. In light of the request by Kaufmann and the Allegheny Conference for a simplified scheme, however, this was a building without a program. The decision to convert the bridges from cantilevers to stayed-cable structures apparently inspired the transformation of the building into a slender tower and broadcast antenna attached to a colossal cable-mooring. Extruded from an arrowhead-shaped plan, this sail-like mass supports a cantilevered observation deck and expressively anchors the cables supporting the bridges and two circular canopies, which shelter the "park bowls."

Scheme 2 was spectacular, and Allen Davison's rendering of the Point at night greatly impressed the delegation from Pittsburgh, but the drawings didn't win them over (see cat. 43). Park Martin's report to Kaufmann, who was ill and convalescing in the recently completed house Neutra had designed for him, was blunt:

> Mr. Wright's second study is dramatic, and while he calls it a "modest" treatment, it was Mr. Richardson's opinion that to do what Mr. Wright has portrayed would cost a minimum of $100,000,000 and would probably run more.
>
> . . . I think we all admitted that the conception and presentation were excellent, but the engineering, in Mr. Richardson's opinion, could not be carried out. The treatment of the traffic was entirely inadequate—in fact, his proposal simply could not be considered as everything was brought into the end of Liberty Avenue [in the Golden Triangle].[28]

The point regarding traffic was well taken, for Wright's scheme did not include the Penn-Lincoln Parkway.

On a more positive note, Martin did acknowledge that the project had some ideas worth pursuing. Wallace Richards elaborated these ideas in his letter to Kaufmann:

> I believe that serious consideration should be given to the possibility of taking his concept for an aquarium, placing it at the tip of the Point, building it below the surface level of the park, and placing above it the Civic Light Opera. The stage would be at the Point where a massive fountain could rise from the rivers behind the stage so that prior to the performance and after it there could be a display of water and color and music. The audience would face the stage and have the Ohio River as a vista. The possibility of a competition for park development plans will have to be given careful consideration, but on the other hand, if Wright were commissioned to do a specific job combining the aquarium and stadium within a specific area of the Park, we might get an even more expressive product of his genius.[29]

Richards seconded Martin's observations about traffic flow but emphasized that cost would be the most serious obstacle to realizing any of the proposals.

Wright's view of the meeting was characteristically upbeat. "Surprised the Allegheny Conference didn't tell you how really enthusiastic they all were on Scheme II," he wrote Kaufmann.[30]

A month later, Kaufmann responded to the reports in a letter to Wright in which he asked for a new proposal limited to an amphitheater for the Civic Light Opera on the site Wright had designated for the aquarium and restaurant. He outlined a specific scope of work including seating for 10,000 spectators facing the Ohio River, a large stage with lifts and a turntable, and provisions for dressing and rehearsal rooms, shops, and administrative offices. He concluded with a strong statement of his belief in Wright:

> I am only suggesting this so that if we are by-passed or delayed with the other projects [Schemes 1 and 2], this Point Park improvement could go forward. It is only because of my great affection for you and for your creative ability, that I want an example of your work in Pittsburgh, and if we can get it no other way, perhaps we can "bore in" as a starter with the above suggestion. What do you think about it?[31]

Kaufmann followed up these specifications with a more detailed list of requirements and other

59

3. Kaufmann, Wright, and Pittsburgh

information provided by the management of the St. Louis Municipal Opera. He had been particularly impressed by the complementary relationship of park setting and theater achieved there.

Wright responded to Kaufmann's proposal by requesting that it be covered by a new financial agreement. Without conceding the matter, Kaufmann sent another payment on the original account, and by April Wright reported that he had begun preliminary work on the amphitheater. On 13 June, he inquired about scheduling a date for the presentation, but two weeks later, Kaufmann asked him to halt work. The project was dead.

Kaufmann did not abandon his dream of a home for the Civic Light Opera. In 1949, he saw an opportunity for building an amphitheater in the East End of Pittsburgh, but this time he did not solicit Wright's assistance. Instead, he commissioned two local architects, Dahlen Ritchey and James Mitchell, to design a facility with a program similar to that which he had described to Wright. Kaufmann had known Ritchey since the 1930s, when the young graduate of the Carnegie Institute of Technology had worked in his store's decoration department. Following World War II, the firm of Mitchell & Ritchey had established itself as an advocate of modern architecture in Pittsburgh and was closely involved with projects sponsored by the Allegheny Conference and the Urban Redevelopment Authority.

Wright learned of Kaufmann's deed in January 1950 and warned him that Mitchell & Ritchey's scheme for the amphitheater would invite ridicule. As he had done in 1946, he lamented the end of their relationship:

> I realize that we will never build anything more together which is a genuine sorrow to me for I conceived a love for you quite beyond the ordinary relationship of client and Architect. That love gave you Fallingwater. You will never have anything more in your life like it because you seem to have changed greatly inside since then.[32]

Kaufmann, well accustomed to such chastisements, ignored these and other more vitriolic tirades and continued to work with Mitchell & Ritchey and with Wright.

In February 1952, Kaufmann agreed to merge his program for an amphitheater with the sports arena that the Urban Redevelopment Authority planned as the centerpiece of its transformation of the Lower Hill, an old residential district adjacent to the Golden Triangle with a large population of low-income African Americans, into "a modern Acropolis to rival the glory of ancient Greece." In addition to the 16,000-seat arena, which at Kaufmann's insistence was to have a retractable roof, the master plan for the area, designed by Mitchell & Ritchey, included apartment and office buildings, a hotel, schools, a symphony hall, theaters, and parking facilities.

The published renderings for the Lower Hill are scarcely less fantastic than those Wright's studio had prepared for the Point, as a local journalist noted, but unlike Wright's projects, the buildings could be developed piecemeal as funds permitted.[33] Despite a lack of private capital for funding the other elements of the plan, a problem that accounts for the acres of parking lots on the Lower Hill today, the Civic Arena, complete with a still-impressive stainless steel retractable dome, opened in 1961 at a cost of $22 million. Edgar Kaufmann donated the first $1 million but did not live to see the building completed. Unfortunately for the Civic Light Opera, the arena proved better suited for the presentation of sporting events than Broadway musicals, and the company used the facility for only six seasons.

The planning of the Lower Hill coincided with the construction of Point State Park and an adjacent commercial development, Gateway Center. The park's gardenlike character is a far cry from Kaufmann's vision of the Point as a populist center where grand opera could be found a few steps away from a hockey game and steel moguls would rub shoulders with mill workers, and he must have been disappointed by the failure of Wright's projects to stimulate sustained discussion and affect the planning of Point Park. Indeed, there are accounts by acquaintances that the plans were a source of embarrassment to him. Nevertheless, he permitted their exhibition when Wright lectured at the Carnegie Institute of Technology in 1949, and he participated in discussions regarding their acquisition by the Carnegie Institute's department of fine arts.

Wright's intellectual investment in the Point projects had less to do with the transformation of Pittsburgh than with giving form to the "automobile

60

objectives" of Broadacre City, his proposal for the resettlement of the United States, first described in the Princeton Lectures of 1930:

> To gratify what is natural and desirable in the get-together instinct of the community, natural places of great beauty—in our mountains, sea-sides, prairies, and forests—will be developed as automobile objectives, and at such recreation grounds would center the planetarium, the race track, the great concert hall, the various units of the national theater, museums, and art galleries. Similar common interests of the many will be centered there naturally, ten such places to the one we have now.[34]

Wright envisioned the "automobile objectives" as the social and cultural hubs of a decentralized America. The Point, with its majestic setting at the headwaters of the Ohio River and its role as a vital highway interchange, offered an ideal place to begin, for it amply accommodated the "get-together in-stinct of the community" yet readily allowed citi-zens to disperse freely in their vehicles across the bridges to their suburban homes.

Like the "automobile objectives" described in the Princeton Lectures, *The Disappearing City,* and Wright's other publications on the city, the Point projects were to be places of entertainment rather

than of government, and their domes marked sports arenas and aquariums rather than law courts and legislative chambers. Wright described the Point to the *Pittsburgh Sun-Telegraph* as "a good time place, a peoples' project."[35] In another description of Scheme 1, Wright stated that it "provides newly spacious means of entertainment for the citizen seated in his motor car Winter or Summer. A plea-surable use of the modern implement is here de-signed instead of allowing it to remain the trouble-some burden it has now become to the City."[36] Unlike the narrow streets of the Golden Triangle, which today, as in the 1940s, are best navigated on foot, Wright planned the Point for the automobile, at least in theory. Had his schemes for merging arte-rial and local traffic from the two bridges and the surface streets within the proposed structures been realized, the resulting traffic snarls likely would have been no less memorable than the architecture, which drivers and passengers would have had ample time to admire.

Wright's proposals for the Point characteristi-cally incorporated programmatic, compositional, and structural ideas explored in other projects. The complex program that Kaufmann presented to him related in various degrees to Wright's own schemes for the Gordon Strong Automobile Objective and Planetarium (fig. 33); the Steel Cathedral project of

61

Fig. 34. Monona Terrace Civic Center project, Madison, Wisconsin, 1938–53. Aerial perspective. Ink, pencil, and color pencil on tracing paper, 17¼ × 40 in. Like Scheme 1 for the Point, this project was located on an ill-used waterfront site and accommodated a complex program of governmental agencies and public amenities within a unifying structure. The Frank Lloyd Wright Foundation, 3909.002.

1926 for New York, which was to contain a "commercial arts festival" on its lower levels; the civic center designed in 1938 for Madison, Wisconsin, which included administrative and judicial facilities for the city and county, a public garden, an auditorium, a railroad station, parking lots, and boathouses (fig. 34); and the Crystal Heights apartments and retail center of the following year for Washington, D.C. The compositional theme of the spiraling ramp issued from the Gordon Strong project and the Guggenheim Museum (1943–59),

and the strategy of arranging functions in a stack of lens-shaped structures appears on a much smaller scale in Wright's project for the Huntington Hartford Play Resort (1947) in Hollywood, California (fig. 35). Furthermore, the office towers of Scheme 1 and the preliminary drawings for Scheme 2 relate closely to the projects for the residential St. Mark's-in-the-Bouwerie Towers (1927–31) in New York, a tower proposed for the *Century of Progress* exposition (1931) in Chicago, and the Rogers Lacy Hotel (1946–47) in Dallas (fig. 36).

Fig. 35. Sports club for Huntington Hartford project, Hollywood, California, 1946–48. Plan and elevation. Ink, pencil, and color pencil on tracing paper, 45⅝ × 74 in. The lens-shaped structures cantilevered from a core are conceptually similar to the theaters, convention center, and arena within the megastructure of Scheme 1; they also are related to the cantilevered observation decks of Scheme 2. The Frank Lloyd Wright Foundation, 4731.001.

62

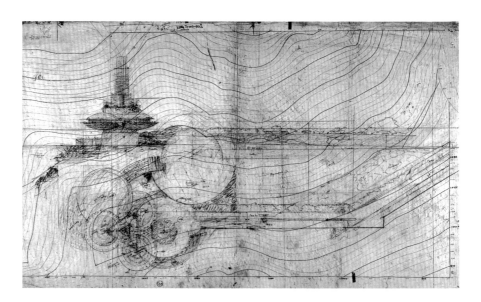

Innovative structural systems were integral to all of these projects. The bridges proposed for the Point, for example, illustrate how Wright's studio actively explored the rapidly developing technologies of reinforced concrete cantilevers and tensile construction in the 1930s and 1940s. They were designed alongside two other bridge projects: a Wisconsin River crossing near Taliesin, and a bridge across San Francisco Bay (fig. 37). All are variants of what Wright termed the "butterfly wing" system, which supported decking from a central, reinforced concrete girder that he likened to a butterfly's thorax supporting its outstretched wings. The Point Scheme 1, Wisconsin River, and San Francisco Bay bridges were conceived as self-supporting cantilevers, whereas the Point Scheme 2 bridges were cable-stayed designs, in which the deck structure was supported by diagonal cables attached to a single pier (the "Bastion"), unlike traditional suspension bridges, which suspended the deck from vertical hangers attached to cables moored by piers on both sides of the span (see cat. 42).

The technology for realizing the precast, prestressed, segmental construction that Wright envisioned had been available for only a decade, and the ideas of cantilevering decks from centrally placed girders and of cable-stayed suspension had become popular only at the end of World War II. A link between Wright's studio and these emerging technologies was the Czech structural engineer, Jaroslav Joseph Polivka (1886–1960).[37] Polivka was a designer of long-span concrete bridges and a specialist on photo-elastic stress analysis who had immigrated to the United States in 1938 and joined the faculty of

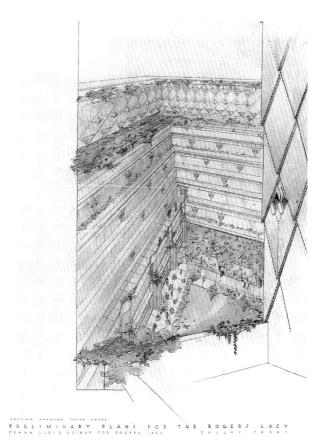

Fig. 36. Hotel for Rogers Lacy project, Dallas, 1946–47. Perspective view of atrium. Pencil and color pencil on tracing paper, 46 × 31 in. Scheme 1 for the Point would have had similar views within the megastructure. The Frank Lloyd Wright Foundation, 4606.011.

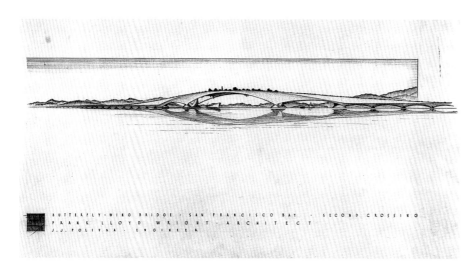

Fig. 37. San Francisco Bay bridge project, 1949–53. Perspective view. Ink, pencil, and color pencil on tracing paper, 23 × 42 in. Wright collaborated with engineer J. J. Polivka on the design of the bridge. The Frank Lloyd Wright Foundation, 4921.027.

63

3. Kaufmann, Wright, and Pittsburgh

the University of California at Berkeley. Around 1946, Wright engaged him to calculate the shell structure of the ramp for the Guggenheim Museum and to assist with the structural design of the Johnson Wax Research Tower and the Rogers Lacy Hotel.

Polivka did more than crunch numbers for Wright. He initiated the San Francisco Bay bridge project, and its design was a collaboration. Moreover, he enriched Wright's intuitive understanding of structure and provided the studio with technical information drawn on his own experience and his network of colleagues in France, Spain, and Germany. In a memoir, he recounted introducing Wright to the Spanish engineer Eduardo Torroja Minet, a pioneer in reinforced-concrete-shell structures. Wright's admiration for both men was such that he saluted them in the legend accompanying the rendering of the Illinois mile-high skyscraper project of 1956.[38]

Wright pursued his interest in unconventional structures based on tensile construction and reinforced concrete in his next large-scale project for Edgar Kaufmann. "Perhaps at last we may be able to have one of your buildings in Pittsburgh," Kaufmann wrote Wright on 25 August 1949. "This would be a great thing after all our attempts. This time we need a really practical job, and need it soon. I think it may appeal to you; and if it does, I know we will have a real opportunity to show people how things can be done properly and beautifully."[39] What Kaufmann had in mind was a structure across the street from his store (the site of the planetarium proposed fifteen years earlier) that would include basement and ground floor sales areas and five levels of parking for more than one thousand cars. The cost was not to exceed $2 million. Kaufmann requested completion of the preliminary designs in four to six weeks and offered Wright a fee of $20,000.

Wright accepted the commission and took the schedule to heart. On 30 September, he informed Kaufmann that a set of drawings was ready for inspection and shortly thereafter sent them to Pittsburgh (see cats. 44–45). He proposed a circular structure consisting of concentric ramps organized into 104,595 square feet of retail space on two levels and parking for 1,106 cars on six levels. The center was a hollow core with a fountain on the ground floor underneath a skylight enclosing the retail levels.

Flanking it were elevator shafts and four slender structural piers rising the full height of the building. Around these elements wrapped a ramp for pedestrians, two ascending ramps linked with parking spaces, and, along the circumference, a descending exit ramp. A waiting room futuristically equipped with a large-screen television accommodated bored family members waiting for shoppers. Pedestrian access to the main store across Forbes Avenue was assured by a tunnel and a bridge.

To reduce obstacles impeding traffic circulation and to maximize the area available for parking and retail sales, Wright employed a tensile structural system in which the reinforced-concrete ramps were supported by steel cables attached to the central piers, thereby eliminating the need for internal columns. Concerns about stabilizing the structure may have led him to develop a variant scheme that added buttressing piers at the corners.

Kaufmann retained engineering and architectural consultants, including Mitchell & Ritchey, to review Wright's plans, and their reports identified numerous problems. Among these were low clearances, awkward layout, and inadequate ventilation in the retail areas; insufficient turning room and hazardous traffic patterns on the parking ramps; and questions about cost. Wright responded to Kaufmann's summary of these issues by reminding him that his drawings represented preliminary thoughts and that the problems would be rectified in the next stage of development. He also rejected Kaufmann's recommendation that he retain Mitchell & Ritchey to manage the project—it was around this time that he learned that Kaufmann had employed the firm for the Civic Light Opera amphitheater—and offered instead to work with Peter Berndtson, a former Taliesin fellow practicing in western Pennsylvania. Kaufmann decided not to pursue the commission, however, and returned the drawings to Wright in March 1950.[40]

Over the following year, the Kaufmanns and Wright exchanged visits, including a trip by the architect to Pittsburgh, where he lectured at the Carnegie Institute and took advantage of the publicity to rebuke the city fathers for ignoring the Point projects. They also designed the Boulder House (see Chapter 2) and, as always, worried about the deflection of beams at Fallingwater. In the late summer

64

Fig. 38. Grandview Avenue, Pittsburgh, 1928. This view is several blocks east of Wright's site for the Point View Residences, but it illustrates the modest character of the neighborhood at the crest of Mount Washington and the steep slope (at left) descending to the Monongahela River. Image courtesy of the Pittsburgh City Photographer Collection, Archives of Industrial Society, University of Pittsburgh.

and fall of 1951, they commissioned the Rhododendron Chapel (see Chapter 2) and also began discussions about a new project for Pittsburgh, the Point View Residences.

This was to be a luxury apartment building located on the crest of Mount Washington that would overlook the central business district and the Point (fig. 38). Unlike the neighboring houses and shops oriented toward Grandview Avenue, it faced away from the street and toward the magnificent prospect that was becoming increasingly visible as a result of recent smoke-control ordinances.

Although the commission was handled personally by Kaufmann and his son, nominally it was an investment venture of the Edgar J. Kaufmann Charitable Foundation and Trust, the family's philanthropic foundation. Among the intended beneficiaries was Wright's own foundation, which was to receive 50 percent of profits realized from apartment rentals.

The Kaufmann Charitable Trust had taken steps to acquire the site by September 1951, and Wright completed a set of presentation drawings the following June (see cats. 46–47). He proposed a fourteen-story reinforced-concrete building clasped to the steep hillside by massive retaining walls and a structural spine from which he cantilevered thirteen

residential units: six duplexes and six flats paired on each side of the spine and a penthouse at the top for the Kaufmanns. Wright's point of departure for the scheme was his project for the Elizabeth Noble Apartments designed in 1929 for a hillside in Los Angeles, but the Pittsburgh site was far steeper.

Distracted by worsening health and marital problems, Edgar Kaufmann was unable to sustain his enthusiasm for and attention to the projects and relied increasingly on his son to work out details with Wright.[41] Kaufmann jr. reviewed the plans for the Point View Residences at his home in New York. Unlike the projects for the Point and the parking garage, which did not advance beyond a schematic level, these plans were sufficiently detailed for him to respond to such specific issues as closet space, lavatory fixtures, and exterior finish materials.[42]

Liliane Kaufmann's death in September 1952 put the project on hold, but the following January, Kaufmann jr. authorized the preparation of working drawings. Wright assured him that they would be completed so that construction could begin in the spring.

Within a few months, however, the prospects for realizing the building had dimmed. Despite the spectacular views it offered, Mount Washington was not a neighborhood favored by the wealthy families the Kaufmanns had hoped to attract as tenants. In an effort to enhance the building's economic viability, they requested Wright to prepare a new design that would conform to construction costs of about $20 a square foot and a budget of $1 million. Wright agreed and cited the contemporary H. C. Price Company Tower (1952–56) in Bartlesville, Oklahoma, as evidence of his ability to work within such constraints.

In the new plans (see cats. 48–49), Wright replaced the orthogonal layout of the earlier scheme with a triangular organization that allowed him to tuck more of the building into the hillside, thereby reducing foundation work and guaranteeing each apartment a view of the Golden Triangle. With the exception of the penthouse, which remained a duplex, each of the eleven other apartments now occupied a single floor with an area of about 3,000 square feet. They would be, Wright assured the Kaufmanns, "the peak of luxurious character in the world."[43]

65

3. Kaufmann, Wright, and Pittsburgh

Discussions about the plans continued through the end of the year, with major issues being the choice of structural materials—reinforced concrete, favored by Wright, or steel, favored by the Kaufmanns' advisors in Pittsburgh—and, typically, disagreements over fees. Specifications and working drawings were completed, but the project was abandoned in 1954 due to unfavorable economic conditions and tensions among family members and the trustees of the Kaufmann Charitable Trust.

While working on the Point View Residences, Wright and Kaufmann flirted with one other project for Pittsburgh. During the summer of 1953, they corresponded about the design of a new building for the Carnegie Institute's art museum. In August, Kaufmann informed Wright, who was in the midst of obtaining building permits for the construction of the Guggenheim Museum, that Gordon Bailey Washburn, the museum's director, was planning a trip to Taliesin to discuss the project. "Washburn," Kaufmann wrote, "has a unique idea of how to present Fine Arts and is interested in your conception of a building following his idea." Kaufmann stated that his charitable trust would pay Wright $15,000 for a preliminary design that Washburn could present to the Mellon Educational and Charitable Trust in October. Despite the initial optimism, the project never got off the ground, and in mid-September, Kaufmann's secretary informed Wright that it had been canceled due to lack of funds.[44]

The more than twenty years of time, energy, and money that the Kaufmanns and Wright invested in their projects for Pittsburgh did not yield a completed building or even a ground-breaking ceremony. Wright chided the family—Edgar Kaufmann, especially— for losing the conviction that had sustained them in realizing Fallingwater, and there was merit to his position in light of the on-again, off-again experiences he had had with the other buildings they proposed for Bear Run. However, the financial dimensions of even the most modest of the Pittsburgh projects, the Point View Residences, were an order of magnitude greater than the work at Fallingwater and required the cooperation of parties outside the Kaufmann family. Had the timing of the Point View Residences project not coincided with the tragedies in the Kaufmanns' personal lives, it is imaginable that the family could have wielded sufficient clout to secure the financing and building permits, but the marketability of the apartments likely would have remained a long-term problem.

The projects themselves occupy a problematic area of Wright's oeuvre and have received mixed reviews from those who have tried to assess them. For example, Robert McCarter's recent monograph on the architect presents the schemes for the Pittsburgh Point as the unfortunate products of a studio environment lacking mechanisms for rigorous self-criticism. Neil Levine, the author of another recent study of Wright, has viewed them in more positive terms alongside the fantastic speculations of other architects about the future of the city in the nuclear age.[45] On McCarter's behalf, it certainly is accurate to note that Wright's attention was divided among many obligations in the studio and elsewhere during the late 1940s and early 1950s, and there is no denying that the Pittsburgh Point projects, which were developed primarily by apprentices, left many important issues unresolved and perhaps unconsidered. Although they do not hold up well under close scrutiny as representations of all-but-realized buildings, they make more sense, as we have seen, as sketches for the idea of Broadacre City and the new way of life it was to offer.

Visionary architecture typically is thought of as a personal creation of the architect. Le Corbusier's projects of the 1920s for Paris and Louis Kahn's schemes of the mid-1950s for Philadelphia, for example, were statements made independently of clients or mandated programs. Wright's projects for Pittsburgh are unusual in that they were commissioned and informed by the active participation of the Kaufmanns. The drawings articulate both his own vision of Broadacre City and Edgar Kaufmann's desire for a more humane Pittsburgh.

"As an 'Idea Man,'" Wright wrote Kaufmann in 1948, "you would soon fashion a new-world, with my help."[46] The making of a new world was beyond the grasp of both the master builder and the merchant prince, but the drawings they created together remain testimonies to their effort.

I. THE KAUFMANNS, WRIGHT, AND GOOD DESIGN

1. Telegram, Wright to Kaufmann jr., 4/16/55: Index K118D04. Correspondence in the collection of the Frank Lloyd Wright Archives at Taliesin West in Scottsdale, Arizona, is identified by the microfiche number published in Anthony Alofsin, ed., *Frank Lloyd Wright: An Index to the Taliesin Correspondence*, 5 vols. (New York: Garland, 1988). All quotations cited herein of the correspondence of Frank Lloyd Wright and the office of Frank Lloyd Wright are © 1999 The Frank Lloyd Wright Foundation. Courtesy The Frank Lloyd Wright Archives.

2. The biography of Wright that best captures his interactions with patrons and clients is Meryle Secrest, *Frank Lloyd Wright* (New York: Knopf, 1992). For accounts of Martin, Barnsdall, and Johnson, see Jack Quinan, *Frank Lloyd Wright's Larkin Building: Myth and Fact* (Cambridge, Mass.: MIT Press and Architectural History Foundation, 1987); Kathryn Smith, *Frank Lloyd Wright: Hollyhock House and Olive Hill* (New York: Rizzoli, 1992); Jonathan Lipman, *Frank Lloyd Wright and the Johnson Wax Buildings* (New York: Rizzoli, 1986).

3. There is no biography of the Kaufmann family and no archive on its members apart from fragmentary collections at the Avery Architectural and Fine Arts Library at Columbia University, New York; Fallingwater; and the Frank Lloyd Wright Archives. Much research on Edgar Kaufmann and his architectural patronage before Fallingwater has been done by Franklin Toker, who shared with me his unpublished manuscript, "Mr. Kaufmann, Mr. Wright, and the Origins of Fallingwater." Toker is the author of the forthcoming book, *Fabricating Fallingwater: How Frank Lloyd Wright and Edgar Kaufmann Conjured Up the Most Famous House in the World*. Kaufmann and his brother-in-law, Irwin Damasius Wolf, were the subjects of a profile titled "Seller's Market: In War Kaufmann's of Pittsburgh, Like All U.S. Department Stores, Has Sold Everything It Could Buy. It Expects to Sell More," in *Fortune* 30, no. 5 (November 1944): 122–31. For a colorful account of Kaufmann's private life, see Leon Harris, *Merchant Princes: An Intimate History of Jewish Families Who Built Great Department Stores* (New York: Harper & Row, 1979), 91–111.

4. I thank Joan K. Mendelsohn, Mary Michaely, and Darthea Speyer for sharing their memories of Liliane Kaufmann with me.

5. Tillie Speyer, Darthea Speyer's mother, was one of Liliane Kaufmann's closest friends. Her son, A. James Speyer, was a friend of Edgar Kaufmann jr. James studied architecture with Ludwig Mies van der Rohe and became a successful architect, curator, and exhibition designer.

See *A. James Speyer: Architect, Curator, Exhibition Designer*, exh. cat. (Chicago: Arts Club of Chicago, 1997).

6. Kaufmann & Baer's was later acquired by Gimbel's.

7. Kaufmann profile in *Fortune*, 124.

8. Ibid., 124.

9. For a well-documented, incisive account of developments in American retailing during the first half of the twentieth century, see William Leach, *Land of Desire: Merchants, Power, and the Rise of a New American Culture* (New York: Random House, 1993). Leach addresses the founding of business research centers and training programs in chap. 6.

10. Leach, 162–63.

11. Ibid., 157–58.

12. The following account is based on information found among papers from the Oliver Kaufmann Estate conserved at Fallingwater.

13. On the topic of design in the United States in the 1920s, see Karen Davies, *At Home in Manhattan: Modern Decorative Arts, 1925 to the Depression*, exh. cat. (New Haven, Conn.: Yale University Art Gallery, 1983); R. Craig Miller, *Modern Design in the Metropolitan Museum of Art 1890–1990* (New York: Metropolitan Museum of Art and Abrams, 1990); Jeffrey L. Meikle, *Twentieth Century Limited: Industrial Design in America, 1925–1939* (Philadelphia: Temple University Press, 1979).

14. Miller, 8–32.

15. The exhibition is documented by photographs and advertising copy conserved by the Media Center of Kaufmann's department store. I thank Carole S. Mazzota for allowing me to work with this material.

16. "Good Design Is Good Business: Not Utility Alone, but Design Befitting the Motif of the Age, Will Determine Products' Selling Success," *Dry Goods Economist* (4 August 1928): 11–12, 82.

17. Isabel Hamilton, "Ignorance & the Right to Modern Art," *Dry Goods Economist* (22 September 1928): 60.

18. "50,000 Pittsburghers Enthuse over Kaufmann's Aircraft Exhibit," *Dry Goods Economist* (7 July 1928): 17.

19. Kaufmann's Media Center, *Storagram*, anniversary issue (June–July 1929).

20. In 1929, for example, Bach's department at the Metropolitan Museum of Art assisted Lamson's department store in Toledo, Ohio, in setting up a program to teach buyers, managers, and salespeople the principles of design. The classes included a session at the art museum and in-store demonstrations of how to apply good design principles in product selection and sales techniques. "Lamson

Executives Cash in on Art in Relation to Merchandise," *Dry Goods Economist* (4 May 1929): 18.

21. By 1931, AUDAC had 114 members, including interior designers, architects, textile designers, ceramists, photographers, and graphic designers. Most of the members were based in the New York area, but the organization had branches in Chicago and Los Angeles. AUDAC presented exhibits of its members' work in 1930 and 1931 and published one book, R. L. Leonard and C. A. Glassgold, eds., *Modern American Design by the American Union of Decorative Artists and Craftsmen* (New York: Ives Washburn, 1930). It contains essays by Lewis Mumford, Kem Weber, Paul Frankl, M. D. C. Crawford, Lee Simonson, Richard Bach, Frank Lloyd Wright, Hugh Ferriss, Norman Bel Geddes, M. F. Agha, Edward Steichen, and Glassgold. On Frankl, see Matthias Boeckl, "Die Reform der Form: New Yorker Art Déco-Design am Beispiel von Paul Theodore Frankl und Wolfgang Hoffmann," in Matthias Boeckl, ed., *Visionäre & Vertriebene: Osterreichische Spuren in der modernen amerikanischen Architektur* (Vienna: Ernst & Sohn, 1995), 86–95; and Davies, 34, 49, 68.

22. Paul T. Frankl, *New Dimensions: The Decorative Arts of Today in Words & Pictures* (1928; reprint, New York: Da Capo, 1975), 15–16.

23. Ibid., 59.

24. Ibid., 58.

25. Ibid., 66–67.

26. The graphic design for this campaign, which ran from approximately 1947–49, was by Paul Rand. See Yusaku Kamekura, ed., *Paul Rand: His Work from 1946 to 1958* (New York: Knopf, 1959), 54–55.

27. Paul T. Frankl, *Form and Re-Form: A Practical Handbook of Modern Interiors* (1930; reprint, New York: Hacker, 1972), 11.

28. The Frank Lloyd Wright Archives hold letters and circulars from AUDAC to Wright. On 9 August 1928, Frankl wrote Wright announcing that AUDAC had named him an honorary member: *Index* F002A04. Dues were the subject of a letter from C. Adolf Glassgold on behalf of Frankl to Wright, 6/25/29: *Index* A005A03. Frank Lloyd Wright, "Principles of Design," in Leonard and Glassgold, *Modern American Design*, 101–4.

29. Wright was the guest of honor at a dinner sponsored by AUDAC on 26 February 1929 and spoke about his exclusion from planning for the upcoming *Century of Progress* exposition in Chicago. Announcement: *Index* A004C01. On 11 October, he was the guest speaker at an AUDAC luncheon. Announcement: *Index* A005D01.

30. I thank Albert M. Tannler for sharing research on the remodeling of Kaufmann's that will appear in chaps. 7–8 of his forthcoming book, *Richardsonian to Modernist: Some Pittsburgh Buildings and Places, 1886–1936*.

31. For Urban, see Randolph Carter and Robert Reed Cole, *Joseph Urban: Architecture, Theatre, Opera, Film* (New York: Abbeville Press, 1992). For Urban's work in Pittsburgh, see Tannler, chap. 7. Urban's projects for Kaufmann's and the William Penn Hotel are preserved in the Joseph Urban Collection, Butler Library, Columbia University.

32. Albert Christ-Janer, *Boardman Robinson* (Chicago: University of Chicago Press, 1946), 51.

33. Ibid., 50–51.

34. For a brief introduction to mural painting from the 1910s to the Depression, see Milton W. Brown, *American Painting: From the Armory Show to the Depression* (Princeton, N.J.: Princeton University Press, 1955), 25–26.

35. Henry Adams, *Boardman Robinson: American Muralist & Illustrator, 1876–1952*, exh. cat. (Colorado Springs: Colorado Springs Fine Arts Center, 1996).

36. The ten murals have the following subjects: *The Persians and Arabs—Before the Christian Era; The Carthaginians on the Mediterranean—Dawn of the Christian Era; Venetians in the Levant—End of the Middle Ages; The Portuguese in India—The Fifteenth Century; The Dutch in the Baltic—The Sixteenth Century; The English in China—The Seventeenth Century; Slave Traders in America—The Eighteenth Century; The Clipper Ships—First Half of the Nineteenth Century; American Internal Trade—Late Nineteenth Century; Trade and Commerce in the United States—The Twentieth Century*.

37. A large-screen television viewing room was a feature of Wright's proposed parking garage of 1949 (see Chapter 3).

38. "'Radical' Is the Only Name for New Kaufmann Layout," *Dry Goods Economist* (10 May 1930): 59.

39. Miscellaneous correspondence regarding the festivities are conserved in Kaufmann's Media Center, file "Boardman Robinson Murals 1931." The essay contest was announced in an advertisement in *Fortune* 1 (June 1930): 30. The winner, Catherine K. Bauer (1905–1964), then closely associated with Lewis Mumford, soon became widely known as a leading advocate for housing reform. Her essay was published as "Prize Essay: Art in Industry," *Fortune* 3 (May 1931): 94–96, 101–2, 104, 109–10.

40. Typed manuscript in Kaufmann's Media Center, file "Art in Industry 1931" (this file contains material from 1926–35). Portions of this text were published in the special "Kaufmann's Supplement" of the *Pittsburgh Sun-*

Telegraph, Sunday, 11 May 1930. Edgar Kaufmann's authorship of the manuscript has not been confirmed.

41. Edgar Kaufmann jr., *Fallingwater: A Frank Lloyd Wright Country House* (New York: Abbeville Press, 1986), 35. On Vally Wieselthier, see Davies, 93.

42. Kaufmann's Media Center, *Storagram,* anniversary issue (June–July 1929), 42.

43. See Maria Welzig, "Entwurzelt: Sobotka, Wlach und Frank in Pittsburgh und New York," in Boeckl, 200–223.

44. Little is known of László Gábor, but anecdotal memories of those who knew him indicate that he was an important conduit of progressive ideas from Europe to Pittsburgh. See Welzig, 202. His influence on A. James Speyer has been noted by Franz Schulze, "Speyer's Life and Career," in *A. James Speyer:* 8–9. See also Bernard Rudofsky, *Architecture Without Architects: A Short Introduction to Non-Pedigreed Architecture* (1964; reprint, Albuquerque: University of New Mexico Press, 1987).

45. See Kristina Wängberg-Erikson, "Life in Exile: Josef Frank in Sweden and the United States, 1933–67," in Nina Stritzler-Levine, ed., *Josef Frank, Architect and Designer: An Alternative Vision of the Modern Home,* exh. cat. (New Haven, Conn.: Yale University Press for Bard Graduate Center for Studies in the Decorative Arts, New York, 1996), 71.

46. I thank my colleague, Christopher Long, for his patient instruction on the *Wiener Wohnkultur.*

47. Christopher Long, "The Wayward Heir: Josef Frank's Vienna Years, 1885–1933," in Stritzler-Levine, 56.

48. Frankl, *Form and Re-Form,* 123.

49. Edgar Tafel, *Years with Frank Lloyd Wright: Apprentice to Genius* (1979; reprint, New York: Dover, 1985), 1–2. The Kaufmanns may have had some familiarity with Wright's ideas from his article, "'Broadacre City': An Architect's Vision," *New York Times Magazine,* 20 March 1932, 8–9.

50. Lewis Mumford gave the model a favorable review in his column, "The Sky Line," *New Yorker* 11 (27 April 1935): 79–80.

51. Following the exhibition in Pittsburgh, the model was displayed at the Corcoran Gallery in Washington, D.C., where it was seen by invitation only.

52. "Home Owners' Utopia! Future Housing Shown," *Pittsburgh Sun-Telegraph,* Tuesday, 18 June 1935, 8; "M'Nair Scoffs at 'Model City,'" *Pittsburgh Post-Gazette,* Thursday, 20 June 1935, 15.

53. See Anthony Alofsin, "Broadacre City: The Reception of a Modernist Vision," *Center: A Journal for Architecture in America* 5 (1989): 5–43. A concise description appears in K. Paul Zygas, "Broadacre City as Artifact," in Herberger Center for Design Excellence, *Frank Lloyd Wright: The Phoenix Papers.* vol. 1. *Broadacre City* (Tempe: Arizona State University, 1995), 16–30. For observations by one of the attending apprentices, see in the same publication John Meunier, "A Model for the Decentralized City: An Interview with Cornelia Brierly," 32–46.

54. L. Frank Baum's books on the Land of Oz became a fixture in popular culture during the first years of the century. See Leach, 248–60.

55. See Christopher Wilk, *Frank Lloyd Wright: The Kaufmann Office* (London: Victoria & Albert Museum, 1993). Following Edgar Kaufmann's death, Kaufmann jr. removed the office from the store and had it reinstalled in the offices of the Edgar J. Kaufmann Charitable Foundation and Trust in the nearby First National Bank Building, which stood on the site of the present Pittsburgh National Bank Building (1972). It remained there until 1963, when Kaufmann jr. had it disassembled and placed in storage. He offered it to the Victoria & Albert Museum in 1972, and the museum created a permanent installation for it in 1993. Wilk, 83–85.

56. Ibid., 42–43.

57. Ibid., 54–55.

58. Ibid., 55.

59. Wolf to Wright, 4/14/38: *Index* K044A09; Wright to Wolf, 4/26/38: *Index* K044B06; Wolf to Wright, 5/17/38: *Index* K044D04.

60. Kaufmann jr. to Eugene Masselink, 8/13/38: *Index* K045D06.

61. Masselink to Kaufmann jr., 8/20/38: *Index* K046A01.

62. Kaufmann jr. to Masselink, 8/25/38: *Index* K046B06.

63. "Eight Houses for Modern Living," *Life* 5 (26 September 1938): 45–67. The traditionalist/modernist pairings were Royal Barry Wills and Frank Lloyd Wright; Richard Koch and Edward D. Stone; H. Roy Kelley and William Wilson Wurster; and Aymar Embury II and Wallace K. Harrison with J. André Fouilhoux.

64. Howard Myers to Wright, 8/3/38: *Index* A054D11. On Wills, see David Gebhard, "Royal Barry Wills and the American Colonial Revival," *Winterthur Portfolio* 27, no. 1 (spring 1992): 45–74.

65. Leach, 473 n. 92.

66. The idea of using exposure in the national press as a means of enhancing a store's local reputation was employed by Neiman-Marcus in Dallas in the mid-1930s. See Stanley Marcus, *Minding the Store: A Memoir* (Boston: Little, Brown, 1974), 72–74.

67. Ruth Goodhue to Wright, 9/23/38: *Index* A056A02.

68. Albert Blackbourn to Wright, 8/25/38: *Index* B059E02. Blackbourn to Wright, 9/20/38: *Index* B060B09.

69. Edgar Kaufmann and A. J. Barone had known each other since the 1920s, when Barone was selling real estate in Pittsburgh's East End. I thank Ray R. Barone, A. J.'s son, for this and other information about the *Life* houses shared in a telephone interview with the author on 20 March 1992. Wright's drawings for the *Life* house in the Frank Lloyd Wright Archives have acc. no. 3919.001–010. The studio planned on using the same set of drawings for the Blackbourns and for Kaufmann's, and one or both names appear on the title blocks.

70. "Work Started on First of 4 Model Houses," *Pittsburgh Sun-Telegraph,* 2 October 1938, pt. 2, 7.

71. "Gertrude Lawrence Helps Open a New *Life* House in Suburban Pittsburgh," *Life* 6 (6 February 1939): 24.

72. See, for example, "Life Houses Open for Inspection," *Life* 5 (12 December 1938): 35–38, 80. A. J. Barone described the financing of the Wills house in his interview with the author.

73. Wright to Kaufmann jr., 1/17/39: *Index* K048A10. In his interview with the author, Ray Barone recounted that Kaufmann jr. and his father visited the Ben Rebhuhn house in Great Neck Estates, New York.

74. Albert Blackbourn to Wright, 11/28/38: *Index* B062A05.

75. In 1944, however, Walter Sobotka sought to interest Kaufmann in supporting his scheme for prefabricated housing. See Welzig, 203.

76. Museum of Modern Art (MoMA) Archives.

77. Kaufmann jr. to Barr, 1/25/40, MoMA Archives, file 148.

78. In addition to Kaufmann's, the stores included L. S. Ayres & Co., Indianapolis; Barker Bros., Los Angeles; Bloomingdale's, New York; Famous-Barr Co., St. Louis; Marshall Field & Company, Chicago; Gimbel Brothers, Philadelphia; Jordan Marsh Company, Boston; The Halle Bros. Co., Cleveland; The J. L. Hudson Company, Detroit; The F. & R. Lazarus & Co., Columbus, Ohio; and Wolf & Dessover, Fort Wayne, Indiana. The Philadelphia Gimbel's and Wolf & Dessover had direct ties to the Kaufmann family: the former was managed by a relative, Arthur Kaufmann, and the latter was owned by the family of Irwin Wolf, Kaufmann's vice president and brother-in-law.

79. Eliot F. Noyes, *Organic Design in Home Furnishings* (1941; reprint, New York: Arno Press, 1969). For photographs of the installations at MoMA and Kaufmann's, see Emrich Nicholson, *Contemporary Shops in the United States* (New York: Architectural Book Publishing, 1945), 148–50, 182–83.

80. Nicholson, 151–53.

81. For a scholarly account of the differences between Kaufmann jr. and Johnson, see Franz Schulze, *Philip Johnson: Life and Work* (New York: Knopf, 1994), 181. For a personal recollection, see Peter Blake, *No Place Like Utopia: Modern Architecture and the Company We Kept* (New York: Knopf, 1993), 129–30.

82. Terence Riley and Edward Eigen, "Between the Museum and the Marketplace: Selling Good Design," in *The Museum of Modern Art at Mid-Century: At Home and Abroad, Studies in Modern Art* 4 (1994): 150–79.

83. Edgar Kaufmann jr., *What Is Modern Design?* (New York: Museum of Modern Art, 1950), 9.

84. Miller, 36–37. For a bibliography of Kaufmann jr.'s writings, see "Edgar J. Kaufmann jr.: Publications 1938–1989," compiled by Alfred Willis, in Edgar Kaufmann jr., *9 Commentaries on Frank Lloyd Wright* (New York: Architectural History Foundation, 1989), 137–56.

2. THE KAUFMANNS' COUNTRY HOUSES AT BEAR RUN AND PALM SPRINGS

1. The principal publications on Bear Run and Fallingwater are Donald Hoffmann, *Frank Lloyd Wright's Fallingwater: The House and Its History,* 2d rev. ed. (New York: Dover, 1993), and Edgar Kaufmann jr., *Fallingwater: A Frank Lloyd Wright Country House* (New York: Abbeville Press, 1986). For recent assessments, see Robert McCarter, *Fallingwater* (London: Phaidon, 1994) and *Frank Lloyd Wright* (London: Phaidon, 1997), 204–20; and Neil Levine, *The Architecture of Frank Lloyd Wright* (Princeton, N.J.: Princeton University Press, 1996), 217–53.

2. Report by Morris Knowles, Inc., Pittsburgh, dated 10 June 1920, in Edgar Kaufmann jr. papers, Avery Architectural and Fine Arts Library, Columbia University (Avery Library).

3. Unpublished preliminary survey of the botanical history of Bear Run by Sean Garrigan and Rene Torres for the Western Pennsylvania Conservancy, 1993.

4. Morris Knowles report, Avery Library.

5. Hoffmann, 7–8.

6. Ibid., 15.

7. Edgar Tafel, *Years with Frank Lloyd Wright: Apprentice to Genius* (1979; reprint, New York: Dover, 1985), 1–7.

8. Hoffmann, 17.

9. Kaufmann jr. to Wright, 27 September 1935, Avery Library.

10. Kaufmann to Wright, 24 November 1935, Avery Library.

11. Knud Lönberg-Holm, "The Weekend House," *Architectural Record* 68 (August 1930): 175–92. Among the examples illustrated in this article is Wright's Ocatilla Desert Camp, 1929.

12. This topic has been examined by Franklin Toker, University of Pittsburgh; see his forthcoming book, *Fabricating Fallingwater*.

13. Hoffmann, 19.

14. The best published account of the construction of the house is ibid., 26–87.

15. "Fallingwater Structural Reinforcing Progress Report," 16 May 1997, prepared by Robert Silman Associates, for the Western Pennsylvania Conservancy, 3.

16. On the plunge pool, see Hoffmann, 37–38; Kaufmann jr. describes this and other changes, 99, 102.

17. Hoffmann, 79.

18. Kaufmann jr., 128. For his account of the family's differences with Wright on the subject of formality, see p. 104.

19. *Architectural Forum* 68 (January 1938); *Life* (17 January 1938), inside cover; *Time* (17 January 1938), color rendering on cover. From 24 January to 1 March, the Museum of Modern Art exhibited twenty photographs of the house.

20. Kaufmann to Wright, 25 January 1938: Avery Library. For the history of the guest house, see Hoffmann, 92–107.

21. Telephone interview with Mary Michaely, 19 June 1998.

22. Kaufmann to Wright, 11/2/45: *Index* K066D10; Wright to Kaufmann, 11/6/45: *Index* K066E07.

23. Kaufmann jr. to Wright, 9/4/46: *Index* K070D09.

24. Wright to Kaufmann, 8/1/47: *Index* K076D05.

25. Sarah E. Beyer, "From Cows to Cantilevers: Kentuck Knob and the Kaufmanns," *Friends of Fallingwater Newsletter*, no. 15 (October 1996): 1–6.

26. Wright to Kaufmann, 4/13/42: *Index* K059D03.

27. Kaufmann to Kaufmann jr., 10 March 1946: Avery Library; Neutra to Kaufmann, 3 March 1947: Neutra Archive, University of California, Los Angeles, quoted in Thomas S. Hines, *Richard Neutra and the Search for Modern Architecture* (New York: Oxford University Press, 1982), 203.

28. Quoted in Hines, 201.

29. Wright to Kaufmann, 6/17/46: *Index* K069C04.

30. Wright to Liliane Kaufmann, 1/15/51: *Index* K093B03.

31. Wright to Kaufmann jr., 2/1/51: *Index* K093C06; Wright to Liliane Kaufmann, 2/9/51: *Index* K093D01.

32. Kaufmann to Wright, 2/12/51: *Index* K093D05; Wright to Kaufmann, 2/14/51: *Index* K093D09.

33. Kaufmann jr. to Wright, 9/2/51: *Index* K098C09.

34. Kaufmann jr. to Wright, 9/25/51: *Index* K098E10.

35. Kaufmann to Wright, 7/3/52: *Index* K104C02.

36. Kaufmann jr. to Wright, 8/2/55: *Index* K120A01.

37. Wright to Kaufmann jr., 8/6/55: *Index* K120A06.

38. Wright to Kaufmann jr., 12/29/55: *Index* K122B02.

39. John Sergeant, *Frank Lloyd Wright's Usonian Houses: The Case for Organic Architecture* (New York: Whitney Library of Design, 1984), 144–45; Frank Lloyd Wright, *The Natural House* (New York: Horizon, 1954), 197–210.

40. Wright to Kaufmann jr., 12/14/56: *Index* K126E10.

41. Kaufmann jr. to Wright, 2/13/57: *Index* K128B04; and 2/15/57: *Index* K128B07.

3. KAUFMANN, WRIGHT, AND PITTSBURGH

1. Quoted in Stefan Lorant, *Pittsburgh: The Story of an American City* (New York: Doubleday, 1964), 168. Edgar Kaufmann commissioned this epic account of the city's history. For further information about the projects Wright and Kaufmann planned for Pittsburgh, see Richard Cleary, "Edgar Kaufmann, Frank Lloyd Wright and the 'Pittsburgh Point Park Coney Island in Automobile Scale,'" *Journal of the Society of Architectural Historians* 52 (June 1993): 139–58; and "Beyond Fallingwater: Edgar J. Kaufmann, Frank Lloyd Wright and the Projects for Pittsburgh," in Narciso G. Menocal, ed., *Wright Studies II* (Carbondale: University of Southern Illinois Press, forthcoming).

2. H. L. Mencken, *Prejudices: Six Series* (New York: Knopf, 1927), 187; quoted in Lorant, 327–28.

3. Lorant, 357.

4. Frank Lloyd Wright, "Broadacres to Pittsburgh," *Pittsburgh Sun-Telegraph*, 24 June 1935, editorial page.

5. "City Target of Architect," *Pittsburgh Post-Gazette*, 1 July 1935, 28.

6. Frank Lloyd Wright, *The Disappearing City* (New York: Payson, 1932).

7. *Pittsburgh Post-Gazette*, 2 July 1935, 8.

8. Franklin Toker describes Edgar Kaufmann as the active party in the design of the original Irene Kaufmann Settlement building in 1909–10 and the addition of 1928 (with tilework designed by Joseph Urban) in his unpublished article, "Mr. Kaufmann, Mr. Wright, and the Origins of Fallingwater," 5. Urban's contribution is noted by Albert M. Tannler, "Another Overlooked Pittsburgh Design by Joseph Urban—Now Gone," in *PHLF News* [newsletter of

the Pittsburgh History & Landmarks Foundation], no. 146 (June 1997): 9.

9. For a concise introduction to planning issues in Pittsburgh, see Roy Lubove, *Twentieth-Century Pittsburgh: Government, Business, and Environmental Change,* vol. 1 (1969; reprint, Pittsburgh: University of Pittsburgh Press, 1995).

10. Authorized by the state legislature on 24 May 1945, the Urban Redevelopment Authority was established by the Pittsburgh City Council on 16 November 1946. On 2 December, Mayor David Lawrence appointed its members. In addition to the mayor, who served as chairman, and Kaufmann, the membership included the attorney and banker Arthur Van Buskirk, steel executive John Lister Perry, and city councilman William Alvah Stewart jr. Published report of the Pittsburgh City Planning Commission, 1946, Hunt Library, Carnegie Mellon University.

11. Kaufmann to Wright, 10/20/34: *Index* K018B06.

12. Kaufmann to Wright, 12/4/34: *Index* K019A01.

13. Wright to Kaufmann, 12/26/34: *Index* K019C01; Kaufmann to Wright, 12/20/34: *Index* K019C05; and 4/5/35: *Index* K020B03.

14. Kaufmann to Wright, 10/20/34: *Index* K018B06; 4/5/35: *Index* K020B03; and 5/4/35: *Index* K020C09.

15. David G. De Long, *Frank Lloyd Wright: Designs for an American Landscape, 1922–1932* (New York: Abrams, in association with the Canadian Centre for Architecture, the Library of Congress, and the Frank Lloyd Wright Foundation, 1996), 92.

16. The Buhl Planetarium and Institute of Popular Science was designed by the Pittsburgh firm of Ingham, Pratt & Boyd and built in 1939. See Walter Kidney, *Landmark Architecture: Pittsburgh and Allegheny County* (Pittsburgh: Pittsburgh History & Landmarks Foundation, 1985), 177.

17. For an introduction to the history of the Point, see Robert C. Alberts, *The Shaping of the Point: Pittsburgh's Renaissance Park* (Pittsburgh: University of Pittsburgh Press, 1980). The Pennsylvania Division of the Carnegie Library of Pittsburgh has a series of newspaper clipping albums titled "Pittsburgh Redevelopment." Point State Park is covered in vol. 2, pt. 1, compiled in 1969. Hereafter, citations from this album are identified as "CL clipping."

18. *Pittsburgh Sun-Telegraph,* 27 October 1935, CL clipping.

19. *Pittsburgh Sun-Telegraph,* 12 March 1939, CL clipping.

20. Robert Moses, *Arterial Plan for Pittsburgh,* report prepared for the Pittsburgh Regional Planning Associa-

tion, November 1939, Hunt Library, Carnegie Mellon University.

21. "Project Declared Within City's Immediate Grasp," *Pittsburgh Post-Gazette,* 15 November 1945, CL clipping.

22. The date of this meeting has not been confirmed. Alberts, *Shaping of the Point,* 91, states that it took place in May 1945, but the year appears to be an error given the sequence of subsequent events. The correspondence between Wright and Kaufmann discusses a trip to Pittsburgh on 18 May 1946 (Kaufmann to Wright, 5/6/46: *Index* K069A01). Wright's studio began work on the project in January 1947. Correspondence in the spring of 1947 between Kaufmann, Allegheny Conference officials, and Wright refers to a meeting long previous to project submissions. See Wright to Kaufmann, 6/27/47: *Index* P089D03; Park Martin to Wright, 5/28/47: *Index* P089A08; Kaufmann to Wright, 7/14/47: *Index* P089D08.

23. Wright to Kaufmann, 7 February 1947, Frank Lloyd Wright Archives, Correspondence P–Q.

24. Kaufmann to Wright, 7 February 1947, Frank Lloyd Wright Archives, Correspondence P–Q.

25. Wright to Robert Moses, 4/4/47: *Index* M160D09; Moses to Wright, 4/9/47: *Index* M161A08; Wright to Moses, 4/15/47: *Index* M161B05.

26. Martin to Wright, 5/28/47: *Index* P089A08; Wright to Martin, 6/15/47, *Index* P089B08.

27. Wright to Martin, 7/19/47: *Index* P089E01.

28. Martin to Kaufmann, 1/15/48: *Index* P093A10.

29. Richards to Kaufmann, 1/20/48: *Index* P093B02.

30. Wright to Kaufmann, 1/23/48: *Index* K078D10.

31. Kaufmann to Wright, 3/3/48: *Index* P094C03.

32. Wright to Kaufmann, 1/23/50: *Index* K088C10.

33. See CL clipping file, "Pittsburgh Redevelopment," vol. 3, pt. 2, "Hill District"; and Charles W. Prine jr., "City Must Decide by End of Year to Get Aid from U.S.," *Pittsburgh Sun-Telegraph,* 4 February 1952, CL clipping.

34. Frank Lloyd Wright, "Modern Architecture (The Princeton Lectures 1930)," in *The Future of Architecture* (New York: Mentor, 1953), 194.

35. *Pittsburgh Sun-Telegraph,* 5 May 1949, Daily Graphic Section.

36. Quoted by Alberts, 95.

37. See Jack Quinan, "L'Ingegneria e gli ingegneri di Frank Lloyd Wright," *Casabella* 52, no. 545 (April 1988): 42–53; and Victor di Suvero, "L'Ingegnere Jaro Joseph Polivka, collaboratore di F. Ll. Wright," *Architettura, cronacha e storia* 45 (July 1959): 203–9. Polivka described his experi-

ences with Wright in an unpublished memoir, "What It's Like to Work with Wright," ca. 1957, University Archives, SUNY at Buffalo.

38. Frank Lloyd Wright Archives, acc. no. 5617.001.

39. Kaufmann to Wright, 8/25/49: *Index* S174C06.

40. The project had a brief coda four years later when Kaufmann raised the possibility of building it near the Carnegie Institute in Oakland, the city's cultural and educational center. Wright sent the drawings to officials in Pittsburgh, but nothing came of the idea. Kaufmann to Wright, 8/30/54: *Index* K114D01.

41. In addition to participating in his parents' projects with Wright in the early 1950s, Kaufmann jr. apparently considered commissions of his own. In January 1950, for example, he and Wright corresponded about building a steel house in San Francisco. Kaufmann jr. to Wright, 5 January 1950; Wright to Kaufmann jr., 10 January 1950, Correspondence K, Frank Lloyd Wright Archives.

42. Kaufmann jr. to Wright, undated letter: *Index* K106D08; and 9/2/52: *Index* K105A07.

43. Wright to Kaufmann, 7/20/53: *Index* K109A09.

44. Kaufmann to Wright, 8/7/53: *Index* K109D04 and Avery Library ST 22.1. Philip Smith for Kaufmann to Wright, 16 September 1953, Avery Library ST 22.1.

45. Robert McCarter, *Frank Lloyd Wright* (London: Phaidon, 1997), chap. 16; Neil Levine, *The Architecture of Frank Lloyd Wright* (Princeton, N.J.: Princeton University Press, 1996), chap. 11.

46. Wright to Kaufmann, 3/10/48: *Index* P094C09.

Catalogue

ABOUT THE DRAWINGS

THE DRAWINGS PRESENTED in this exhibition and catalogue are a sampling of the more than six hundred known drawings documenting the projects commissioned from Frank Lloyd Wright by the Kaufmanns (see Drawings for Projects). The drawings have been selected to illustrate the stages of project development and points of interaction between architect and client. They can be classed in five broad categories: schematic design, client presentation, design development, working drawings, and construction documentation.

Schematic drawings, such as cats. 1 and 13, are those in which Wright and his assistants set out the basic ideas for a project. They worked in pencil and color pencil on tracing paper, drawing freehand and with a parallel rule and triangle.

Drawings may be reviewed by clients at any stage during the design process. Edgar Kaufmann, for example, viewed rough schematic designs for Fallingwater when he paid Wright a surprise visit in September 1935 (see Chapter 2; cat. 3), but the studio generally prepared finished plans, elevations, and perspective renderings in color pencil for presentation at key decision points (see cats. 31, 37). Wright's chief delineator during the years of the Kaufmann projects was John H. Howe (see cat. 27). Allen Lape Davison, a Pittsburgh native, produced some of the studio's most spectacular renderings (see cat. 43). As his assistants neared completion of a drawing, Wright often added his own touches of architectural detail, foliage, and color (see cat. 46).

Design development drawings (see cats. 10–11) are those in which details of composition, function, materials, and structure are resolved. They usually were prepared by members of the studio and reviewed by Wright, who would add notes and redraw problematic areas. Design development drawings precede working drawings (see cat. 9), which, along with written specifications, are the instructions architects furnish contractors so that they can prepare bids and proceed with construction.

During the construction of Fallingwater, Wright relied on apprentices Bob Mosher and Edgar Tafel to observe the work and ensure that the builders realized his intentions. They prepared field drawings (see cat. 7) documenting what had been done and identifying unresolved issues.

Few of the drawings for the Kaufmann projects have inscribed dates, but most can be assigned at least a year on the basis of their relationship to dated drawings or other documentation such as correspondence. In an era before inexpensive photomechanical copying and computer-aided design, the reproduction of drawings was expensive and time-consuming, and Wright's studio routinely used an existing drawing as a base for developing a new scheme (see cat. 49). Thus, a given sheet might have been worked on by a number of hands at various times during the planning of a project.

1 Fallingwater

Mill Run, Pennsylvania

Superimposed plans
1935
Pencil and color pencil on tracing paper
27½ × 32 in.
The Frank Lloyd Wright Foundation,
3602.166

This drawing is believed to be the first surviving sketch for Fallingwater. Wright drew it over a site plan prepared by his apprentices. The topographical features he recorded are Bear Run and the waterfall (drawn in blue pencil), the hearth boulder (drawn in pencil and red pencil), and a few elevations. He sited the house on a roughly triangular shelf on the right bank (the northern side) and aligned it approximately parallel to the flow of the stream at an angle of 30 degrees east of south. Lightly drawn pencil guidelines indicate that he laid out the house using a 30-60-90-degree triangle placed with reference to a horizontal baseline.

The drawing establishes the essential features of the house through superimposed plans of the foundation piers and the three floors above. The foundation piers, or "bolsters," as Wright termed them, are drawn in pencil. He adjusted their number and dimensions in subsequent drawings. In addition to their structural role as foundations, the bolsters defined a series of regular bays that guided the layout of rooms and the dimensioning of the terraces.

The first floor plan is also drawn in pencil. Some features, such as the portion of the living room cantilevered over the stream, are drawn very lightly; others have been worked repeatedly, indicating hesitations or changes of thought, such as in the shape of the fireplace. The entire drawing conveys a vivid sense of Wright's mind at work as he transferred his idea for the house from his imagination to paper. Faint marks at the edge of the living room, for example, record a thought about the direction windows would open, a sketch at the lower right of the sheet examines the longitudinal elevation of the living room cantilever, and simply drawn furnishings suggest how the kitchen could be organized.

The second and third floors and the outlines of the roofs are drawn in red pencil. Simple labels and lightly sketched furnishings identify the distribution of bedrooms, bathrooms, and the sleeping porch. There is no indication of the terraces adjacent to

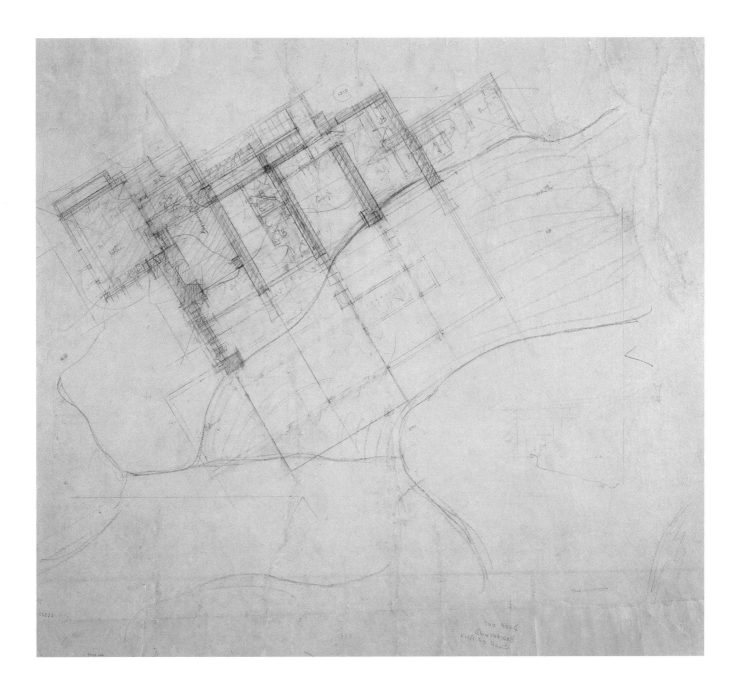

Edgar Kaufmann's room on the second floor or of Edgar Kaufmann jr.'s room on the third floor, both of which appear in subsequent drawings.

Among the other prominent features that Wright would revise is the location of steps at the entrance to the house. The floor of the living room is elevated two steps above ground level, and in this drawing Wright placed the steps at the edge of the slab that includes the living room and its terraces. Visitors arriving at the house would step up onto the slab, as onto a plinth, and cross to the entry door. In the final version of the house, the steps were located inside the entry vestibule.

Another significant change would be made to the fenestration of the masonry wall on the north and west sides of the living room. Here, Wright sketched glazing between slender piers, a device employed in the concrete-block Richard Lloyd Jones house (1928–31) in Tulsa, Oklahoma. He later eliminated the northern windows and, on the west side, applied the same system of mullions and glazing that he used for the terrace facades.

2 Fallingwater

Mill Run, Pennsylvania

Preliminary first floor plan
1935
Pencil and color pencil on tracing paper
31 × 41 in.
The Frank Lloyd Wright Foundation,
3602.044

The first floor has been crisply drawn and embellished with such details as paving stones, furnishings, and plants, but superimposed freehand sketches investigate unresolved issues regarding the relationship of the house to its immediate setting and, at the top of the sheet, a connection detail. The topographic map that the Kaufmanns had provided to Wright marked the locations of six trees on the shelf of land where he sited the house, and the three largest—an 18-inch-diameter tulip on the east side of the house, a 28-inch-diameter oak in the vicinity of the kitchen, and a 30-inch-diameter oak to the west—are drawn here.

Evidently, there was some confusion in Wright's studio regarding the precise locations of the tulip and the smaller oak—the former is drawn in three locations around the eastern retaining wall, and the latter appears both within and outside the kitchen. A portion of the trunk of the oak has been drawn in addition to the diameter of the base, indicating that the tree was being considered in elevation and plan.

Another issue under study was the location of the large boulder immediately to the west of the kitchen. Its high point, defined by measurement, was used as a datum for a series of measurements in the kitchen. During construction, problems arising from the proximity of the boulder, the basement stairs, and the oak tree resulted in the removal of the tree (see cat. 7).

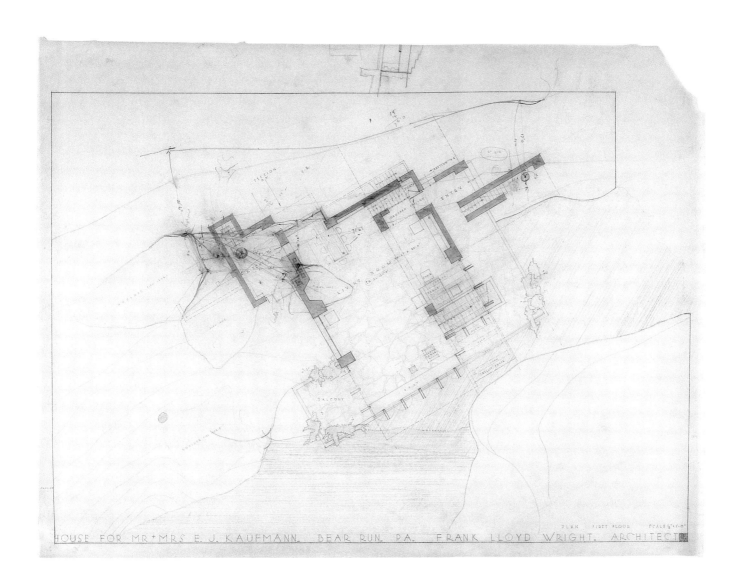

HOUSE FOR MR + MRS E. J. KAUFMANN.   BEAR RUN. PA.   FRANK LLOYD WRIGHT. ARCHITECT

3 Fallingwater

Mill Run, Pennsylvania

Preliminary second floor plan
1935
Pencil and color pencil on tracing paper
28½ × 40½ in.
The Frank Lloyd Wright Foundation,
3602.047

This preliminary study for a more polished drawing (3602.043; see Drawings for Projects, p. 175) accompanied cat. 2. Red pencil outlines the cliff alongside the driveway and indicates the large boulder adjacent to Edgar Kaufmann's room. Orange pencil marks the center lines of the bolsters and the outlines of the roof canopies. Beds, major pieces of cabinetry, and bathroom fixtures are indicated, as well as suggestions of the flagstone paving of the master bedroom terrace and plantings on the trellis. The tulip tree rises through the sleeping porch, and the oak rises through a small terrace bridging Edgar Kaufmann's room and the large boulder.

The south facade consists of regularly spaced windows and glass doors across the master bedroom, the master bathroom, and the guest room. Wright subsequently adjusted the fenestration to reflect the different uses of these spaces.

Another area subsequently revised was the sleeping porch. As drawn here, it is set seven or eight steps below the level of the second floor bedrooms. In the definitive plan, it was raised so as to be only two steps lower. The change likely was driven by the compositional balance of the sleeping porch, the master bedroom terrace, and Edgar Kaufmann's terrace.

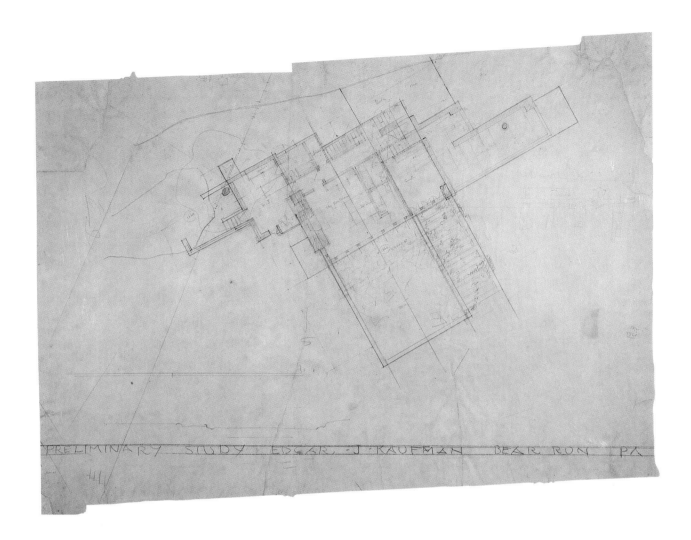

PRELIMINARY STUDY EDGAR J KAUFMAN BEAR RUN PA

4 Fallingwater

Mill Run, Pennsylvania

Longitudinal section
ca. 1935
Pencil on tracing paper
26¾ × 36 in.
The Frank Lloyd Wright Foundation,
3602.060

The dimensioning of the heights of the floors, ceilings, and balcony parapets was the object of considerable study by Wright's studio. Other drawings (for example, 3602.128; see Drawings for Projects, p. 176) demonstrate that Wright used a 17-inch unit to organize these features but readily departed from it, as seen here, to satisfy visual, programmatic, and technical requirements. In this instance, the critical issues appear to have been the relative visual weight of the balconies and canopies and the relationship of human scale (indicated by figures) to the masonry piers on the ground floor and the height of the third floor.

The drawing also includes information about proposed interior finishes, such as the vertical graining of the passage doors. In the living room, the rock at the hearth projects slightly above the floor but has been cropped to create a level surface. (Following Kaufmann's subsequent suggestion, the rock was not cropped.) The fireplace is shown with its hanging kettle, but its masonry differs from what was realized. The stones are much larger than those used for the piers, and two of them are set on edge, similar to what was achieved in the third floor bedroom fireplace. To the left of the fireplace, a cabinet displaying objets d'art stands in the space now occupied by seating. On the second floor, the fireplace in the master bedroom indicates features evident in the realized version: asymmetry and ledges for the display of objects such as candlesticks.

In addition to the section, the sheet has many dimensional calculations and small sketches. At upper right is a small elevation of the bolsters and first floor cantilever, and at lower right is a sketch of stone laid on a concrete slab.

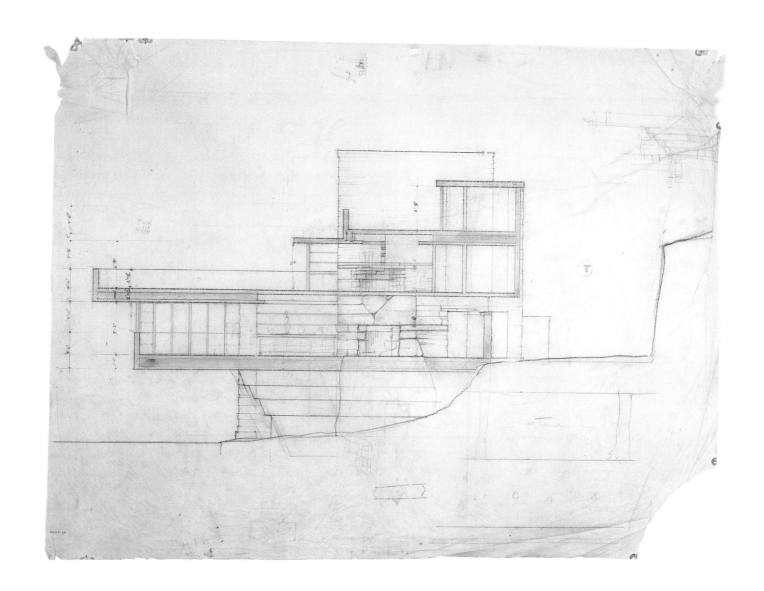

5 Fallingwater

Mill Run, Pennsylvania

East, west, and south elevations
ca. 1935
Pencil and color pencil on tracing paper
32 × 41 in.
The Frank Lloyd Wright Foundation,
3602.045

Of the different types of drawings that Wright's studio prepared for presentation to clients, the perspective renderings generally have the greatest artistic appeal, but as this drawing demonstrates, orthogonal elevations can be no less elegant. The three principal elevations—south, west, and east—have been arranged in an artful composition that conveys important information about the natural setting and the scale of the house relative to the human figures sketched on the living room terrace and on the platform above Bear Run.

The east and west elevations indicate how the house is anchored on the bank of the stream and cantilevered from it. The south elevation relates the horizontal lines of the terraces, roofs, and retaining walls to the stratified topography and the vertical masonry piers to the trunks of the oak on the west side of the house and the tulip to the east. Their canopies frame the composition from above as the stream does from below.

The erasures and redrawing of the second floor windows in the vicinity of the master bathroom and guest room respond to changes in the interior layout.

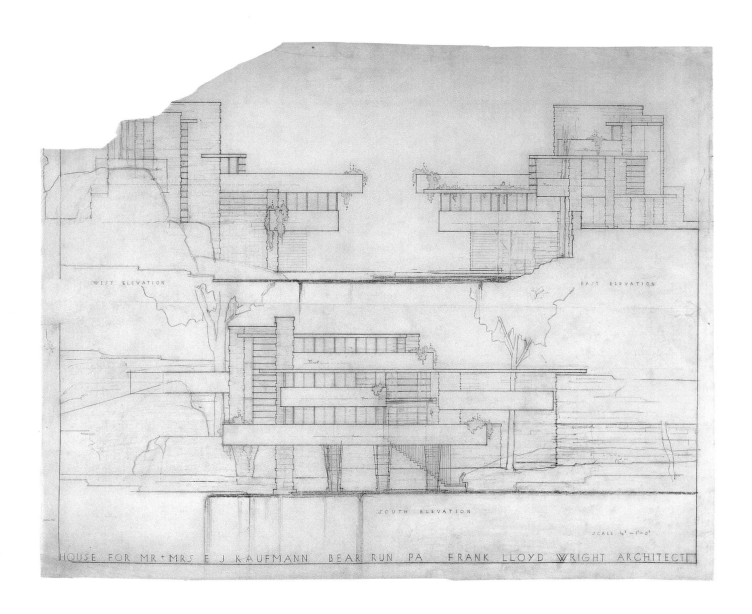

WEST ELEVATION   EAST ELEVATION

SOUTH ELEVATION

SCALE ⅛" = 1'-0"

HOUSE FOR MR + MRS E J KAUFMANN   BEAR RUN PA   FRANK LLOYD WRIGHT ARCHITECT

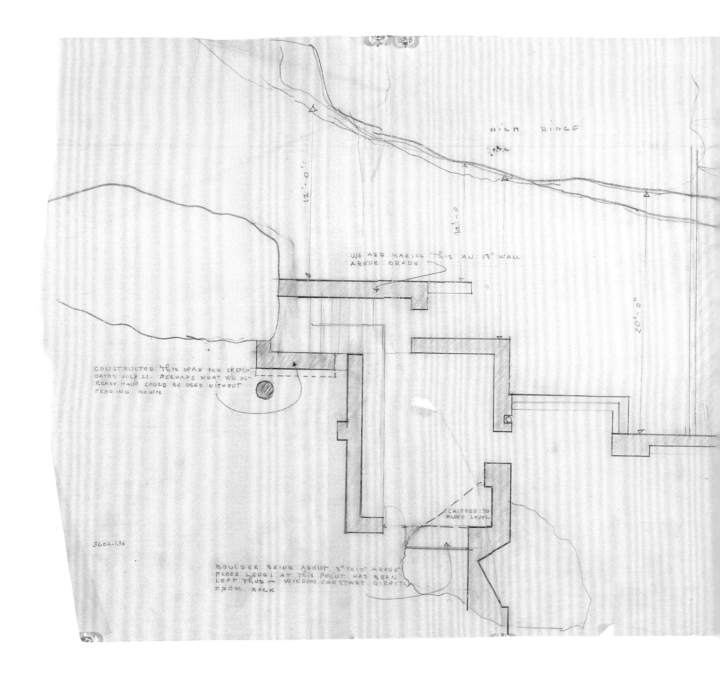

HIGH RIDGE

12'-0"

10'-0"

WE ARE MAKING THIS AN 18" WALL
ABOVE GRADE

20'-0"

CONSTRUCTED THIS WAX PER SKETCH
DATED JULY 21. PERHAPS WHAT WE ALREADY HAVE COULD BE USED WITHOUT
TEARING DOWN

CHIPPED TO
FLOOR LEVEL

3602.136

BOULDER BEING ABOUT 8"TO10" ABOVE
FLOOR LEVEL AT THIS POINT HAS BEEN
LEFT THUS — WINDOW CAN START DIRECTLY
FROM ROCK

6 Fallingwater

Mill Run, Pennsylvania

First floor, north wall plan
1936
Pencil and color pencil on tracing paper
13½ × 32¼ in.
Drawn by Bob Mosher (1909–1992)
The Frank Lloyd Wright Foundation,
3602.136

This drawing by Bob Mosher, the apprentice Wright assigned as his field representative at the beginning of construction, reports on the progress of work along the northern perimeter of the house. Issues noted for Wright's consideration are the location of trees, the design of the small quarter-circle basin just outside the entrance, the optimal way to hang the front door, and the construction of the walls framing the basement stairs.

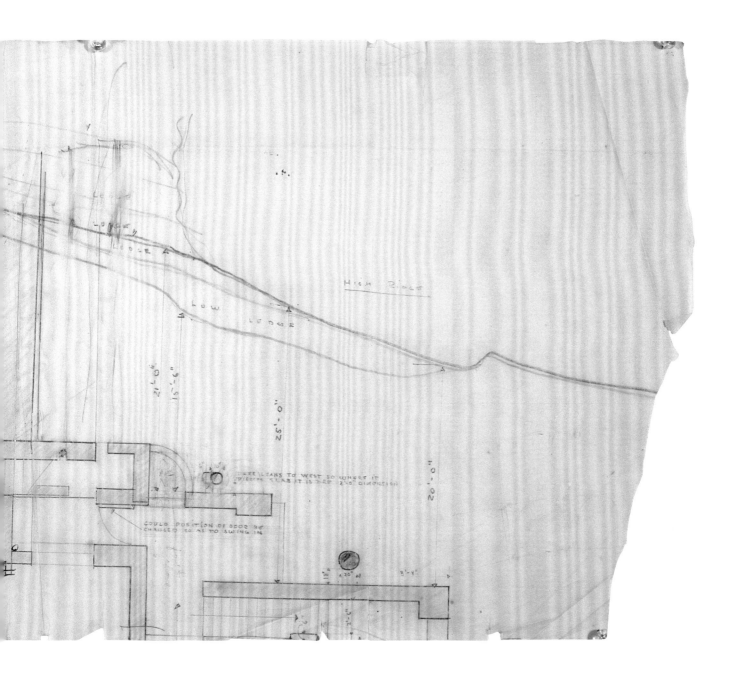

HIGH RIDGE

LOW LODGE

7 Fallingwater

Mill Run, Pennsylvania

Basement stairwell
1936
Pencil and color pencil on tracing paper
17¾ × 17 in.
Drawn by Bob Mosher (1909–1992)
The Frank Lloyd Wright Foundation,
3602.110

This drawing documents an exchange between Wright and the apprentice on site, Bob Mosher, who presented a problem encountered in the construction of the stairwell from the kitchen to the basement. Wright had called for the installation of a window in the stairwell between the foundation wall and a boulder, but the wall had been built without it. Mosher's drawing shows how the wall could be rebuilt but notes that it would have to be constructed around the roots of the 28-inch-diameter oak, a tree that had played an important role in Wright's initial conception of the house (see cats. 2, 5). Wright recorded his decision to leave the wall in place.

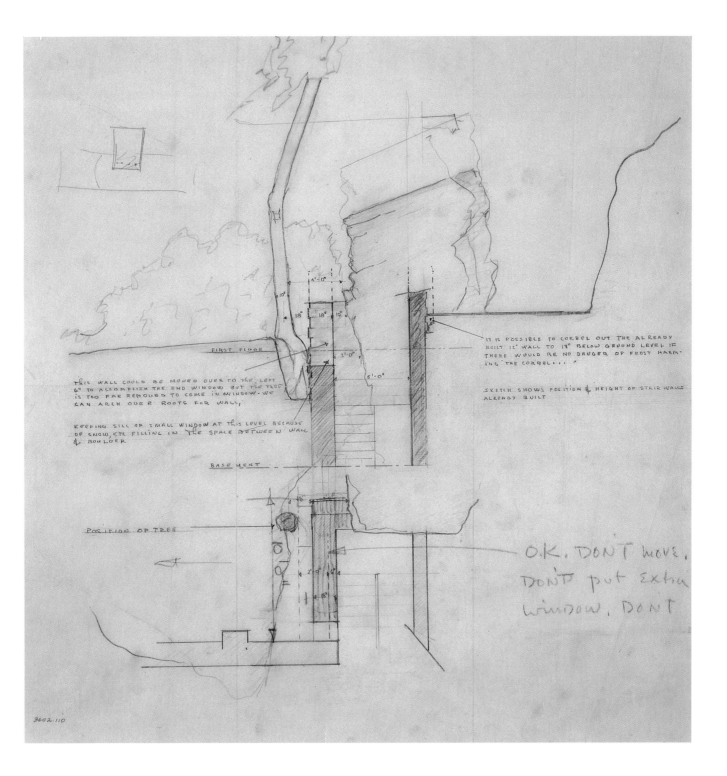

FIRST FLOOR

THIS WALL COULD BE MOVED OVER TO THE LEFT
6" TO ACCOMPLISH THE END WINDOW BUT THE TREE
IS TOO FAR REMOVED TO COME IN WINDOW. WE
CAN ARCH OVER ROOTS FOR WALL,

KEEPING SILL OR SMALL WINDOW AT THIS LEVEL BECAUSE
OF SNOW, ETC FILLING IN THE SPACE BETWEEN WALL
& BOULDER

BASEMENT

POSITION OF TREE

IT IS POSSIBLE TO CORBEL OUT THE ALREADY
BUILT 12" WALL TO 18" BELOW GROUND LEVEL IF
THERE WOULD BE NO DANGER OF FROST HARM-
ING THE CORBEL...

SKETCH SHOWS POSITION & HEIGHT OF STAIR WALLS
ALREADY BUILT

O.K. DON'T MOVE,
DON'T PUT EXTRA
WINDOW, DON'T

3602.110

8 Fallingwater

Mill Run, Pennsylvania

Bathroom layouts for Liliane Kaufmann's
room and guest room
1936
Ink, pencil, and color pencil on tracing paper
10¼ × 8½ in.
Drawn by Bob Mosher (1909–1992)
The Frank Lloyd Wright Foundation,
3602.108

The Kaufmanns closely monitored the construction of the house and didn't hesitate to offer their suggestions. Apprentice Bob Mosher and his successor, Edgar Tafel, often had the responsibility of communicating these ideas to Wright. In this drawing, Mosher relays questions regarding the layout of the master bathroom and the small guest bathroom. Wright returned the drawing with the following reply: "Dear Bob— / Tub arrangement OK / But tell E.J that 6'-0 tubs / are special now as a 5'-6 is / equal to all emergencies and / it was found that the 6'-0 tubs / consume altogether too much / hot water— In other words / the upkeep again / Everything from boiler up must / be enlarged— / If he thinks it worth the extra / price—OK. But I can't see anything / coming back for it. / FLLW."

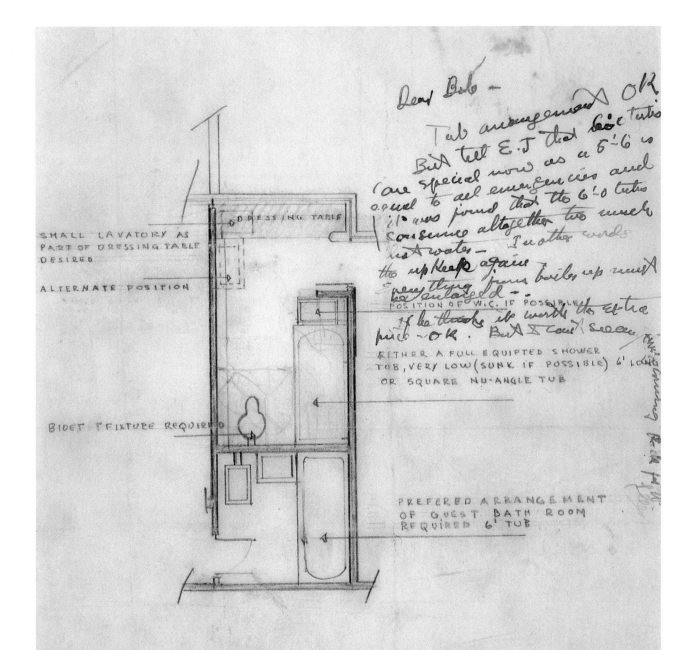

SMALL LAVATORY AS
PART OF DRESSING TABLE
DESIRED

ALTERNATE POSITION

BIDET FFIXTURE REQUIRED

DRESSING TABLE

Dear Bob —

Tub arrangement ✗ OK.
But tell E.J that *two* tubs
one special now as a 5'-6 is
equal to all emergencies and
it was found that the 6'-0 tubs
consume altogether too much
hot water — In other words
the up keep again
Everything from boilers up must
be enlarged —

POSITION OF W.C. IF POSSIBLE

if he thinks its worth the extra
price — OK. But I can't *see* any

EITHER A FULL EQUIPTED SHOWER
TUB, VERY LOW (SUNK IF POSSIBLE) 6' LONG
OR SQUARE NU-ANGLE TUB

PREFERED ARRANGEMENT
OF GUEST BATH ROOM
REQUIRED 6' TUB

PROPOSED REARRANGEMENT OF
BATH ROOMS —

9 Fallingwater

Mill Run, Pennsylvania

Details of second floor steel reinforcing
1936
Pencil on tracing paper
30¾ × 42 in.
The Frank Lloyd Wright Foundation,
3602.090

Poured concrete allowed Wright to almost seamlessly mold integral floors and ceilings varying in depth from the thin slabs in the bedrooms to the deep beams and parapets of the cantilevered porches. Steel reinforcing bars embedded in the concrete greatly improve the material's resistance to the tensile, or bending, forces that would cause the longer spans and cantilevers to droop. The quantity and location of the reinforcing bars within the concrete are critical factors determined in the case of complex structures such as Fallingwater by quantitative analysis.

This drawing translates the analysis of Wesley Peters and Mendel Glickman, who supervised the engineering of Wright's buildings, into instructions for the Kaufmanns' contractor, Walter Hall. It and related drawings became the object of controversy when an independent engineering firm hired by Edgar Kaufmann concluded that the reinforcing was insufficient (see Chapter 2). Matters were complicated further by difficult working conditions at Bear Run.

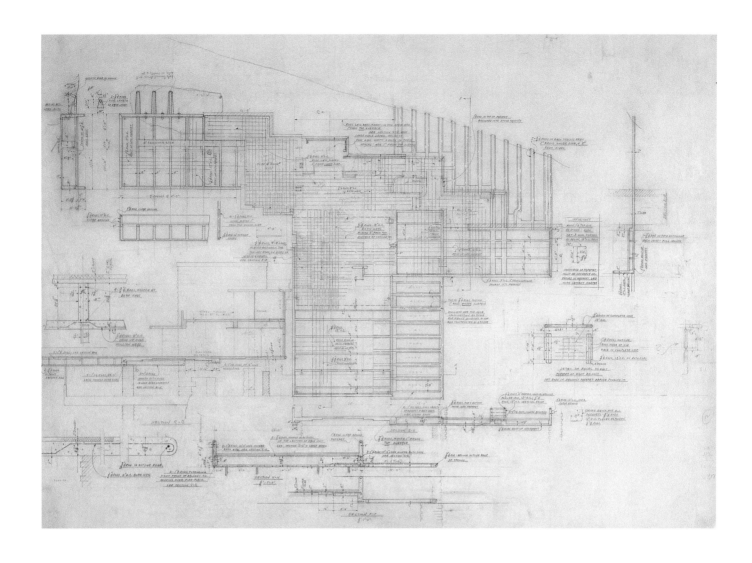

10 Fallingwater

Mill Run, Pennsylvania

*Details of flashing and sound deafening
for concrete floors and roofs
1936
Pencil on tracing paper
36 × 42 in.
The Frank Lloyd Wright Foundation,
3602.083*

The flooring at Fallingwater consists of paving stones laid on a wooden subfloor—a note changes the specification from pine to more-water-resistant redwood. The wood was intended to span the beams of the cantilever and help deaden the transmission of sound so that footsteps would not become drumbeats. Both the flooring diagram and the smaller roof sketches also study flashing and water seals, unglamorous but formidable challenges.

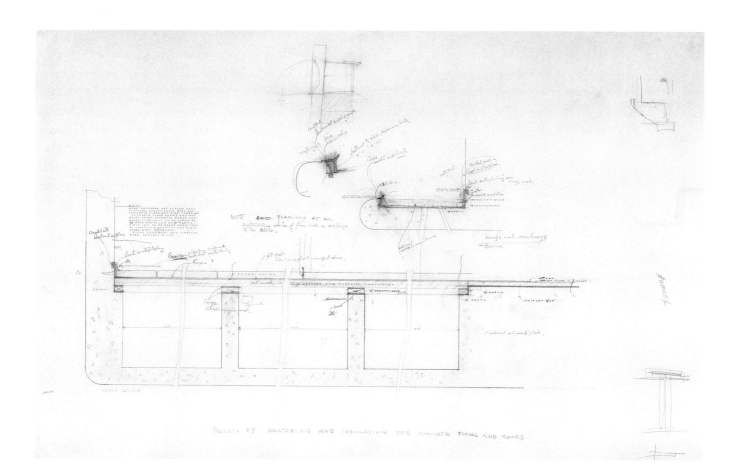

DETAIL OF WEATHERING AND INSULATION FOR CONCRETE FLOORS AND ROOFS

11 Fallingwater

Mill Run, Pennsylvania

Living room furnishing plan
ca. 1936
Pencil and color pencil on tracing paper
26¾ × 36 in.
The Frank Lloyd Wright Foundation,
3602.078

The furnishings were an integral component of Wright's design for Fallingwater. Drawings and correspondence demonstrate that their design was closely scrutinized in the studio and by the Kaufmanns. This plan includes many annotations by Wright, including the following comment referring to the intimate reading area adjacent to the entry: "Note / Same seat as / elsewhere / Absolutely necessary ensemble and the / best one in the house."

The focus of attention is the tall pole lamp, highlighted in blue pencil, studied at enlarged scale in plan and elevation on the right half of the drawing. Wright proposed distributing these lamps around the room. In his memoir of Fallingwater, Edgar Kaufmann jr. wrote that the family rejected the design because the lamps suggested a solemnity unsuited to the informal character they sought for the house.

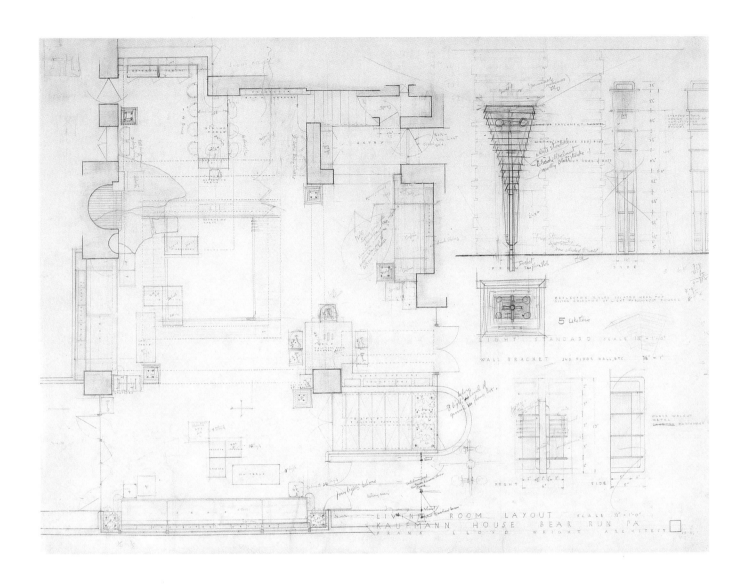

LIVING ROOM LAYOUT   SCALE ½" = 1'-0"
KAUFMANN HOUSE   BEAR RUN PA
FRANK   LLOYD   WRIGHT   ARCHITECT

LIGHT   STANDARD   SCALE 1½" = 1'-0"

WALL BRACKET   2ND FLOOR HALL, ETC.   ⅜" = 1'

FRONT   SIDE

12 Fallingwater

Mill Run, Pennsylvania

East and south living room elevations
ca. 1936
Pencil and color pencil on tracing paper
24½ × 36 in.
The Frank Lloyd Wright Foundation,
3602.141

Throughout his career, Wright was attentive to the natural and artificial lighting of his interiors. He designed fixtures that complemented the architecture and carefully considered the quality of the light they produced: direct or indirect, harsh or soft. At Fallingwater, the artificial lighting is indirect and diffused. In this drawing, Wright studied the arrangement of the fixtures in the ceiling coves and the distribution of reflected light from the pole lamp.

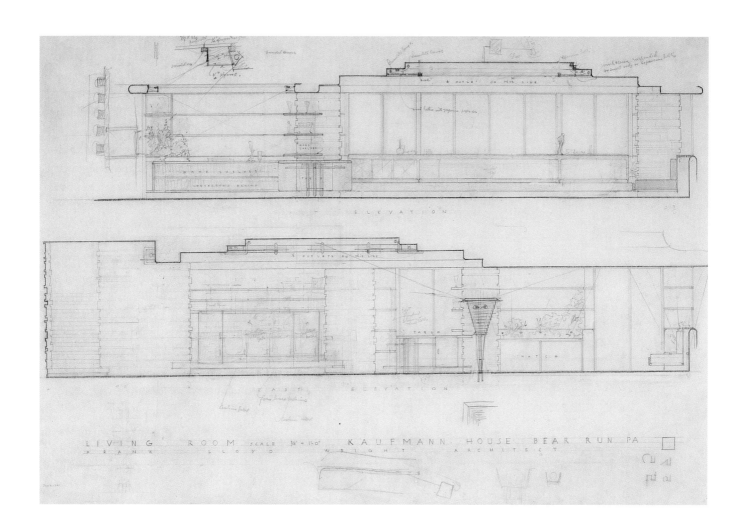

ELEVATION

EAST ELEVATION

LIVING ROOM SCALE 3/4" = 1'0" KAUFMANN HOUSE BEAR RUN PA
FRANK LLOYD WRIGHT ARCHITECT

13 Fallingwater Guest House and Servants' Quarters

Mill Run, Pennsylvania

Preliminary plan
ca. 1938
Pencil and color pencil on tracing paper
11 × 8½ in.
The Frank Lloyd Wright Foundation,
3812.007

This study likely was drawn in the spring of 1938. The footprint of the guest house and servants' quarters is similar to what the Kaufmanns would build in 1939, but there are significant differences in the organization of the exterior and interior spaces. The garage is oriented eastward, toward a courtyard from which guests would begin an elaborate entry sequence recalling the turns and stairs of Taliesin, Wright's home in Wisconsin. The path continues past the guest house along a covered walk to a bridge entering the main house on the third floor.

The guest house consists of a sitting room, three bedrooms, and a bathroom linked by a corridor running along the north side. The ceiling of much of the corridor is drawn as a trellis, presumably glazed like the trellis on the east side of the living room of the main house.

Existing trees played an important role in the layout of the servants' wing and guest house. A hickory tree adjacent to the courtyard marks the beginning of the entrance and requires the first turn. The sitting room is aligned with a large oak that would continue to be a critical element in all subsequent studies.

Above the plan is a small section sketch. The verso of the drawing has numerous small freehand sketches for unidentified building parts and, curiously, a pair of eyeglasses.

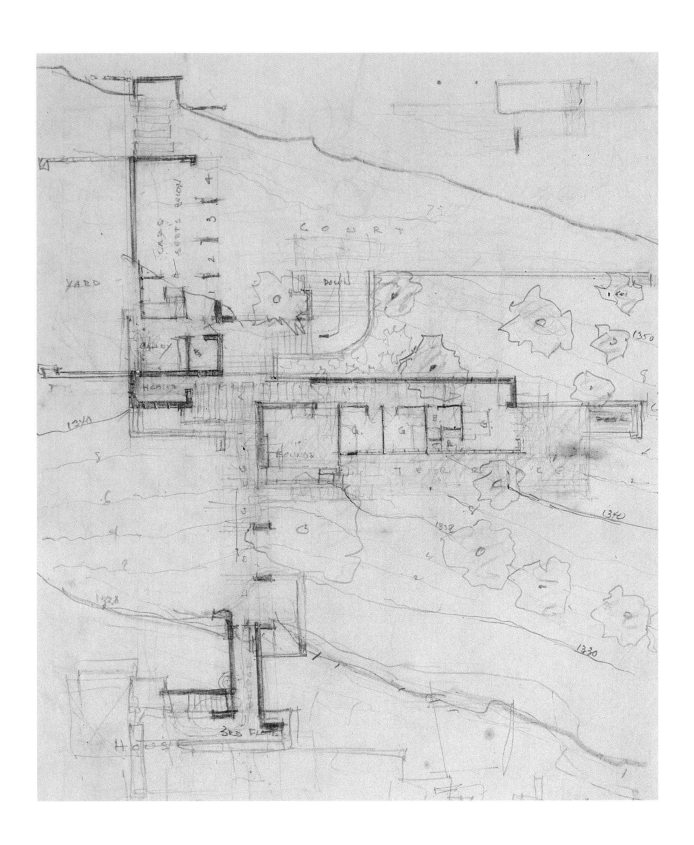

Study for Kaufmann Guest House '39

14 Fallingwater Guest House and Servants' Quarters

Mill Run, Pennsylvania

Preliminary scheme, bird's-eye perspective
from the southeast
May 1938
Pencil and color pencil on tracing paper
12¾ × 29¾ in.
The Frank Lloyd Wright Foundation,
3812.040

This rendering, initialed "OK FLLW" at lower left, was presented to the Kaufmanns along with a plan (see cat. 15). Their correspondence with Wright states that they thought that the layout of the rooms was too formal, and they asked him to simplify it. This view shows how the guest house and adjacent servants' wing would be nestled among the trees, much as the main house engaged trees, such as the large tulip rising through the driveway trellis in the foreground. The drawing also suggests the experience guests would have of being partially inside and partially outside as they made their way under the canopies from the guest house, to the curved walkway, to the bridge entering Fallingwater.

15 Fallingwater Guest House and Servants' Quarters

Mill Run, Pennsylvania

Preliminary plan
18 May 1938
Pencil and color pencil on tracing paper
33¼ × 36 in.
The Frank Lloyd Wright Foundation,
3812.029

This plan accompanied the perspective view presented to the Kaufmanns in May 1938 (see cat. 14). As in the proposal drawn earlier that spring (see cat. 13), the guest house contains three bedrooms linked by a corridor. A second bathroom has been added, and the sitting room has become an extension of the corridor but reduced in size. Its southern wall has been curved to broaden the passageway between the guest house and servants' wing. In contrast to the earlier scheme, the garage faces west, as it does today, and the area behind the guest house is designated as a laundry yard rather than an entry court. The Kaufmanns rejected the scheme, and the drawing was labeled "void."

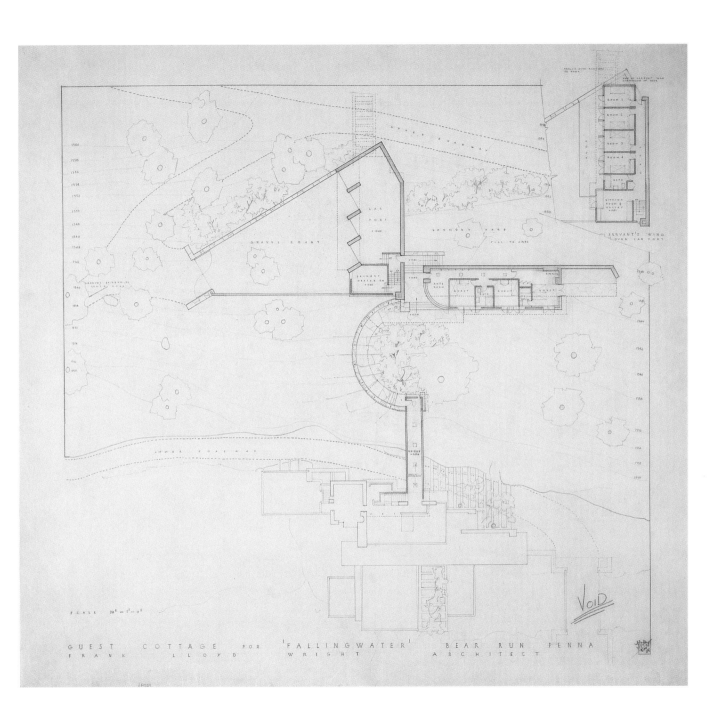

VOID

SCALE ⅛' = 1'-0'

GUEST   COTTAGE   FOR   'FALLINGWATER'   BEAR RUN PENNA
FRANK   LLOYD   WRIGHT   ARCHITECT

16 Fallingwater Guest House and Servants' Quarters

Mill Run, Pennsylvania

Plans and section
January 1939
Pencil and color pencil on tracing paper
24 × 36 in.
The Frank Lloyd Wright Foundation,
3812.033

Wright's studio completed the schematic drawings for the definitive design of the guest house and servants' quarters at the end of January 1939. A note on this drawing from Wright to Kaufmann reads, "EJ. Here it is at last. / Is it OK? If so / put yours here," and points to where Kaufmann was to indicate his approval.

Wright had responded to the family's reservations about the previous schemes by replacing the three boxy bedrooms with a single, large bedroom and a generous living room. He indicated how a second bedroom could be added in a separate pavilion to the east. The plan also included a swimming pool, something the family desired for their own use as much as for their guests.

The drawing reflects the Kaufmanns' decision to shift the bridge entering the main house from the third floor to the second floor. This change required Wright to add a curved staircase from the bridge to the canopied walkway, but it also allowed him to reduce the length of the bridge and make it a less conspicuous feature on the site.

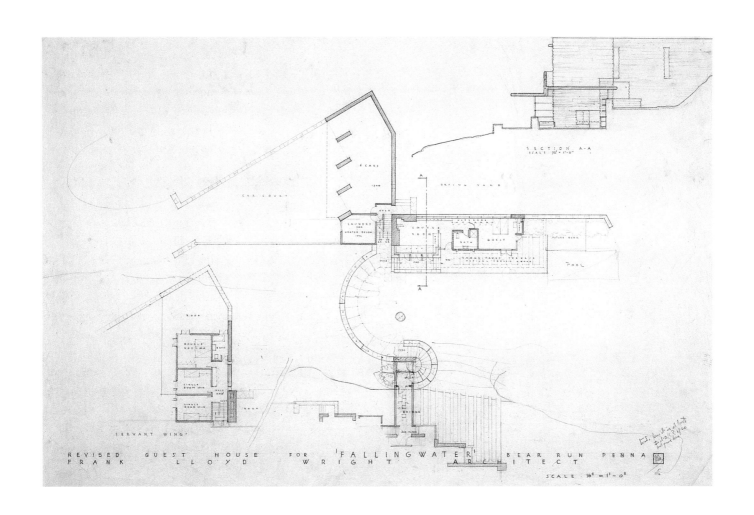

SECTION A-A
SCALE ¼" = 1'-0"

CAR COURT   6 CARS

LAUNDRY
HEATER BELOW

LOUNGE
ROOM

BATH   GUEST

STONE PAVED TERRACE

POOL

OPEN

DOUBLE
BEDROOM   BATH

SINGLE
ROOM

SINGLE
ROOM

SERVANT WING

BRIDGE

REVISED GUEST HOUSE FOR 'FALLINGWATER' BEAR RUN PENNA
FRANK LLOYD WRIGHT ARCHITECT

SCALE ⅛" = 1'-0"

17 Fallingwater

Mill Run, Pennsylvania

Plan for proposed Shady Lane entrance, guest house, and dining room extension
1947
Pencil, color pencil, and ink on tracing paper
44¼ × 36¼ in.
The Frank Lloyd Wright Foundation, 3812.013

In 1947, the Kaufmanns commissioned Wright to study ways of enlarging the dining room and improving the approach to the house from Shady Lane, the road running above the guest house. The magnitude of the changes proposed in this plan and a series of related drawings (see cats. 18–20) indicates that patron and architect were considering a fundamental transformation of the way guests would be introduced to Fallingwater.

Guests would arrive by car via Shady Lane and first view Fallingwater from above while standing at the head of the broad stairs connecting the servants' wing and guest house. They would then descend the covered walk and enter the main house through the bridge on the second floor. This sequence elaborates ideas sketched in the first studies for the guest house in 1938 (see cat. 13).

The scheme called for the demolition of the eastern wall of the servants' wing to allow the extension of the parking bays toward Shady Lane. It also relocated the staircase leading to the servants' living quarters to provide room for the widening of the stairs from the parking area to the beginning of the covered walk.

Alterations were planned for Fallingwater as well. A portion of the driveway on the north side of the house was to be filled in with an addition containing a double-height dining room interlocked with the bridge, which on one side would become an indoor gallery and on the other would connect to a cloakroom and lavatory.

Loose fine granite gravel on roofs ...

A L T E R A T I O N S   "F A L L I N G W A T E R"   F O
F R A N K   L L O Y D   W R I G H T   A R C H I

I find this Mass is essential to Entrance feature

MR AND MRS. EDGAR J. KAUFMANN

E C T

18 Fallingwater Guest House and Servants' Quarters

Mill Run, Pennsylvania

*Bird's-eye view of proposed Shady Lane
entrance from the northeast
20 October 1947
Pencil, color pencil, and ink on tracing paper
24¼ × 36 in.
The Frank Lloyd Wright Foundation,
4702.001*

This view of the servants' wing and guest house
shows Wright's proposal for reorienting the entrance
and garage toward Shady Lane (see cat. 17). One of
the two notes initialed by Wright specifies "Loose
Red granite gravel on roofs and Drive." The other,
referring to the masonry encasing the relocated
staircase to the servants' living quarters states,
"I find this Mass is essential to Entrance feature."

19 Fallingwater

Mill Run, Pennsylvania

Plan of proposed dining room addition
1947
Pencil on tracing paper
20½ × 36 in.
The Frank Lloyd Wright Foundation,
3602.096

Fallingwater was built (and remains) without a formal dining room. Evidently, by the late 1940s the Kaufmanns found themselves using the house for more elaborate parties and turned to Wright for suggestions for accommodating larger numbers of dinner guests. His proposed enlargement of the bridge linking the Shady Lane entrance (see cat. 17) and the second floor of the main house included a cloakroom and lavatory facilities for those who would not be staying as overnight guests. This addition is indicated here by the dotted line adjacent to the driveway trellis.

On the first floor, Wright proposed an addition that would fill the driveway. It included a double-height dining room and an adjacent sitting area tucked underneath the bridge. Although the placement of the new dining table as an extension of the old one provided a degree of spatial continuity with the living room, the dining room essentially would have been a discrete space that would have permitted the Kaufmanns' staff to set and clear a meal while the family entertained guests in the living room or on the terraces. These large-scale changes were not realized, but the drawing also indicates the servants' sitting room that was added by enclosing an area under Edgar Kaufmann's balcony between the kitchen and a large boulder.

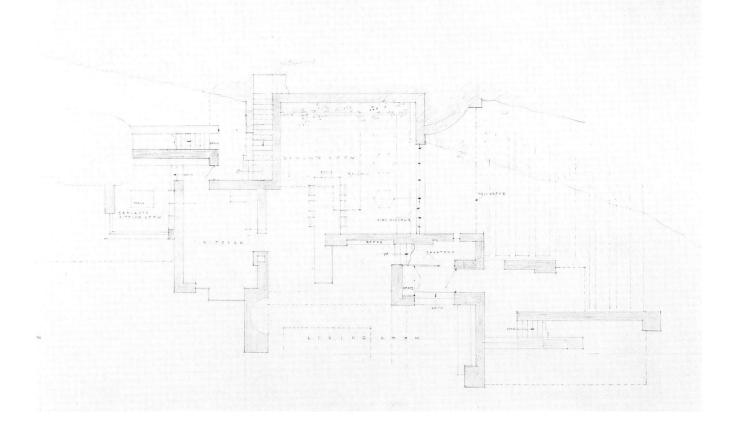

20 Fallingwater

Mill Run, Pennsylvania

*Section showing proposed dining room
addition*
1947
Pencil on tracing paper
18½ × 29¼ in.
*The Frank Lloyd Wright Foundation,
3602.106*

The dining room addition would have been a space unlike any other at Fallingwater. If the other rooms in the house might be likened to rock shelters by virtue of their relatively low ceilings, horizontal orientation, and outward prospects to the surrounding landscape, the dining room might be thought of as a chamber deep within a cave—isolated, vertically oriented, and illuminated from above by a skylight during the day and indirect cove lighting at night. Such an inwardly focused space could be very appropriate for dinner parties, and this design for Fallingwater recalls the character of the original theater—known as the kiva or hogan—at Taliesin West, Wright's home in Arizona, built around 1938.

This drawing also studies the installation of horizontal slats on the west-facing living room window, which may have been intended as sunshades.

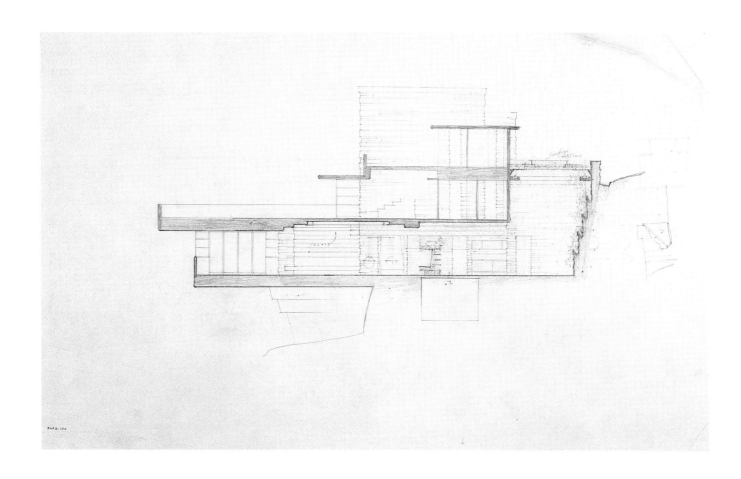

21 Gate Lodge Project

Mill Run, Pennsylvania

Bird's-eye perspective from approach road
1942
Pencil and sepia ink on tracing paper
29 × 36 in.
The Frank Lloyd Wright Foundation,
3713.005

The driveway from the township road (Route 381) to Fallingwater that was used by the Kaufmanns began north of the present entrance and crossed Bear Run from the right bank to the left (see fig. 20, p. 39). This crossing was the site for the gate lodge project Edgar Kaufmann commissioned in 1942.

Wright conceived the house as part of a high wall of coursed stone extending from the far bank of the stream, across the driveway, and into the woods. The house was to have been elevated enough to allow the caretakers views from the windows and terrace, but the broad, flat, overhanging roof assures a low profile in keeping with the horizontal lines of the wall.

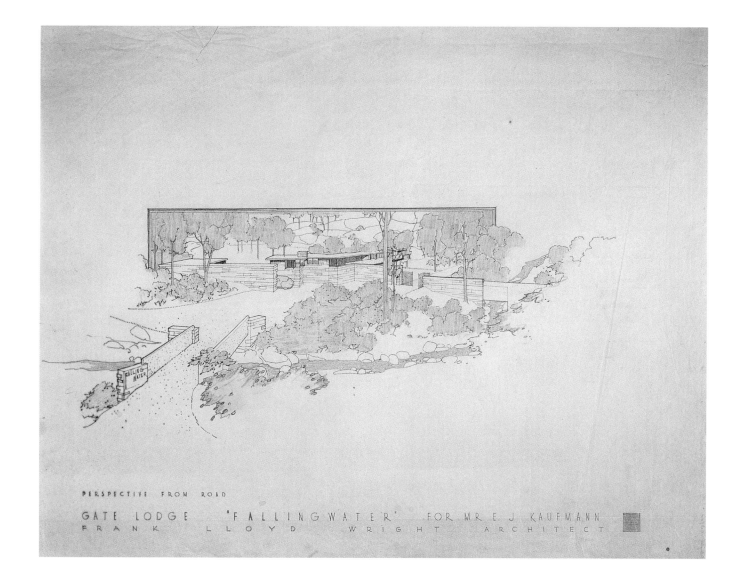

PERSPECTIVE FROM ROAD

GATE LODGE   'FALLINGWATER'   FOR MR E J KAUFMANN
FRANK   LLOYD   WRIGHT   ARCHITECT

22 Gate Lodge Project

Mill Run, Pennsylvania

Plan and section
1942
Pencil and color pencil on tracing paper
29½ × 36 in.
The Frank Lloyd Wright Foundation,
3713.001

This drawing studies the relationship of the gate lodge complex (wall, house, and toolshed) to its site. At upper right is a sketch of the course of Bear Run through the Kaufmanns' property. The section at the bottom examines the profile of the buildings with respect to the site's topography, which rises gradually from the streambed to an abrupt, rocky outcropping.

Wright's interest in these features went beyond the exigencies of security to establish expressive connections between architecture and landscape, a theme that he pursued throughout his career. Here, the complex engages the site in three directions: the wall and its water gate span Bear Run, the toolshed wing lays claim to the woods, and the bedroom wing extends into the face of the outcropping. Views from the house were no less important. The entrance side was like a battlement commanding the approach road under the shelter of the overhanging roof. The living room and especially the semicircular dining room offered panoramic views of the woods and glimpses of wildlife behind the house.

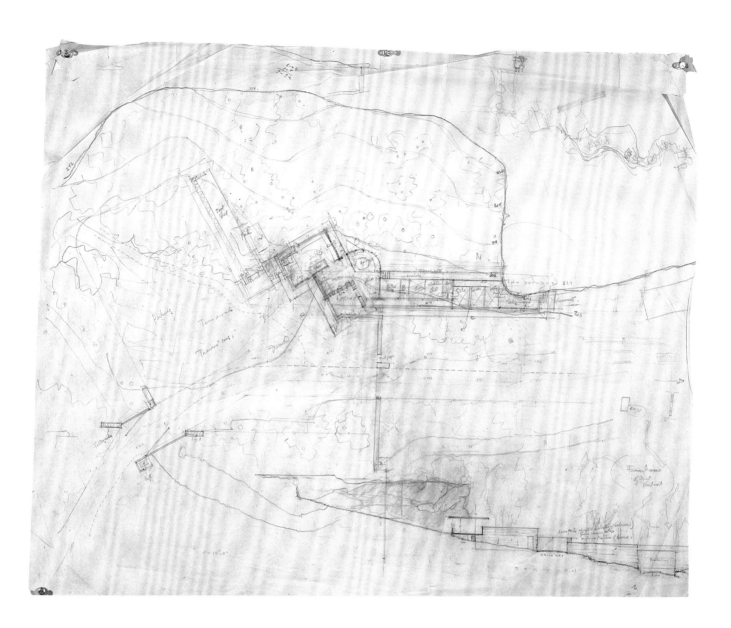

23 Gate Lodge Project

Mill Run, Pennsylvania

Perspective view from approach road
1956
Ink, pencil, and color pencil on tracing paper
25 × 34½ in.
The Frank Lloyd Wright Foundation,
5715.001

In 1956–57, Wright and Edgar Kaufmann jr. developed two schemes for a gate lodge and guest quarters near the site of the present ticket booth. This location reflects a change from the older driveway, used as the basis for the gate lodge project of 1942, to the existing drive. Wright and Kaufmann jr. planned the project as a demonstration of Wright's concrete-block Usonian Automatic houses, which promised ease of construction and modest cost.

The schemes differ only in the number of houses proposed for the site and in their orientation. This first scheme called for three houses arranged around a courtyard and an L-shaped service wing at the rear for parking and equipment storage. In contrast to the perspective view of the gate lodge project of 1942 (see cat. 21), which renders the building as an integral feature of the wooded site, the projects of the 1950s have a suburban appearance. The houses are set apart from the trees on a broad lawn and make no reference to features of the site. The apparent autonomy may have been a strategy to promote the idea of the houses as a flexible type.

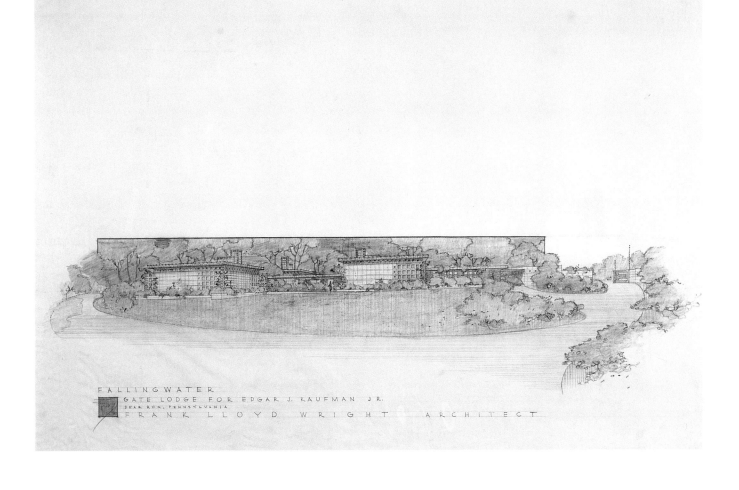

FALLINGWATER
GATE LODGE FOR EDGAR J. KAUFMAN JR.
BEAR RUN, PENNSYLVANIA
FRANK LLOYD WRIGHT ARCHITECT

24 Gate Lodge Project

Mill Run, Pennsylvania

Plan
20 December 1956
Ink, pencil, and color pencil on tracing paper
25½ × 35 in.
The Frank Lloyd Wright Foundation,
5715.003

Wright's reinforced-concrete-block Usonian Automatic houses issue from the "textile block" construction system that he had developed in the 1920s. The houses designed for Edgar Kaufmann jr. are ordered horizontally and vertically by a 2-foot module projected across the entire building site to coordinate their layout with the courtyard and the service wing.

The houses have identical plans. The ground floor has a double-height living and dining room, kitchen (labeled "workspace"), master bedroom, bathroom, and utility room. Wrapping around the living room above the smaller rooms is a balcony that could be subdivided as needed to create additional bedrooms or storage areas.

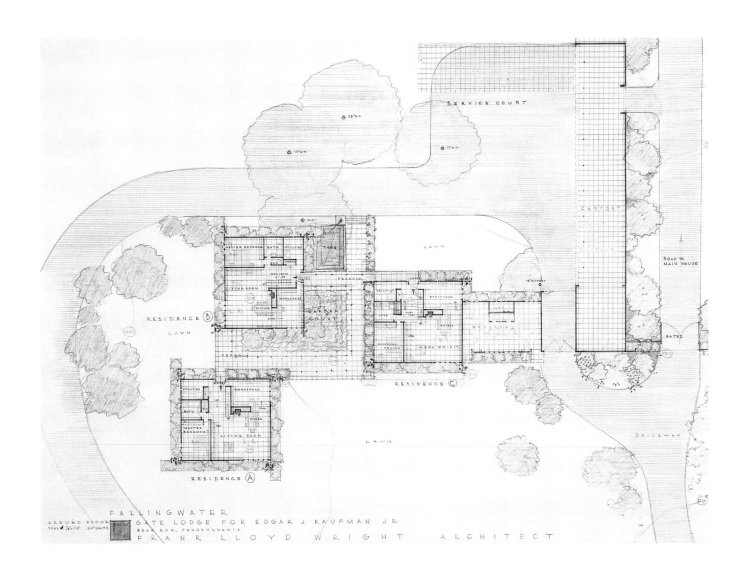

FALLINGWATER
GATE LODGE FOR EDGAR J. KAUFMAN JR.
BEAR RUN, PENNSYLVANIA
FRANK LLOYD WRIGHT ARCHITECT

GROUND FLOOR
SCALE

SERVICE COURT

LAWN

CARPORT

ROAD TO
MAIN HOUSE

RESIDENCE B

LAWN

MASTER BEDROOM   BATH   UTILITIES

LIVING ROOM

WORKSPACE

DINING

PERGOLA

GARDEN
COURT

PERGOLA

LIVING ROOM

WORKSPACE

DINING

RESIDENCE C

GATE

DRIVEWAY

RESIDENCE A

UTILITIES   WORKSPACE

BATH

MASTER BEDROOM   LIVING ROOM   DINING

LAWN

25 Farm Cottage Project
Mill Run, Pennsylvania

Perspective view of front
1941
Ink and pencil on tracing paper
29 × 36 in.
The Frank Lloyd Wright Foundation,
3711.002

In 1941, as part of his effort to develop a dairy herd, Edgar Kaufmann asked Wright to design a farmhouse (see Chapter 2). The intended site has not been verified, but the hillside depicted in the perspective view and the springhouse included in the plan (see cat. 26) suggest that it might have been in the vicinity of Kaufmann's dairy barn on the east side of Route 381.

26 Farm Cottage Project

Mill Run, Pennsylvania

Plan and side elevation
1941
Pencil on tracing paper
29 × 36 in.
The Frank Lloyd Wright Foundation,
3711.001

This plan is based on a 3-foot unit and consists of an L-shaped wing containing bedrooms, bathroom, kitchen (labeled "workspace"), toolroom, and springhouse set two steps above a rectangular living/dining room and porch. A broad shed roof with a pronounced return unifies the composition. The profile makes sense in the Laurel Highlands, where winter snowfalls can be heavy, but is rare in Wright's oeuvre. (A related example is the 1946 project for the Oboler Studio in Los Angeles.) Wright's more typical response to such a site was to treat the stepped elements of the house as terraces.

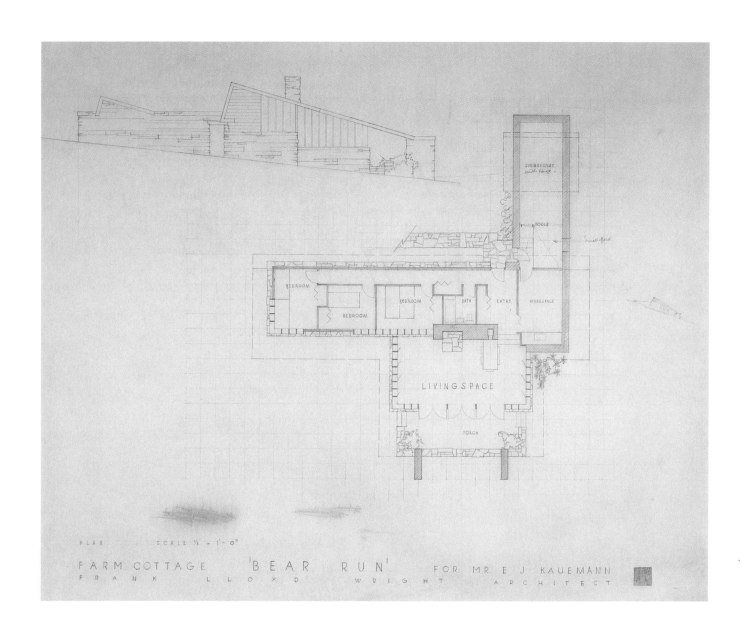

PLAN   SCALE ½" = 1'-0"

FARM COTTAGE   'BEAR RUN'   FOR MR E J KAUFMANN
FRANK   LLOYD   WRIGHT   ARCHITECT

27 Rhododendron Chapel Project

Mill Run, Pennsylvania

Perspective view of rear
8 June 1952
Pencil, color pencil, and ink on illustration board
18 × 34 in.
Drawn by John H. Howe (1913–1997)
The John H. Howe Collection, The State Historical Society of Wisconsin

Edgar Kaufmann jr. and his mother, Liliane Kaufmann, commissioned Wright to design a "place of prayer" at Bear Run in September 1951. A sheet of schematic drawings is dated 28 April 1952 (see cat. 28), and a set of renderings for presentation, including this drawing by John H. Howe, Wright's chief draftsman, is dated 8 June 1952. Kaufmann jr.'s correspondence with Wright indicates that he and his mother had sites in mind for the building, but the locations are not known. Howe's renderings indicate a setting consistent with an area on the right bank of Bear Run where the family mausoleum was later built.

RHODODENDRON CHAPEL · FOR MR. E. J. KAUFMANN
FRANK LLOYD WRIGHT · ARCHITECT

NOTE: THESE DRAWINGS OR THE SUBMITTED TO MR. KAUFMANN

DRAWN BY G.H.M.

28 Rhododendron Chapel Project

Mill Run, Pennsylvania

Plan and elevations
28 April 1952
Pencil and color pencil on illustration
board and tracing paper
28 × 35 ¼ in.
The John H. Howe Collection, The State
Historical Society of Wisconsin

Wright named the building the Rhododendron Chapel after the shrub common along the banks of Bear Run. An inscription explicates the building's purpose: "Private to the Beauty of Thought" / (Temple to poetry / for EJ Kaufman)." This much-worked drawing includes numerous annotations indicating materials and furnishings and an overlay of details for the roofline and the doorway.

Wright planned the building for a gently sloping site, which he mediated with a broad, stepped platform. It was to have two rooms laid out on a 2½-foot grid—a hall seating thirty under a steep gable roof and a more intimate low-ceilinged reading area with a large fireplace. The walls were to be stone, like those of Fallingwater, and the eaves of the flat roof were to be faced with copper.

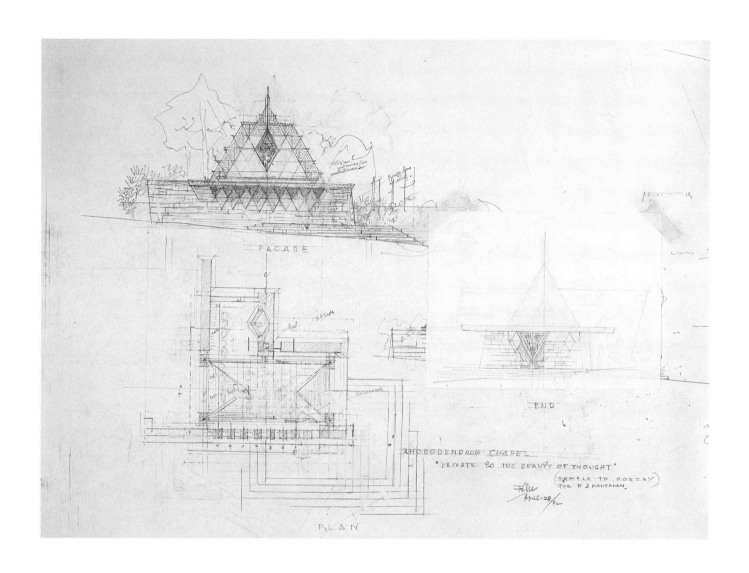

FACADE

END

PLAN

RHODODENDRON CHAPEL

"PRIVATE TO THE BEAUTY OF THOUGHT"

(TEMPLE TO POETRY
FOR E J KAUFMANN.)

April 28/5L

29 Rhododendron Chapel Project

Mill Run, Pennsylvania

Interior perspective
ca. 1952
Pencil and color pencil on tracing paper
18 × 34¾ in.
The Frank Lloyd Wright Foundation,
5308.002

This view cuts away the rear wall to reveal the reading area and the main hall, shown with an audience seated before a podium. The gable roof was to have two layers of clear, reflective, and perhaps colored glass set into frames and separated by an airspace. The scheme recalls the roof that Wright had proposed for the Steel Cathedral project of 1926 and that he would subsequently develop in 1954 for the Beth Sholom Synagogue in Elkins Park, Pennsylvania.

30 Boulder House Project

Palm Springs, California

Bird's-eye perspective
15 January 1951
Pencil, color pencil, and ink on tracing paper
25¼ × 35¼ in.
The Frank Lloyd Wright Foundation,
5111.001

Wright designed Boulder House during the winter of 1950–51 as a vacation residence for the Kaufmanns. He viewed it as a corrective for what he considered to be the family's blunder in building a house by Richard Neutra in Palm Springs in 1946.

Boulder House takes its name from the site's rocky terrain in the California desert, and the rendering indicates that Wright planned to embed boulders in the coursed masonry of the lower walls and chimneys. A plan has not come to light, but this view shows a main house flanked by two satellites and a long carport linked by curved passageways. A swimming pool, complete with a water gate into Liliane Kaufmann's bedroom, wraps around the house.

The elliptical forms of the plan and the roof profiles represent Wright's strong interest in curvilinear geometry in the late 1940s and 1950s. Realized examples of such forms include the houses he built for his sons David Wright (Phoenix, 1950–52) and Robert Llewellyn Wright (Bethesda, Maryland, 1953–57).

"BOULDER HOUSE" FOR LILIANE AND E·J·KAUFMANN
PALM SPRINGS···CALIFORNIA···DESERT BOULDER FIELD
FRANK LLOYD WRIGHT   ARCHITECT

31 Boulder House Project

Palm Springs, California

Rendered elevation
15 January 1951
Pencil and color pencil on tracing paper
16½ × 36 in.
The Frank Lloyd Wright Foundation,
5111.003

Edgar Kaufmann's initials next to Wright's in the signature block indicate his acceptance of this scheme. Between January and April 1951, the family purchased a lot for the house and hired a contractor to begin some preliminary work, but the project went no further.

Wright's design contrasted dramatically with the house Neutra had built for the Kaufmanns. Whereas the Neutra house engaged nature through the opposition of its rectilinear geometry and precisely composed manufactured materials, Wright sought to anchor his building in the particularities of the place—materially, through the use of local stone, and representationally, by echoing the profiles of the distant mountains with the undulating rooflines.

32 Edgar J. Kaufmann's Private Office

Pittsburgh

Perspective view from entrance
ca. 1936
Pencil on tracing paper
15½ × 18 in.
The Frank Lloyd Wright Foundation,
3704.023

Wright made the first studies for Edgar Kaufmann's private office during the summer of 1935. Construction did not begin until January 1937, however, and was not completed until the beginning of 1938. Originally installed on the northwest corner of the tenth floor of Kaufmann's department store, the office is now in the Victoria & Albert Museum, London.

This undated perspective study views the interior from the side of the entrance. Wright transformed the raw space into a work of cypress plywood cabinetry with a low ceiling, louvers screening the windows along the wall to the right, and a louvered clerestory above a row of storage cabinets at the rear. Edgar Kaufmann's desk extends from the wall at the left.

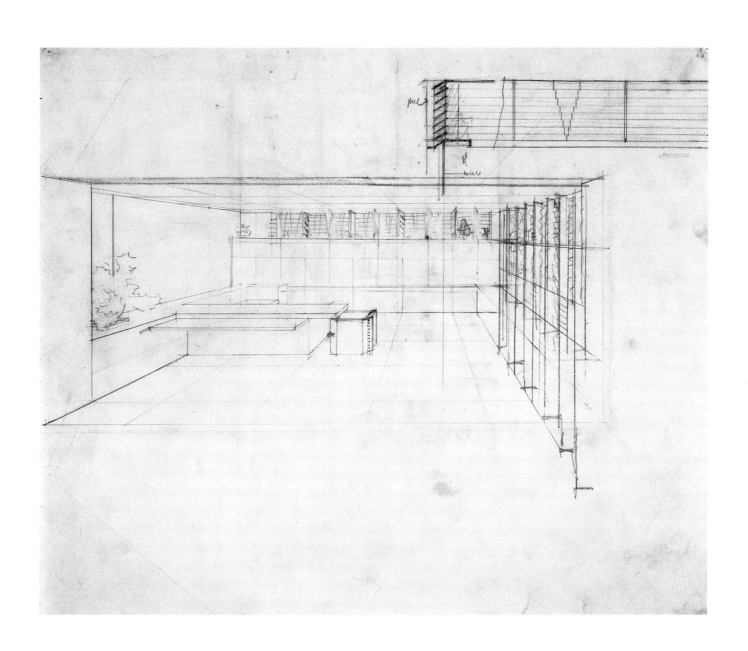

33 Edgar J. Kaufmann's Private Office

Pittsburgh

Elevation of mural and desk
ca. 1936
Pencil and color pencil on tracing paper
20 × 29 in.
The Frank Lloyd Wright Foundation,
3704.002

The focal point of the office is a mural alongside Edgar Kaufmann's desk made of the same plywood cypress used for the walls and ceiling. It is composed of up to six ¼-inch layers with carefully chosen grains arranged in a geometrical design playing 30-, 60-, and 120-degree angles against horizontal lines. The triangular form pointing downward from the top of the drawing is a glass light fixture. The drawing indicates dimensional adjustments and Wright's intention, later abandoned, of staining some of the wood in muted shades of red, blue, purple, and yellow.

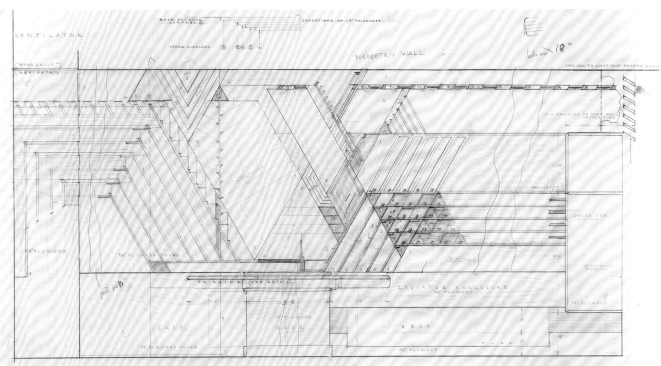

VENTILATOR

MARQUETRY WALL

CEILING TO CONTINUE BEYOND LOUVR

RADIATOR ENCLOSURE

SCALE 1½" — 1'-0"

34 Edgar J. Kaufmann's Private Office

Pittsburgh

Plan, elevations, and section for a curved-back chair
ca. 1936
Pencil on tracing paper
23½ × 28½ in.
The Frank Lloyd Wright Foundation,
3704.011

Decorative arts historian Christopher Wilk has noted in his book on Kaufmann's office (see Further Reading) that this unrealized design for a curvilinear, four-legged chair is strikingly different from the heavy, cubic forms of the other furnishings that Wright designed for Edgar Kaufmann's office and suggests that it may have been intended for the adjacent reception area. The chair was to have been built of the same materials used throughout the office: solid red cypress for the curved frame and spindles, and plywood for the horizontal elements. The drawing shows numerous erasures marking adjustments to the location and angles of the arms and the curve of the seat. It is initialed alongside Wright's name by Manuel J. Sandoval, the Nicaraguan-born cabinetmaker who built the office.

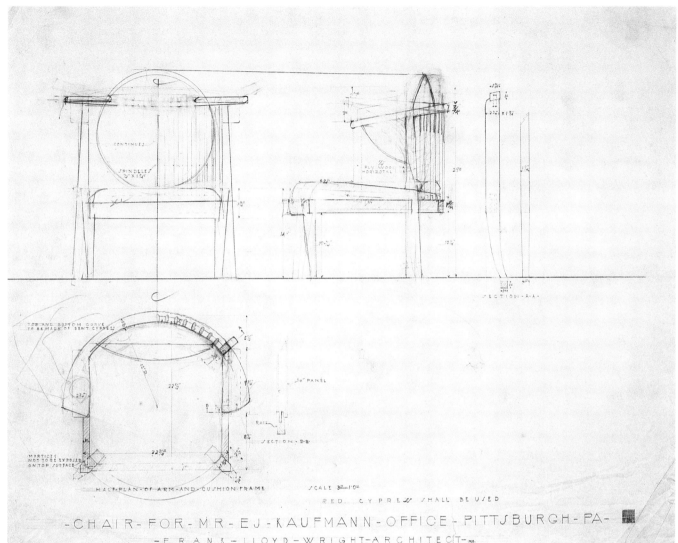

SECTION-A-A-

HALF-PLAN-OF-ARM-AND-CUSHION-FRAME

SECTION-B-B-

SCALE 3"=1'0"

RED CYPRESS SHALL BE USED

-CHAIR-FOR-MR-EJ-KAUFMANN-OFFICE-PITTSBURGH-PA-

-FRANK-LLOYD-WRIGHT-ARCHITECT-

35 Point Park Civic Center Project

Pittsburgh

*Scheme 1: bird's-eye view from
Mount Washington*
1947
Sepia ink and pencil on tracing paper
31½ × 35¾ in.
*The Frank Lloyd Wright Foundation,
4821.004*

Breaking with the prevailing sentiment to transform the Pittsburgh Point from an industrial site into a park, Edgar Kaufmann commissioned Wright to develop the site as a civic center offering a wide range of amenities that would bring together Pittsburghers of all social classes and interests.

The center's principal components are a megastructure containing a variety of entertainment facilities (theaters, arenas, and so on) wrapped by a spiral ramp; one tall and two low office buildings housing social service agencies; a round building at the tip of the Point containing an aquarium, restaurants, and a swimming pool; and two cantilevered reinforced concrete bridges spanning the Allegheny and Monongahela Rivers. The remainder of the site was to be developed with a zoo, an outdoor amphitheater, and an intricate, layered system of traffic circulation separating pedestrians, automobiles, and trucks.

This bird's-eye view looks eastward past the Point and the Golden Triangle (Pittsburgh's central business district) to the tower of the Cathedral of Learning at the University of Pittsburgh on the horizon. The drawing dramatically contrasts the traditional pattern of block-by-block piecemeal urban development with Wright's notion of consolidating a complex array of building types and transportation patterns into a unified scheme. Issues of technological and programmatic feasibility aside, the project was premised on a radically different way of thinking that gave priority to collective interests. Wright's understanding of the unique public-private partnerships responsible for postwar planning in Pittsburgh may have given him some hope that his vision would be received favorably.

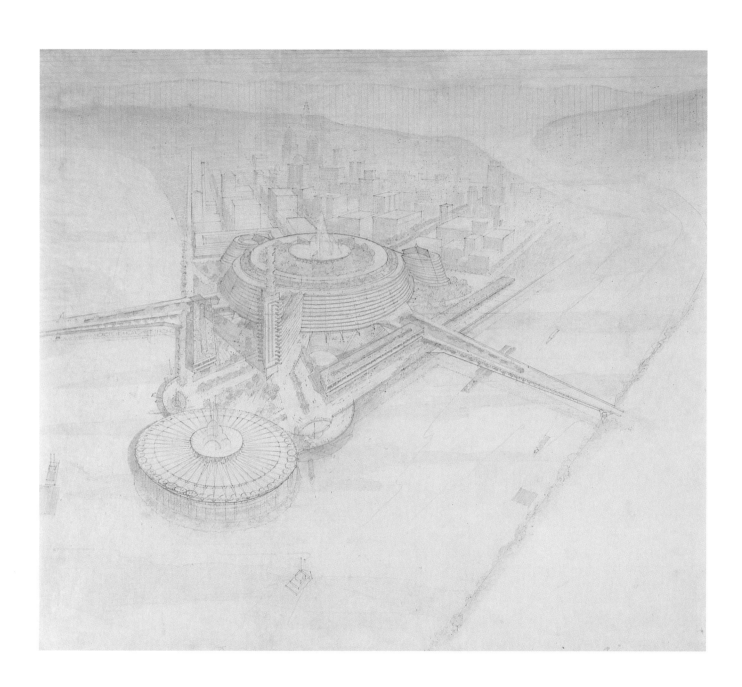

36 Point Park Civic Center Project

Pittsburgh

Scheme 1: plan at parking level
20 April 1947
Pencil and color pencil on tracing paper
18 × 21½ in.
The Frank Lloyd Wright Foundation,
4821.040

This scheme would have directed traffic from the cantilevered bridges to a below-grade traffic interchange under the megastructure. Above, at ground level, most of the site was to be given over to parking. Within the megastructure, separate parking areas would serve the convention hall, opera house, and the three cinemas. Wright termed the adjacent circular structures "fast ramps," which were to provide express connections to the longer ramp wrapping around the megastructure.

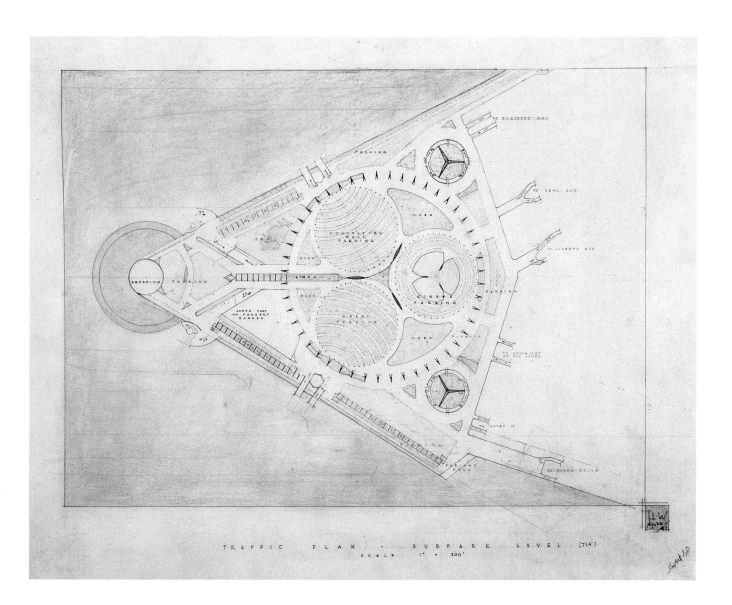

TRAFFIC PLAN — SUBPARK LEVEL (714')
SCALE 1" = 200'

SOUTH ELEVATION

37 Point Park Civic Center Project

Pittsburgh

Scheme 1: south elevation
1947
Ink, pencil, and color pencil on tracing paper
40 × 88 in.
The Frank Lloyd Wright Foundation,
4821.036

This large, delicately rendered elevation viewed from the Monongahela River evokes the festive "get-together" atmosphere Wright and Kaufmann sought for the civic center. The center was to have been a permanent fair, animated night and day by tens of thousands of people arriving by automobile, boat, and even dirigible. The drawing also indicates the importance of greenery throughout the project—on rooftops and balconies as well as at ground level.

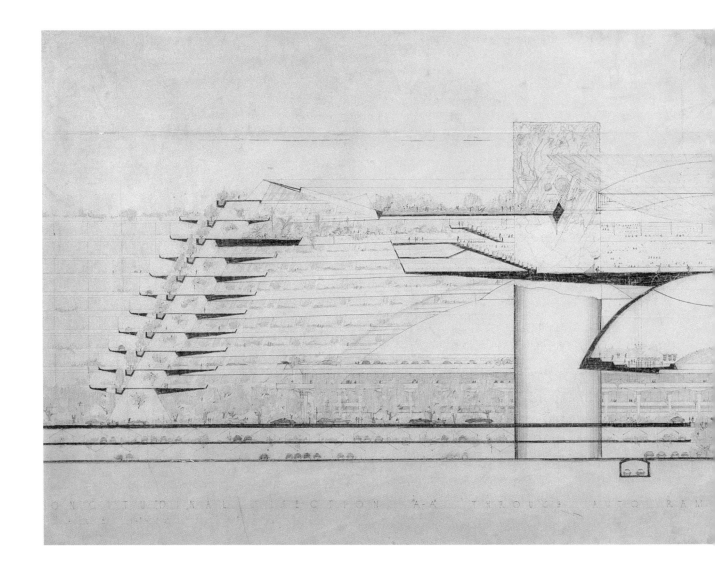

38 Point Park Civic Center Project

Pittsburgh

Scheme 1: longitudinal section through exhibition hall and arena within megastructure

1947
Ink, pencil, and color pencil on tracing paper
31 × 81½ in.
The Frank Lloyd Wright Foundation,
4821.005

The spiral ramp wrapping the megastructure was to be cantilevered from thin, reinforced-concrete piers recalling the structure of the Guggenheim Museum, which was on the drawing boards in Wright's studio when the Pittsburgh projects were being designed. The outer edge of the ramp was a roadway, and the inner portion provided space for parking and small shops.

The ramp was to have enclosed a vast atrium-like space, illuminated by skylights around the perimeter of the rooftop garden and occupied by a variety of structures of reinforced-concrete cantilever and shell construction. Shown in this view are,

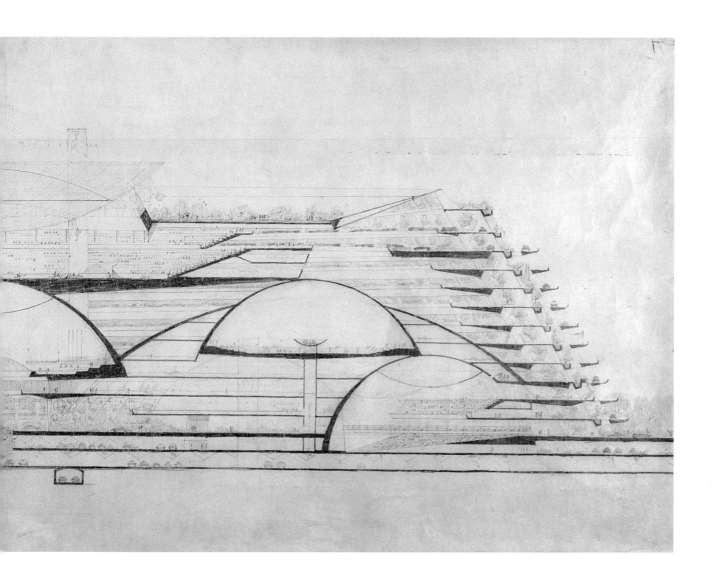

at center, a sports arena and a domed exhibition hall
and, at right, a planetarium and one of three large
cinemas. The arrival and lobby area left of center
is framed by the distinctive columns Wright in-
vented for the Johnson Wax Administrative Building
(1936–39) in Racine, Wisconsin.

39 Point Park Civic Center Project

Pittsburgh

Scheme 1: longitudinal section through aquarium
1947
Pencil and color pencil on tracing paper
32 × 58½ in.
The Frank Lloyd Wright Foundation,
4821.021

The center of the building at the tip of the Point was to house an aquarium displaying its major specimens in two glass spheres that could be viewed from all sides. At the right is a large restaurant, and at the left are swimming pools that would have offered views down the Ohio River. At the top of the drawing is a partial plan of the roof, showing a detail of the trellis along the perimeter.

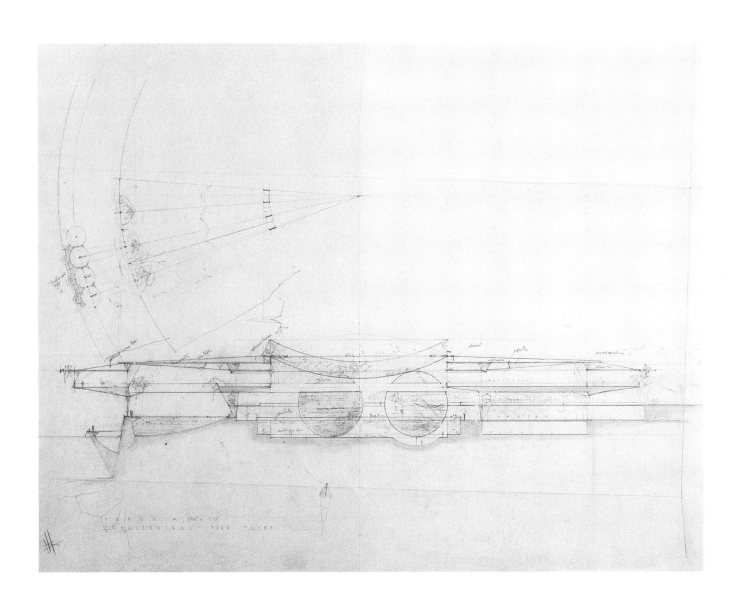

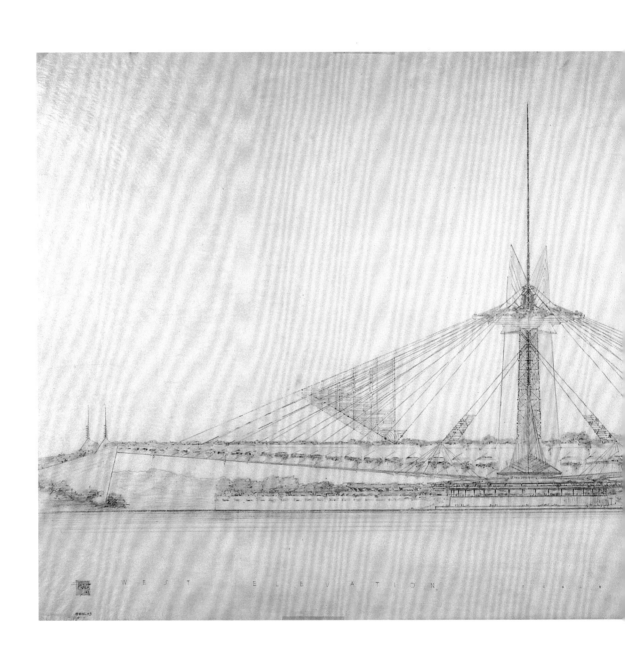

40 Point Park Civic Center Project

Pittsburgh

Scheme 2: west elevation
20 October 1947
Color pencil on tracing paper
28⅜ × 56¼ in.
Carnegie Museum of Art, Pittsburgh.
Museum purchase: gift of Women's Committee, Carnegie Treasures Cookbook Fund, 86.24
Frank Lloyd Wright Foundation reference 4836.003

Wright's second proposal retained the aquarium at the tip of the Point but replaced the megastructure with a colossal pier anchoring triple-decked cable-stayed bridges spanning the Monongahela and Allegheny Rivers. Large round disks suspended from the bridges shaded garden areas, which Wright termed "park bowls."

41 Point Park Civic Center Project

Pittsburgh

Scheme 2: perspective view from the east
1947
Ink, gouache, pencil, and color pencil on tracing paper
29 × 44 in.
The Frank Lloyd Wright Foundation, 4836.004

Wright once described Pittsburgh as a "disappearing city." In this view, attributed to apprentice Allen Lape Davison (1913–1974), all references to the urban context of the Pittsburgh Point have been eliminated to dramatically present Wright's scheme in relation to its natural setting of the Monongahela, Allegheny, and Ohio Rivers.

The drawing indicates that the Point was to be separated from the streets of the central business district (the Golden Triangle) by a broad berm that loosely recalls the earthen ramparts of Fort Pitt, the eighteenth-century fortress that once stood on the site. Wright may have alluded to this association in naming this scheme the "Bastion."

The two round structures that flank the pier anchoring the bridges are office buildings. The structure in the background on the left side of the drawing is an observation tower clasping the side of Mount Washington. The image gives form to an idea Wright had proposed in his first meeting with the members of the Allegheny Conference on Community Development in 1946.

42 Point Park Civic Center Project

Pittsburgh

Scheme 2: longitudinal and cross sections through Monongahela River bridge
20 October 1947
Ink, pencil, and color pencil on tracing paper
32 × 57 in.
The Frank Lloyd Wright Foundation,
4836.007

The cable-stayed bridges that Wright proposed in his second scheme for the Point are a type of suspension bridge in which the deck is supported by cables anchored by a single pier. Cable-stayed construction was an emerging technology in the years following World War II, as was the segmental, prestressed concrete construction that Wright proposed for the deck. The structure accommodated pedestrians, automobiles, and trucks on three levels contained within a giant truss. The lowest member of this structure (the truck deck) was to have been a cantilever supported by a deep beam. It was an application of Wright's "butterfly" system, which he likened to the way a butterfly's broad wings spring from its thorax. Such analogies from forms appearing in nature frequently were at the heart of Wright's structural inventions.

The longitudinal section is drawn to include a portion of one of the two "park bowls." Unlike the other garden areas in Wright's scheme, such as the promenade deck on the bridges, which were planned to take advantage of the river views, these parks within the park would have been internally focused landscapes sheltered by the canopies suspended from the bridges.

LONGITUDINAL   SECTION   THROUGH   MONONGAHELA   BRIDGE   CROSS   SECTIONS   THROUGH
SCALE   MONONGAHELA   BRIDGE

SECTIONS

43 Point Park Civic Center Project

Pittsburgh

*Scheme 2: perspective view at night from
the Ohio River*
1947
Paint on posterboard
25 × 38 in.
*The Frank Lloyd Wright Foundation,
4836.009*

Taliesin apprentice Allen Lape Davison (1913–1974) was a native of Pittsburgh. He mastered Wright's style for handling color pencil and also developed a spectacular technique for portraying buildings at night: he prepared posterboard with matte black paint and then rendered the buildings using tiny dabs of bright color.

Provisions for nocturnal illumination were an integral part of Wright's design for the Point. The tall, slender tower attached to the sail-like anchor pier, for example, was to have been equipped to present sound and light shows.

44 Kaufmann's Parking Garage Project

Pittsburgh

Perspective from Smithfield Street and
Fourth Avenue
20 September 1949
Ink, pencil, and color pencil on tracing paper
35½ × 46¾ in.
The Frank Lloyd Wright Foundation,
4923.053

Wright's parking garage for Kaufmann's department store (at left) was to have been built on the site of the present garage. The lower levels were to have contained retail space with display windows facing Smithfield Street. The big corner buttresses anchored the outer ring of the cantilevered parking ramp.

Although Edgar Kaufmann had been optimistic about building the structure when he initiated the commission with Wright, he abandoned it in the wake of structural, functional, and building-code problems identified by his consultants.

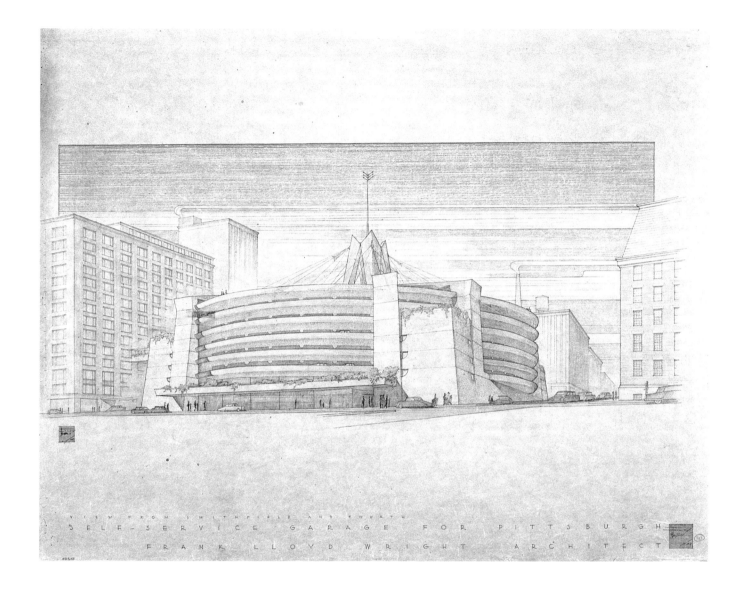

VIEW FROM SMITHFIELD AND FOURTH
SELF-SERVICE GARAGE FOR PITTSBURGH
FRANK LLOYD WRIGHT ARCHITECT

45 Kaufmann's Parking Garage Project

Pittsburgh

Section
20 September 1949
Ink, pencil, and color pencil on tracing paper
36 × 46¾ in.
The Frank Lloyd Wright Foundation,
4923.048

The reinforced-concrete structure was to have had two ramps: an outer ramp stabilized by piers at the corner of the building, and an inner ramp attached to tall slender piers, which also anchor cables supporting the extremities of the cantilevers. The center piers frame a lightwell, which becomes an enclosed atrium with fountain and plants in the retail areas. Adjacent to the entrance is a theater-like waiting room equipped with television to provide entertainment for family members awaiting shoppers.

SECTION ON CENTER LINE FROM CHERRY WAY TO SMITHFIELD STREET PARKING SYSTEM

SELF SERVICE GARAGE FOR PITTSBURGH

FRANK LLOYD WRIGHT ARCHITECT

46 Point View Residences Project

Pittsburgh

Scheme 1B: perspective view from northeast
June 1953
Ink, pencil, and color pencil on tracing paper
35 × 30 in.
The Frank Lloyd Wright Foundation,
5222.001

The Point View apartment building planned for Grandview Avenue on Mount Washington was to have been a speculative venture by the Edgar J. Kaufmann Charitable Foundation and Trust with a portion of the building's profits to be donated to the Frank Lloyd Wright Foundation.

Wright based his first project on the unrealized apartment building that he had designed in 1929 for Elizabeth Noble in Los Angeles. The version for Pittsburgh included a penthouse for the Kaufmanns and luxurious duplex apartments cantilevered from a structural spine.

In drawings such as this, Wright generally relied on John Howe, Allen Davison, or other apprentices to lay out the building and begin the rendering in color pencil. He would then add his own touches, such as the foliage on the hillside.

VIEW FROM NORTHEAST
POINT VIEW RESIDENCES
FOR THE EDGAR J. KAUFMANN CHARITABLE TRUST
FRANK LLOYD WRIGHT ARCHITECT

47 Point View Residences Project

Pittsburgh

Scheme 1A: plan at street level
8 June 1952
Ink, pencil, and color pencil on tracing paper
34½ × 30½ in.
The Frank Lloyd Wright Foundation,
5222.004

An inscription on Wright's signature square reads "1927–1952," a reference to this scheme's origins in the unrealized Elizabeth Noble apartments planned for Los Angeles. Wright planned to erect the building on a concrete perch set on the steep slope of Mount Washington. He laid out the apartments with the kitchens and dining rooms closest to the hillside and the living rooms and terraces opening toward views of the Ohio River and the Golden Triangle, the central business district. The apartments on the western side of the building would have had more restricted views than those on the east, however, because of a bearing wall that rises the full height of the building at the outer corner of the living rooms.

PLAN AT STREET LEVEL
LIVING ROOM LEVEL FOR APARTMENTS ⒡ AND ⒢   GRANDVIEW AVENUE   SCALE: ⅛"=1'-0" - UNITS 5'-6"X5'-0"

APARTMENTS FOR THE EDGAR J. KAUFMANN CHARITABLE TRUST

FRANK LLOYD WRIGHT
ARCHITECT

48 Point View Residences Project

Pittsburgh

Scheme 2: perspective view from northwest
11 April 1953
Ink, pencil, and color pencil on tracing paper
34½ × 29 in.
The Frank Lloyd Wright Foundation,
5310.001

The cost estimates for the first scheme for the Point View apartments exceeded the anticipated return from rentals, so Edgar Kaufmann jr. requested that Wright design an alternative. Wright responded by pulling the building closer to the crest of Mount Washington to reduce the dimensions of the foundations and by laying out the apartments as flats instead of duplexes. In making these changes, he switched from an orthogonal geometry to a diagonal composition that provided all units with unobstructed views of the Golden Triangle.

Although the site had not changed, in this drawing it appears gentler and greener than in the rendering of the first scheme, which more closely approximated the barren slopes of Mount Washington before the implementation of clean-air regulations. The more bucolic setting may have been intended to win over officers of the Kaufmann Charitable Trust who were skeptical of the viability of luxury apartments on Grandview Avenue in the 1950s.

VIEW FROM NORTHWEST
POINT VIEW RESIDENCES
FOR THE EDGAR J. KAUFMANN CHARITABLE TRUST
FRANK LLOYD WRIGHT ARCHITECT   SHEET

49 Point View Residences Project

Pittsburgh

Scheme 2B: site plan
ca. 1952–53
Ink, pencil, and color pencil on tracing paper
35 × 32½ in.
The Frank Lloyd Wright Foundation,
5310.002

This sheet was originally laid out to present a variant of the first scheme for the Point View Residences. Its plan, drawn in red pencil, has been rotated northward from the original position and shifted slightly to the east. Superimposed on it is the triangular plan of the second scheme. Its primary axis runs parallel to the topographic contours so that more of the building is tucked into the hillside than in the first scheme. Among the issues under study are room layouts—more spacious than in the first scheme—and vehicular circulation from Grandview Avenue to the parking garage.

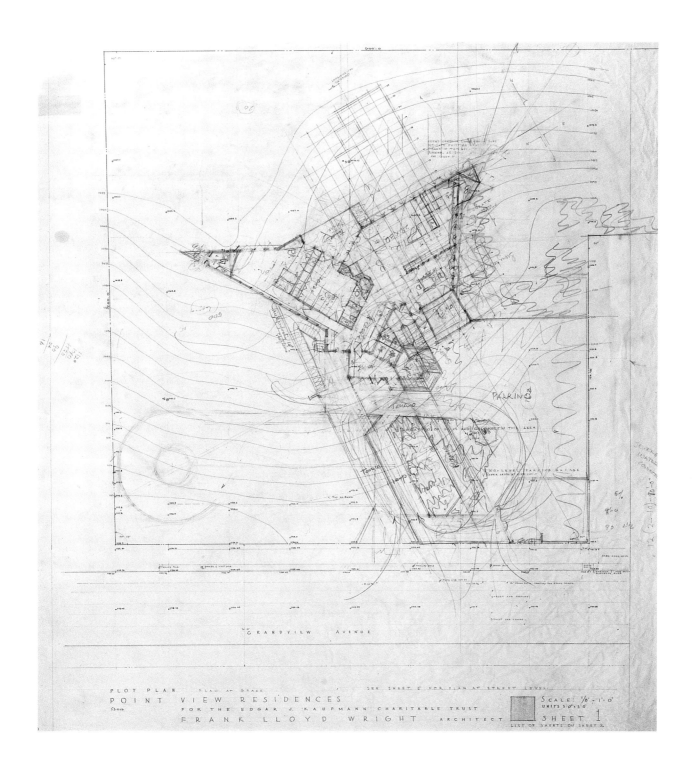

GRANDVIEW AVENUE

PLOT PLAN   PLAN AT GRADE   SEE SHEET 5 FOR PLAN AT STREET LEVEL
POINT VIEW RESIDENCES   SCALE: 1/8" = 1'-0"
    FOR THE EDGAR J. KAUFMANN CHARITABLE TRUST   UNITS 5'-0" x 5'-0"
FRANK LLOYD WRIGHT ARCHITECT   SHEET 1
                                            LIST OF SHEETS ON SHEET 2

Drawings for Projects Commissioned by the Kaufmann Family from Frank Lloyd Wright, 1935–57

Although many drawings produced by Frank Lloyd Wright's studio have been published, there is no master list allowing scholars to situate these drawings within the larger corpus of his unpublished drawings—a necessary task for understanding the genesis of projects and realized buildings. The closest thing to such a compilation is the inventory of the Frank Lloyd Wright Archives, which lists the more than 22,000 drawings in that collection. Its primary function, however, is as a tool for collection management.

The drawings in the Wright archives are organized by project number. This filing system does not differentiate variant schemes for a given project, and this matter is further complicated by the studio's practice of dating only presentation drawings and working drawing sets and of reusing drawings at various stages of project development.

The following list itemizes the known drawings for the projects the Kaufmann family commissioned from Wright. Most are in the collection of the Frank Lloyd Wright Archives. The second largest collection was donated by Edgar Kaufmann jr. to the Avery Architectural and Fine Arts Library at Columbia University. The State Historical Society of Wisconsin possesses the most extensive set of drawings for the Rhododendron Chapel project, and the Canadian Centre for Architecture owns two perspective views of Fallingwater. One perspective view of the house is in a private collection.

This list offers a preliminary sorting of the Kaufmann projects based on inscribed dates, identifiable schemes, and obvious preliminary drawings for sets in those categories. The remaining drawings for each project are listed by type, such as perspective views, plans, elevations, sections, and details. Each entry includes the following elements:

- Subject.
- Inscription (if any), noting date and signatures. *FLLW* = Frank Lloyd Wright; *EJK* = Edgar J. Kaufmann.
- Medium and dimensions.
- Collection. FLLWF = The Frank Lloyd Wright Foundation; Avery = Avery Architectural and Fine Arts Library.
- Inventory number. Usually the project number of the Frank Lloyd Wright Archives.
- Publication. *Monograph = Frank Lloyd Wright: Monograph, Preliminary Studies, Renderings* (see Further Reading); cat. = *Merchant Prince and Master Builder.*
- Notes.

Fallingwater and Related Projects

Fallingwater (1936–38)

PUBLICATION PLANS

First floor plan. Ink on tracing paper, 17¾ × 24½ in. FLLWF, 3602.162.

Second floor plan. Ink on tracing paper, 16¾ × 27½ in. FLLWF, 3602.163.

Longitudinal section. Ink on tracing paper, 16¼ × 25¾ in. FLLWF, 3602.164.

Guest house plan. Ink on tracing paper, 22½ × 29¾ in. FLLWF, 3602.165.

PERSPECTIVE VIEWS

Bird's-eye view from the south. Pencil and color pencil on tracing paper, 18½ × 29⅝ in. Canadian Centre for Architecture, 3602.001. *Monograph*, 11: 48.

Bird's-eye view from the north. Pencil and color pencil on tracing paper, 14⅜ × 31½ in. Canadian Centre for Architecture, 3602.002. *Monograph*, 11: 49.

View from waterfall. Pencil and color pencil on tracing paper, 15 × 32 in. Private collection, 3602.003. *Monograph*, 11: 47.

View from waterfall. Pencil on tracing paper, 17¼ × 36 in. FLLWF, 3602.050. *Monograph*, 11: 46. Preliminary drawing for 3602.003.

View from waterfall. Inscr. *1936*. Pencil and color pencil on tracing paper, 15⅜ × 27¼ in. FLLWF, 3602.004. *Monograph*, 12: 98.

View from waterfall. Pencil on tracing paper, 24¼ × 35½ in. FLLWF, 3602.051.

View from waterfall. Pastel on paper, 15½ × 27¾ in. FLLWF, unnumbered. Preliminary study.

View from south. Pencil on tracing paper, 23 × 36 in. FLLWF, 3602.056. Preliminary study.

30° SERIES

Note: Drawn in the fall of 1936, with plans laid out to indicate the building's orientation 30 degrees east of south

Superimposed plans. Pencil and color pencil on tracing paper, 27½ × 32 in. FLLWF, 3602.166. *Monograph*, 11: 44. Cat. 1.

Foundation plan. Pencil and color pencil on tracing paper, 31 × 41 in. FLLWF, 3602.036.

First floor plan. Pencil and color pencil on tracing paper, 31 × 41 in. FLLWF, 3602.044. Cat. 2.

First floor plan. Pencil and color pencil on tracing paper, 28 × 43 in. FLLWF, 3602.048. *Monograph*, 11: 45. Preliminary drawing for 3602.044.

Second floor plan. Pencil and color pencil on tracing paper, 30½ × 41 in. FLLWF, 3602.043.

Second floor plan. Pencil and color pencil on tracing paper, 28½ × 40½ in. FLLWF, 3602.047. Cat. 3. Preliminary drawing for 3602.043.

Third floor plan and section. Pencil and color pencil on tracing paper, 31¼ × 41 in. FLLWF, 3602.040.

Third floor plan. Pencil and color pencil on tracing paper, 16 × 26 in. FLLWF, 3602.046. Preliminary drawing for 3602.040.

North elevation and section. Pencil and color pencil on tracing paper, 31½ × 41½ in. FLLWF, 3602.042. *Monograph*, 5: 275.

South elevation. Pencil and color pencil on tracing paper, 18½ × 34 in. FLLWF, 3602.049. *Monograph*, 11: 50. Preliminary layout.

West, east, and south elevations. Pencil and color pencil on tracing paper, 32 × 41 in. FLLWF, 3602.045. Cat. 5.

Elevations. Pencil on tracing paper, 31½ × 40½ in. FLLWF, 3602.041. Preliminary drawing for 3602.045.

DRAWINGS INSCRIBED 27 MAY 1936

Plot plan. Inscr. *27 May 1936, FLLW*. Pencil on tracing paper, 30 × 36 in. FLLWF, 3602.005, no. 1.

Foundation plan. Inscr. *27 May 1936, FLLW*. Pencil and color pencil on tracing paper, 30 × 36 in. FLLWF, 3602.006, no. 2.

First floor plan. Inscr. *27 May 1936, FLLW*. Pencil and color pencil on tracing paper, 30 × 36 in. FLLWF, 3602.007, no. 3. See p. 181, "Fallingwater Additions."

Second floor plan. Inscr. *27 May 1936, FLLW*. Pencil and color pencil on tracing paper, 30 × 36 in. FLLWF, 3602.008, no. 4. Drawing has been reworked to study the guest house bridge connection at the second floor.

Third floor and roof plan. Inscr. *27 May 1936, FLLW*. Pencil and color pencil on tracing paper, 30 × 36 in. FLLWF, 3602.009, no. 5.

North and south elevations. *Inscr. 27 May 1936, FLLW*. Pencil and color pencil on tracing paper, 30 × 36 in. FLLWF, 3602.010, no. 6. 17 vertical units indicated.

East and west elevations, sections. Inscr. *27 May 1936, FLLW*. Pencil on tracing paper, 30 × 36 in. FLLWF, 3602.011, no. 7. *Monograph*, 5: 270.

East and west elevations, sections. Pencil on tracing paper, 29½ × 36 in. FLLWF, 3602.031. Preliminary drawing for 3602.011.

Sections. Inscr. *27 May 1936, FLLW*. Pencil on tracing paper, 30 × 36 in. FLLWF, 3602.012, no. 8. *Monograph*, 5: 271.

Details. Inscr. *27 May 1936, FLLW*. Pencil on tracing paper, 30 × 36 in. FLLWF, 3602.013, no. 9.

Heating and wiring diagram, first floor. Pencil on tracing paper, 30 × 36 in. FLLWF, 3602.014. Preliminary
layout.

Heating and wiring diagram, second and third floors.
Pencil on tracing paper, 30 × 36 in. FLLWF, 3602.015.
Preliminary layout.

Glass schedule. Inscr. *27 May 1936.* Pencil on tracing
paper, 30 × 36 in. FLLWF, 3602.016, no. 11.

UNDATED PLANS

Plot plan. Pencil on tracing paper, 15 × 36 in. FLLWF,
3602.089. Indicates contours, major rocks, and first
floor plan.

Plot plan, including first floor. Pencil on tracing paper,
24¼ × 36 in. FLLWF, 3602.158.

Plot plan, including first floor. Pencil on tracing paper,
24½ × 36 in. FLLWF, 3602.123. Gridded plan.

Topographic plan. Pencil and ink on tracing paper, 29½ ×
36 in. FLLWF, 3602.124. Indicates contours, boulders,
and trees.

Topographic plan. Pencil on tracing paper, 18¾ × 36 in.
FLLWF, 3602.129. Shows hearth boulder, other boulders to west and south, and 28-inch-diameter
oak tree.

Foundation plan. Pencil on tracing paper, 30½ × 36 in.
FLLWF, 3602.066. Preliminary layout.

Plunge pool plan. Pencil on tracing paper, 22½ × 16 in.
FLLWF, 3602.087.

First floor plan. Pencil and color pencil on tracing paper,
27¼ × 35¾ in. FLLWF, 3602.055. Preliminary study.

First floor, north wall plan. Pencil and color pencil on
tracing paper, 13½ × 32¼ in. FLLWF, 3602.136. Cat. 6.
Drawing by Bob Mosher, noting construction progress
along north side of house.

Second floor plan. Pencil on tracing paper, 28¾ × 36 in.
FLLWF, 3602.059. Examines Edgar Kaufmann's terrace
and adjacent boulder.

Second floor plan. Inscr. *void.* Pencil on tracing paper,
28½ × 36. FLLWF, 3602.061. Erasures and redrawing
of the bathroom and guest room windows and Edgar
Kaufmann's bathroom; freehand drawing of masonry
pier added to the east balcony.

Third floor plan and roof plan. Inscr. *Bach chromatic Fant.
& Fugue / Chopin—2 Preludes / Ravel—Sanatine* [sic]
/ Brahms—2 Cappriccio op 76, 116. Pencil on tracing
paper, 30½ × 36 in. FLLWF, 3602.125.

UNDATED ELEVATIONS AND SECTIONS

North and south elevations. Pencil on tracing paper,
30½ × 36 in. FLLWF, 3602.057.

West and south elevations, second and third floor plans.
Pencil on tracing paper, 24½ × 36½ in. FLLWF,
3602.157. *Monograph,* 5: 268.

Longitudinal section, showing living room and bedroom
fireplaces. Pencil on tracing paper, 26¾ × 36 in. FLLWF,
3602.060. *Monograph,* 11: 51. Cat. 4. Includes numerous marginal sketches and notations.

Longitudinal and transverse sections. Inscr. *not final.*
Pencil on tracing paper, 28¼ × 36 in. FLLWF, 3602.080.
Preliminary layouts.

Section across rear of house. Pencil and color pencil on
tracing paper, 14½ × 25 in. FLLWF, 3602.113.

Terrace sections. Pencil and color pencil on tracing paper,
28¾ × 36 in. FLLWF, 3602.058.

Elevation and sectional studies, bedroom plan sketches.
Pencil and color pencil on tracing paper, 16¼ × 36 in.
FLLWF, 3602.128. Indication of 17-inch unit.

CASEWORK DRAWINGS, NUMBERED SERIES

Door frames. Inscr. *FLLW.* Pencil on tracing paper, 21 ×
36 in. FLLWF, 3602.145, no. 1. *Monograph,* 5: 290.

Living room: casework. Pencil on tracing paper, 28 × 36 in.
FLLWF, 3602.018, no. 2.

Living room: details for convector grilles. Pencil on tracing
paper, 24½ × 36 in. FLLWF, 3602.134, no. 3.

Guest room: plan and elevations. Pencil on tracing paper,
26 × 36 in. FLLWF, 3602.019, no. 4.

Liliane Kaufmann's bedroom: layout and casework.
Pencil and color pencil on tracing paper, 26¼ × 36 in.
FLLWF, 3602.135, no. 5. *Monograph,* 5: 295.

Wardrobes. Pencil on tracing paper, 27½ × 36 in. FLLWF,
3602.020, no. 6.

Edgar Kaufmann's room: casework details. Pencil on tracing paper, 26 × 34 in. FLLWF, 3602.021, no. 7.

Edgar Kaufmann jr.'s bathroom: elevations. Pencil on
tracing paper, 28 × 34 in. FLLWF, 3602.022, no. 8.

Dining area casework: elevation, plan, and detail. Pencil
on tracing paper, 27 × 36 in. FLLWF, 3602.079.

Dining area casework: elevation, plan, and detail. Pencil
on tracing paper, 27 × 36 in. FLLWF, 3602.081. Preliminary drawing for 3602.079, no. 9.

Dining area casework. Pencil on tracing paper, 30 × 26 in.
FLLWF, 3602.082. Study for 3602.079.

Edgar Kaufmann's bathroom: elevations. Pencil on tracing
paper, 28 × 34½ in. FLLWF, 3602.023, no. 10.

Liliane Kaufmann's bathroom: elevations. Pencil on tracing paper, 26½ × 34½ in. FLLWF, 3602.024, no. 11.

Stairway bookshelves. Pencil on tracing paper, 26 × 35 in.
FLLWF, 3602.025, no. 12. *Monograph,* 5: 294.

Edgar Kaufmann jr.'s bedroom: casework. Pencil on tracing paper, 25 × 36 in. FLLWF, 3602.133, no. 13.

Third floor casework. Pencil on tracing paper, 24 × 36 in. FLLWF, 3602.064. Preliminary study.

Wardrobe details. Pencil on tracing paper, 24 × 35 in. FLLWF, 3602.026. No. 14. Full-size details.

Third-floor hall bookshelves. Inscr. *2 July 1937*. Pencil on tracing paper, 21 × 34 in. FLLWF, 3602.027, no. 15.

Liliane Kaufmann's bathroom: dressing table. Inscr. *2 July 1937*. Pencil on tracing paper, 21½ × 34½ in. FLLWF, 3602.028, no. 16.

Guest bathroom: towel case. Inscr. *2 July 1937*. Pencil on tracing paper, 22½ × 30 in. FLLWF, 3602.029, no. 17.

CASEWORK AND FURNISHINGS

Wardrobe schedule. Inscr. *FLLW*. Pencil on tracing paper, 28 × 36 in. FLLWF, 3602.038.

Bedroom swivel light: elevation and plans. Pencil and color pencil on tracing paper, 36 × 19½ in. FLLWF, 3602.103. Full-size.

BASEMENT

Plan and elevations. Pencil and color pencil on tracing paper, 20½ × 36 in. FLLWF, 3602.152.

Plan and elevations. Pencil on tracing paper, 25¼ × 36 in. FLLWF, 3602.151. Preliminary drawing for 3602.152.

Basement stairwell. Pencil and color pencil on tracing paper, 17¾ × 17 in. FLLWF, 3602.110. *Monograph*, 11: 58. Cat. 7. Drawn by Bob Mosher, with annotations by Wright.

LIVING ROOM AND DINING AREA

Plan. Inscr. *27 October 1937, FLLW*. Pencil and color pencil on tracing paper, 27½ × 35 in. FLLWF, 3602.033. Indicates color for upholstery and layout of rugs.

Plan. Inscr. *FLLW*. Pencil and color pencil on tracing paper, 26¾ × 36 in. FLLWF, 3602.078. Cat. 11. Preliminary drawing for 3602.033; more detailed and larger scale than 3602.054; annotated by Wright.

Plan. Pencil and color pencil, 26¼ × 30 in. FLLWF, 3602.054. Preliminary layout for rugs and furniture.

Plan and elevation of west wall. Pencil and color pencil on tracing paper, 19½ × 42 in. FLLWF, 3602.076. Corresponds to 3602.073.

Elevations. Pencil and color pencil on tracing paper, 25 × 36 in. FLLWF, 3602.073.

East and south elevations. Pencil and color pencil on tracing paper, 24½ × 36 in. FLLWF, 3602.141. Cat. 12. Similar to 3602.073.

Section cut through the hatch. Inscr. *void*. Pencil on tracing paper, 13¾ × 36 in. FLLWF, 3602.138.

Reflected ceiling plan. Pencil on tracing paper, 25 × 36 in. FLLWF, 3602.067.

Reflected ceiling plan. Pencil on tracing paper, 20¾ × 33 in. FLLWF, 3602.070. Preliminary drawing for 3602.067.

Fireplace. Inscr. *26 August 1936*. Pencil on tracing paper, 20½ × 25 in. FLLWF, 3602.069. Office copy of drawing sent to Mill Run.

Fireplace accessories. Pencil on tracing paper, 25¾ × 36 in. FLLWF, 3602.153. *Monograph*, 5: 285, 11: 54. Drawings on recto and verso.

Casework: plan, elevation, and section. Pencil and color pencil on tracing paper, 15½ × 30½ in. FLLWF, 3602.074.

Casework: Inscr. *void*. Pencil and color pencil on tracing paper, 17 × 36 in. FLLWF, 3602.137. Includes sketch of guest house and service buildings.

Studies for dining table and a living room chair. Pencil and color pencil on tracing paper, 21½ × 36 in. FLLWF, 3602.097.

Dining area extension tables: plan, elevation, and section. Inscr. *10 July 1936*. Pencil on tracing paper, 22¼ × 36 in. FLLWF, 3602.155.

Furniture: studies. Pencil on tracing paper, 20½ × 36 in. FLLWF, 3602.105.

Furniture: details. Inscr. *27 October 1937, FLLW*. Pencil and color pencil on tracing paper, 19½ × 36 in. FLLWF, 3602.077.

Metal shelves: elevation, plan, and full-size section. Pencil and color pencil on tracing paper, 22 × 35½ in. FLLWF, 3602.146. Includes freehand sketches for zinc planter boxes.

Lamps: elevation and plan. Inscr. *4 July 1938*. Pencil on tracing paper, 18 × 15 in. FLLWF, 3602.112. Preliminary study.

Light fixture: detail. Pencil on tracing paper, 11 × 8½ in. FLLWF, 3602.052. *Monograph*, 11: 55. Fixture height correlated to 17-inch vertical unit and 5-foot, 8-inch human figure.

Pole lamp. Inscr. *10 September 1939, FLLW*. Pencil on tracing paper, 29 × 21 in. FLLWF, 3602.100. Elaborated version of lamp in 3602.052.

Lighting cove: full-size section. Pencil and color pencil on tracing paper, 17¼ × 36 in. FLLWF, 3602.149.

Trellis lighting. Inscr. *27 October 1937, FLLW*. Pencil and color pencil on tracing paper, 20 × 36 in. FLLWF, 3602.071.

Details: hatch, parapet, and skylight. Pencil on tracing paper, 31½ × 36 in. FLLWF, 3602.126.

Details: parapet, glazing, and sectional studies. Pencil on tracing paper, 27 × 36 in. FLLWF, 3602.127.

LIVING ROOM HATCH AND STAIRS

Living room hatch. Pencil on tracing paper, 23½ × 31 in. FLLWF, 3602.035. *Monograph*, 5: 284.

Living room hatch: glazing. Inscr. *25 November 1936*. Pencil on tracing paper, 15¼ × 17¾ in. FLLWF, 3602.111.

Living room hatch: details. Pencil on tracing paper, 19 × 21¾ in. FLLWF, 3602.116.

Living room hatch stairs. Pencil on tracing paper, 20 × 37½ in. FLLWF, 3602.150. Revised drawing sent to Bob Mosher.

LIVING ROOM HATCH STAIRS RECONSTRUCTION, JULY 1955

Plan, elevation, and details. Inscr. *14 July 1955, FLLW.* Pencil and color pencil on paper, 35 × 36 in. FLLWF, 3602.093.

Plan, elevation, and details. Pencil and color pencil on tracing paper, 25½ × 25½ in. FLLWF, 3602.121. *Monograph*, 11: 56. Preliminary drawing for 3602.93.

Plan, elevation, and details. Pencil and color pencil on tracing paper, 25½ × 25½ in. FLLWF, 3602.122.

KITCHEN

Kitchen: plan and elevations. Pencil on tracing paper, 25½ × 34½ in. FLLWF, 3602.030. *Monograph*, 5: 280.

Kitchen: plan and elevations. Pencil on tracing paper, 26 × 36 in. FLLWF, 3602.130.

Kitchen casework. Pencil and color pencil, 26¼ × 36 in. FLLWF, 3602.034.

LILIANE KAUFMANN'S BEDROOM AND BATHROOM

Bedroom casework: plan and elevation. Pencil on tracing paper, 25½ × 36 in. FLLWF, 3602.037.

Bedroom and bathroom: plan and elevations. Pencil on tracing paper, 25¼ × 36 in. FLLWF, 3602.039.

Bedroom: plan and elevation of fireplace wall and plan. Pencil and color pencil on tracing paper, 16 × 27¾ in. FLLWF, 3602.140. Shows statue of the Madonna and objets d'art.

Bathroom vanity mirror: details. Pencil on tracing paper, 21½ × 36 in. FLLWF, 3602.062.

Bathroom and guest bathroom: layouts. Ink, pencil, and color pencil on tracing paper, 10¼ × 8½ in. FLLWF, 3602.108. Cat. 8. Drawn by Bob Mosher, with note by Wright.

GUEST ROOM

Guest room: plan and elevations. Pencil on tracing paper, 24½ × 34½ in. FLLWF, 3602.032.

EDGAR KAUFMANN'S BEDROOM

Plan. Inscr. *void*. Pencil on tracing paper, 26 × 36 in. FLLWF, 3602.132.

Plan. Pencil on tracing paper, 21½ × 36 in. FLLWF, 3602.139. Definitive scheme, annotated by Wright.

Plan and elevation. Pencil and color pencil on tracing paper, 12 × 19 in. FLLWF, 3602.107. Drawing by Bob Mosher showing the terrace stairs.

Section. Pencil and color pencil on tracing paper, 14 × 10 in. FLLWF, 3602.109. Drawn by Bob Mosher; same scheme as 3602.107.

Wardrobes, for Edgar Kaufmann's bedroom and Kaufmann jr.'s bedroom. Pencil and color pencil on tracing paper, 25 × 36 in. FLLWF, 3602.143.

Wardrobes, for Edgar Kaufmann's bedroom and Kaufmann jr.'s bedroom: elevations and plan. Pencil on tracing paper, 25¼ × 36 in. FLLWF, 3602.141A. Preliminary drawing for 3602.143.

EDGAR KAUFMANN JR.'S BEDROOM

Plan and three elevations. Pencil on tracing paper, 25½ × 36 in. FLLWF, 3602.154. Preliminary scheme, without outside entrance.

Third floor fireplace. Pencil on tracing paper, 17¼ × 32 in. FLLWF, 3602.120. Specifies that stone be set on end.

Third floor fireplace: elevation and plan. Pencil on tracing paper, 17½ × 30 in. FLLWF, 3602.118. Preliminary drawing for 3602.120.

MISCELLANEOUS INTERIOR DETAILS

Interior stairs. Pencil on tracing paper, 14½ × 21¼ in. FLLWF, 3602.053. Six risers and eleven treads.

Stair rods. Pencil on tracing paper, 24½ × 35 in. FLLWF, 3602.017.

Shower. Pencil on tracing paper, 23½ × 18½ in. FLLWF, 3602.065.

EXTERIOR LIGHTING DETAILS

Exterior trellis. Pencil and color pencil on tracing paper, 24 × 36 in. FLLWF, 3602.072.

Trellis skylights and lighting fixtures. Inscr. *FLLW.* Pencil and color pencil on tracing paper, 16 × 41½ in. FLLWF, 3602.095.

Trellis skylights and lighting fixtures. Pencil and color pencil on tracing paper, 24¼ × 36 in. FLLWF, 3602.104.

Fixtures for bridge and living room hatch. Pencil on tracing paper, 19½ × 36 in. FLLWF, 3602.160.

STRUCTURAL DETAILS

Foundation piers. Inscr. *1 July 1936*. Pencil on tracing paper, 17¼ × 33 in. FLLWF, 3602.161. Specifies location of reinforcing rods.

Foundations: elevation. Pencil on tracing paper, 18 × 26½ in. FLLWF, 3602.119. Denies Bob Mosher's request to raise the height of the masonry piers.

First floor steel reinforcement. Pencil on tracing paper, 31½ × 42 in. FLLWF, 3602.091.

First floor formwork. Pencil and color pencil on tracing paper, 16½ × 33 in. FLLWF, 3602.102.

Second floor reinforcing. Pencil on tracing paper, 30¾ × 42 in. FLLWF, 3602.090. Cat. 9.

Floor and roof construction. Inscr. *10 January 1936*. Pencil and color pencil on tracing paper, 33½ × 36 in. FLLWF, 3602.085.

Roof slabs and calculations. Pencil on tablet paper, 11 × 8½ in. FLLWF, unnumbered.

Exterior stairs. Inscr. *FLLW*. Pencil on tracing paper, 31 × 36 in. FLLWF, 3602.092.

Roof flashing. Pencil on tracing paper, 21 × 20½ in. FLLWF, 3602.068. Preliminary study.

Cornice: full-size elevation. Pencil on tracing paper, 29¾ × 36 in. FLLWF, 3602.147.

Trellis flashing: full-size details. Pencil on tracing paper, 19 × 36 in. FLLWF, 3602.148. Annotated by Wright.

Flashing and sound-deafening of floors and roofs. Inscr. *10 January 1936*. Pencil on tracing paper, 26½ × 42 in. FLLWF, 3602.086.

Flashing and sound-deafening of floors and roofs. Pencil on tracing paper, 36 × 42 in. FLLWF, 3602.083. Cat. 10. Preliminary drawing for 3602.086.

Flashing and sound-deafening of floors and roofs. Pencil on tracing paper, 29¾ × 38 in. FLLWF, 3602.094. Preliminary drawing for 3602.086.

Roof flashing revisions. Inscr. *FLLW*. Pencil on tracing paper, 24½ × 35 in. FLLWF, 3602.117.

GUEST HOUSE BRIDGE

Elevation. Pencil and color pencil on tracing paper, 25½ × 42 in. FLLWF, 3602.098. Engages second and third floors.

Slab construction. Pencil on tracing paper, 23½ × 25 in. FLLWF, 3602.131. Engages second and third floors.

Side elevation. Pencil and color pencil on tracing paper, 19 × 33 in. FLLWF, 3602.114. Connection at third floor.

North elevation. Inscr. *August 1936*. Pencil and color pencil on tracing paper, 18 × 36 in. FLLWF, 3602.115.

BRIDGE ACROSS BEAR RUN

Plan, elevation, and section. Pencil and color pencil on tracing paper, 26 × 42 in. FLLWF, 3602.142.

Plan. Pencil on blue line print, 20¼ × 39 in. FLLWF, 3602.159. Print dated 12 September 1936.

Steel reinforcement. Pencil and color pencil on tracing paper, 21¾ × 36 in. FLLWF, 3602.144.

Plan and elevation. Inscr. *12 September 1936*. Pencil on tracing paper, 19¼ × 38 in. FLLWF, 3602.063.

Plan and east elevation. Pencil on tracing paper, 15¼ × 18½ in. FLLWF, 3602.075.

Parapets: steel reinforcing diagram. Pencil and color pencil on tracing paper, 20¾ × 36 in. FLLWF, 3602.088.

EAST TERRACE REINFORCEMENT

Slab reinforcement. Inscr. *24 August 1954, FLLW per M.G.* [Mendel Glickman]. Pencil on tracing paper, 16½ × 24¼ in. FLLWF, 3602.084.

Reinforcing grilles. Inscr. *25 May 1951, FLLW*. Pencil on tracing paper, 17 × 36 in. FLLWF, 3602.099.

Reinforcing grilles. Inscr. *1 August 1951, FLLW*. Pencil on tracing paper, 19 × 36 in. FLLWF, 3602.101.

AVERY LIBRARY HOLDINGS

146 photomechanical reproductions, including blueprints, blue line prints, and black line prints. Some are annotated in pencil and color pencil. 35¼ × 43¼ in. or smaller. Series begins with acc. no. NYDA.1972.001.00001.

Topographic surveys of Bear Run site from 1920s–30s in binders among boxed items, ST 22.1.

Topographic maps from 1940s. Set of 11 photomechanical reproductions. 44 × 80¼ in. or smaller. Series begins with acc. no. NYDA.1972.001.00216.

Fallingwater Guest House and Servants' Quarters (1938–39)

SPRING 1938

Plan. Inscr. *FLLW, EJK*. Pencil and color pencil on tracing paper, 11 × 8½ in. FLLWF, 3812.007. *Monograph*, 11: 59. Cat. 13. Verso has numerous small sketches, including a pair of eyeglasses; three bedrooms, one bath.

Plan. Pencil and color pencil on tracing paper, 11 × 8½ in. FLLWF, 3812.008. *Monograph*, 11: 60. Variant of 3812.007; three bedrooms, one bath.

Plan. Pencil on tracing paper, 28 × 36 in. FLLWF, 3812.024. Similar to 3812.007, with freehand studies of the canopy and rearrangement of the parking area.

Plan and south elevation. Pencil and color pencil on tracing paper, 25 × 36 in. FLLWF, 3812.006. Three bedrooms, two baths, no living room.

Section and south elevation. Pencil and color pencil on tracing paper, 23½ × 36 in. FLLWF, 3812.005-1. *Monograph*, 11: 63. Left-hand side of torn sheet; corresponds to 3812.007 series.

Section and south elevation. Pencil and color pencil on tracing paper, 23 × 18¾ in. FLLWF, 3812.005-2. Right-hand side of torn sheet; includes many small sketches and calculations.

Section through guest house and details. Pencil and color pencil on tracing paper, 8½ × 11 in. FLLWF, 3812.009. *Monograph*, 11: 62. Drawings also on verso; corresponds to 3812.007 series.

MAY 1938

Bird's-eye view from southeast. Inscr. *ok FLLW*. Pencil and color pencil on tracing paper, 12¾ × 29¾ in. FLLWF, 3812.040. *Monograph*, 11: 66. Cat. 14. Corresponds to 3812.003.

Bird's-eye view from southeast. Inscr. *1938, FLLW*. Pencil on tracing paper, 15 × 36 in. FLLWF, 3812.004.

Bird's-eye view from southeast. Pencil and color pencil on tracing paper, 9½ × 36 in. FLLWF, 3812.001. *Monograph*, 11: 65. Preliminary drawing for 3812.004, 3812.040.

Plan and elevation. Pencil and color pencil on tracing paper, 27½ × 36 in. FLLWF, 3812.003. See 3812.027 for additional elevations; three bedrooms, two baths, curved lounge.

Plan and section. Pencil and color pencil on tracing paper, 13¾ × 22½ in. FLLWF, 3812.002. *Monograph*, 11: 64. Preliminary drawing for 3812.003.

Plan of guest house and servants' quarters. Inscr. *18 May 1938, FLLW, void*. Pencil and color pencil on tracing paper, 33¼ × 36 in. FLLWF, 3812.029. Cat. 15. Same as 3812.003.

Plan of servants' rooms. Pencil on tracing paper, 11 × 8½ in. FLLWF, 3812.010. *Monograph*, 11: 61. Corresponds to 3812.003.

West, east, and south elevations. Inscr. *18 May 1938, FLLW*. Pencil on tracing paper, 33 × 36 in. FLLWF, 3812.027. *Monograph*, 5: 308. Same as 3812.003; bridge connects to third floor of house.

1939

Plans and section of guest house and servants' quarters. Inscr. *FLLW* and *EJK*. Pencil and color pencil on tracing paper, 24 × 36 in. FLLWF, 3812.033. *Monograph*, 5: 305. Cat. 16. Final scheme.

Plan. Pencil on tracing paper, 20 × 36 in. FLLWF, 3812.038. Preliminary drawing for 3812.033.

Plans of guest house and servants' quarters and canopy details. Pencil and color pencil on tracing paper, 20¾ × 36 in. FLLWF, 3812.025. Preliminary drawing for 3812.033.

Plan. Pencil and color pencil on tracing paper, 20½ × 36 in. FLLWF, 3812.026. Same as 3812.025.

Plan. Blueprint of 3812.033 with pencil and color pencil, 24 × 36 in. FLLWF, 3812.039. Has sketches of details and swimming pool.

Plan of servants' rooms. Pencil and color pencil on tracing paper, 27¾ × 36 in. FLLWF, 3812.035.

Elevations and sections. Inscr. *26 January 1939, FLLW*. Pencil on tracing paper, 36 × 52 in. FLLWF, 3812.020.

Section and north elevation. Pencil on tracing paper, 30 × 36 in. FLLWF, 3812.016.

West and south elevations and section. Pencil on tracing paper, 28 × 36 in. FLLWF, 3812.028. Fenestration corresponds to final scheme, but bridge connects to third floor of main house.

South elevation and section. Pencil on tracing paper, 20 × 36 in. FLLWF, 3812.037. Preliminary drawing for final scheme.

Site section. Inscr. *FLLW*. Pencil and color pencil on tracing paper, 21½ × 36 in. FLLWF, 3812.017.

Car court wall. Inscr. *20 February* [1939]. Pencil on tracing paper, 10 × 36 in. FLLWF, 3812.011.

Bridge entrance: details. Inscr. *20 February* [1939]. Pencil on tracing paper, 36 × 49¾ in. FLLWF, 3812.014. *Monograph*, 5: 309. Connects to second floor of main house; sheet includes a small bird's-eye view.

Bridge: sections. Inscr. *20 February* [1939]. Pencil on tracing paper, 25 × 36 in. FLLWF, 3812.015.

Bridge entrance: plan and sections. Pencil and color pencil on tracing paper, 28½ × 36 in. FLLWF, 3812.018.

Canopy: structural details. Pencil on tracing paper, 35½ × 51 in. FLLWF, 3812.031. *Monograph*, 5: 304.

Canopy: plan, elevation, and section. Pencil on tracing paper, 36 × 39½ in. FLLWF, 3812.012.

Canopy: plan, elevation, and details. Pencil on tracing paper, 29 × 36 in. FLLWF, 3812.021. Details indicate steel reinforcement.

Canopy: plan and section. Pencil on tracing paper, 21½ × 36 in. FLLWF, 3812.023. Plan superimposed on section used for 3812.017.

Garage doors. Inscr. *13 January 1939*, [illegible signature]. Pencil on tracing paper, 36 × 41½ in. FLLWF, 3812.019. Wooden accordion doors with piano hinges.

Garage door: details. Pencil on tracing paper, 31 × 36 in. FLLWF, 3812.032. Includes sketches of a bell mounted on a stone pier.

Fireplace: details. Inscr. *14 March 1939, FLLW*. Pencil on tracing paper, 33 × 36 in. FLLWF, 3812.034.

Staircase: details. Inscr. *10 June 1939*. Pencil on tracing paper, 15 × 21½ in. FLLWF, unnumbered.

Shop drawing for guest house shelving. Blueprint, 42 × 47 in. FLLWF, unnumbered. Filed with 3602 series drawings.

Plan. Ink, pencil, and color pencil on tracing paper, 44¼ × 36¼ in. FLLWF, 3812.013. See p. 181, "Fallingwater Additions."

Servants' rooms: plan. Pencil and color pencil on tracing paper, 27 × 36 in. FLLWF, 3812.036. See p. 181, "Fallingwater Additions."

Topographic plan, with guest house plan. Blueprint with color pencil, 18 × 24¾ in. FLLWF, 3812.030. Topographic survey by F. Eng. Co. dated 22 January 1936; yellow pencil marks a grid and the plan of the guest house, canopy, and bridge.

Topographical section, with section and elevations for guest house. Pencil on blueprint, 27½ × 24¾ in. FLLWF, unnumbered. Filed with 3812.005; drawings on recto and verso.

Topographic plan of Bear Run. Photostat, 12½ × 23 in. FLLWF, unnumbered. Prepared by A. J. Opperman, Uniontown, Pennsylvania, 24 April 1947.

Topographic plan of Shady Lane Road, east of Fallingwater. Photostat, 12½ × 23 in. FLLWF, unnumbered.

Fallingwater Additions (1947)

Shady Lane entrance, bird's-eye view from northeast. Inscr. *20 October 1947, FLLW.* Pencil, color pencil, and ink on tracing paper, 24¼ × 36 in. FLLWF, 4702.001. Cat. 18.

Shady Lane entrance, bird's-eye view from northeast. Pencil on tracing paper, 22 × 36¼ in. FLLWF, 4702.002. Preliminary drawing for 4702.001.

Plan of Shady Lane entrance, guest house, and dining room extension. Pencil, color pencil, and ink on tracing paper, 44¼ × 36¼ in. FLLWF, 3812.013. Cat. 17.

First floor plan. Inscr. *27 May 1936, FLLW.* Pencil and color pencil on tracing paper, 30 × 36 in. FLLWF, 3602.007. Drawing has been reworked ca. 1947 to study the kitchen and dining room extensions.

Kitchen addition: plan and elevation. Inscr. *11 August 1945, FLLW.* Blue line print, 17¾ × 36 in. FLLWF, 3602.156.

Dining room addition: plan. Pencil on tracing paper, 20½ × 36 in. FLLWF, 3602.096. Cat. 19.

Dining room addition: section. Pencil on tracing paper, 18½ × 29¼ in. FLLWF, 3602.106. Cat. 20.

Plan. Pencil on tracing paper, 41 × 46¾ in. FLLWF, 3812.022.

Servants' rooms: plan. Pencil and color pencil on tracing paper, 27 × 36 in. FLLWF, 3812.036. Indicates changes to provide access to the new parking bays.

Farm Cottage (1941)

Perspective view of front. Ink and pencil on tracing paper, 29 × 36 in. FLLWF, 3711.002. *Monograph,* 6: 416. Cat. 25.

Plan and side elevation. Pencil on tracing paper, 29 × 36 in. FLLWF, 3711.001. *Monograph,* 6: 417. Cat. 26. At right is a small sketch of the side elevation.

Plan. Ink and pencil on tracing paper, 28½ × 36 in. FLLWF, 3711.003.

Plan. Pencil on drawing paper, 19 × 32 in. FLLWF, 3711.005. Preliminary drawing for 3711.003.

Elevation. Pencil on tracing paper, 9¾ × 21½ in. FLLWF, 3711.004.

Gate Lodge

Scheme 1 (1942)

Bird's-eye view from road. Pencil and sepia ink on tracing paper, 29 × 36 in. FLLWF, 3713.005. *Monograph,* 6: 414. Cat. 21.

Plan and section through site. Pencil and color pencil on tracing paper, 29½ × 36 in. FLLWF, 3713.001. Cat. 22. Numerous annotations and details; at upper right is a schematic site plan of Bear Run.

Plot plan. Pencil and color pencil on tracing paper, 29 × 36 in. FLLWF, 3713.003.

Plot plan. Ink on tracing paper, 28¾ × 36 in. FLLWF, 3713.006. Ink version of 3713.003.

Plan. Pencil and color pencil on tracing paper, 27¼ × 36 in. FLLWF, 3713.002. Preliminary drawing for 3713.003.

North and south elevations. Pencil and color pencil on tracing paper, 29 × 36 in. FLLWF, 3713.004. *Monograph,* 6: 415.

Scheme 2 (1956)

Perspective view from road. Inscr. *1956, FLLW.* Ink, pencil, and color pencil on tracing paper, 25 × 34½ in. FLLWF, 5715.001. *Monograph,* 8: 494. Cat. 23.

Plot plan. Inscr. *20 December 1956, FLLW.* Ink, pencil, and color pencil on tracing paper, 26½ × 35 in. FLLWF, 5715.002.

Ground floor plan. Inscr. *20 December 1956, FLLW.* Ink, pencil, and color pencil on tracing paper, 25½ × 35 in. FLLWF, 5715.003. *Monograph,* 8: 495. Cat. 24.

Mezzanine plan. Inscr. *20 December 1956, FLLW.* Ink, pencil, and color pencil on tracing paper, 26¼ × 35 in. FLLWF, 5715.004.

Elevation. Inscr. *20 December 1956, FLLW.* Ink, pencil, and color pencil on tracing paper, 25 × 35 in. FLLWF, 5715.005.

Scheme 3 (1957)

Plot plan. Inscr. *10 April 1957, FLLW.* Ink, pencil, and color pencil on tracing paper, 27¼ × 36 in. FLLWF, 5715.007.

Plot plan. Inscr. *10 April 1957, FLLW.* Ink, pencil, and color pencil on tracing paper, 27½ × 36 in. FLLWF, 5715.011.

Ground floor plan. Inscr. *10 April 1957.* Ink, pencil, and color pencil on tracing paper, 27¼ × 36 in. FLLWF, 5715.008. *Monograph,* 8: 498.

Mezzanine plan. Inscr. *10 April 1957.* Ink, pencil, and color pencil on tracing paper, 27¼ × 36 in. FLLWF, 5715.009.

Elevation. Inscr. *10 April 1957, Ekjr* [Edgar Kaufmann jr.] *as changed.* Ink, pencil, and color pencil on tracing paper, 27½ × 36 in. FLLWF, 5715.006. *Monograph,* 8: 497.

Elevation. Inscr. *10 April 1957, FLLW.* Ink, pencil, and color pencil on tracing paper, 27¼ × 36 in. FLLWF, 5715.010.

Plot plan. Inscr. *1 September 1957, FLLW, Ekjr.* Ink, pencil, and color pencil on tracing paper, 36 × 51 in. FLLWF, 5715.012, no. 1.

Residence A: mat and heating plan; Residence B mezzanine: plan. Inscr. *1 September 1957, FLLW, Ekjr.* Ink, pencil, and color pencil on tracing paper, 26 × 42½ in. FLLWF, 5717.013, no. 2A.

Residence A ground floor and mezzanine: plans. Inscr. *1 September 1957, FLLW, Ekjr.* Ink, pencil, and color pencil on tracing paper, 26 × 42 in. FLLWF, 5715.014, no. 3A. Includes layout of major furnishings.

Residence A: elevations. Inscr. *1 September 1957, FLLW, Ekjr.* Ink, pencil, and color pencil on tracing paper, 26 × 42 in. FLLWF, 5715.015, no. 4A.

Residence A: sections. Inscr. *1 September 1957, FLLW, Ekjr.* Ink, pencil, and color pencil on tracing paper, 26 × 42 in. FLLWF, 5715.016, no. 5A.

Residence A: structural plans. Inscr. *1 September 1957, FLLW, Ekjr.* Ink, pencil, and color pencil on tracing paper, 26¾ × 42 in. FLLWF, 5715.017, no. 6A.

Residence A workspace [kitchen]: plan. Inscr. *1 September 1957, Ekjr.* Ink, pencil, and color pencil on tracing paper, 25¾ × 42 in. FLLWF, 5715.018, no. 7A.

Residence B workshop and storage building: mat plan and heating. Inscr. *1 September 1957, FLLW, Ekjr.* Ink, pencil, and color pencil on tracing paper, 26 × 42½ in. FLLWF, 5715.019, no. 2B.

Residence B workshop and storage building: ground floor plan. Inscr. *1 September 1957, FLLW, Ekjr.* Ink, pencil, and color pencil on tracing paper, 26 × 42½ in. FLLWF, 5715.020, no. 3B.

Residence B workshop and storage building: elevations. Inscr. *1 September 1957, FLLW, Ekjr.* Ink, pencil, and color pencil on tracing paper, 26 × 42½ in. FLLWF, 5715.021, no. 4B. *Monograph,* 8: 496.

Residence B: sections. Inscr. *1 September 1957, FLLW, Ekjr.* Ink, pencil, and color pencil on tracing paper, 26 × 42 in. FLLWF, 5715.022, no. 5B.

Residence B workshop and storage building: structural plan. Inscr. *1 September 1957, FLLW, Ekjr.* Ink, pencil, and color pencil on tracing paper, 26 × 42½ in. FLLWF, 5715.023, no. 6B.

Gate, tower, and pool: details. Inscr. *1 September 1957, FLLW, Ekjr.* Ink, pencil, and color pencil on tracing paper, 26½ × 42½ in. FLLWF, 5715.024, no. 8.

AVERY LIBRARY HOLDINGS

Working drawings: 42 blue line prints on paper, 35⅜ × 51 in. or smaller. Series begins with acc. no. NYDA.1972.001.00261.

Rhododendron Chapel (1952)

Perspective view of front. Inscr. *8 June 1952, FLLW.* Pencil, color pencil, and ink on illustration board, 18 × 34 in. Del. John H. Howe; John H. Howe Collection, State Historical Society of Wisconsin. Annotated black line print in Avery, NYDA.1972.001.00256.

Perspective view of rear. Inscr. *8 June 1952, FLLW.* Pencil, color pencil, and ink on illustration board, 18 × 34 in. Del. John H. Howe; John H. Howe Collection, State Historical Society of Wisconsin. Cat. 27. Annotated black line print in Avery, NYDA.1972.001.00257.

Interior perspective. Pencil and color pencil on tracing paper, 18 × 34¾ in. FLLWF, 5308.002. Cat. 29.

Plan and elevations. Inscr. *28 April 1952, FLLW.* Pencil and color pencil on illustration board; overlay on trace, 28 × 35¼ in. John H. Howe Collection, State Historical Society of Wisconsin. Cat. 28.

Plan. Inscr. *8 June 1952, FLLW, J.H.H.* Pencil, color pencil, and ink on illustration board, 18 × 34 in. Del. John H. Howe, John H. Howe Collection, State Historical Society of Wisconsin.

Plan. Inscr. *8 June 1952, FLLW.* Sepia print with color pencil on illustration board, 18 × 32½ in. FLLWF, 5308.003. Annotated black line print in Avery, NYDA.1972.001.00260.

Front and rear elevations. Inscr. *8 June* [1952]*, FLLW.* Sepia print with pencil and color pencil on illustration board, 17¾ × 32¼ in. FLLWF, 5308.005. Annotated black line print in Avery, NYDA.1972.001.00258.

Rear elevation and section. Inscr. *8 June* [1952], *FLLW.* Sepia print with pencil and color pencil on illustration board, 17¾ × 32¼ in. FLLWF, 5308.004. Annotated black line print in Avery, NYDA.1972.001.00259.

Boulder House, Palm Springs, California (1950–51)

Bird's-eye view. Inscr. *15 January 1951, FLLW.* Pencil, color pencil, and ink on tracing paper, 25¼ × 35¼ in. FLLWF, 5111.001. *Monograph,* 8: 38. Cat. 30.

Bird's-eye view. Pencil on tracing paper, 18¼ × 34⅜ in. FLLWF, 5111.004. Preliminary drawing for 5111.001.

Perspective view. Inscr. *15 January 1951, FLLW.* Pencil, color pencil, and ink on tracing paper, 25¼ × 35⅛ in. FLLWF, 5111.002. *Monograph,* 8: 40, 12: 163c.

Perspective view. Pencil and ink on tracing paper, 17½ × 36 in. FLLWF, 5111.005. Preliminary drawing for 5111.002.

Elevation. Inscr. *15 January 1951, FLLW, EJK.* Pencil and color pencil on tracing paper, 16½ × 36 in. FLLWF. 5111.003. *Monograph,* 8: 39. Cat. 31.

Kaufmann Office and Projects for Pittsburgh

Kaufmann Office (1936–38)

PERSPECTIVE VIEWS

View from entrance. Pencil on tracing paper, 15½ × 18 in. FLLWF, 3704.023. Cat. 32.

View from entrance. Pencil and color pencil on tracing paper, 19¼ × 29 in. FLLWF, 3704.024. Similar to 3704.023.

PLANS AND ELEVATIONS

Plan and elevation of site for office. Pencil on tracing paper, 19¼ × 20 in. FLLWF, 3704.022. Shows location of windows, doors, and structural columns.

Plan. Inscr. *10 January 1937, FLLW.* Pencil and color pencil on tracing paper, 18 × 24 in. FLLWF, 3704.026. This scheme extends the office toward the adjacent waiting room.

Plan and elevations. Pencil on tracing paper, 20 × 36 in. FLLWF, 3704.004. Preliminary layout for a final drawing.

Plan and elevations. Pencil on tracing paper, 17¾ × 25¾ in. FLLWF, 3704.001. Preliminary drawing for 3704.004.

Plan and elevations. Pencil on tracing paper, 19 × 35 in. FLLWF, 3704.003. This scheme is one 4-foot unit deeper than 3704.004.

Plan and elevations. Pencil and color pencil on tracing paper, 19 × 35 in. FLLWF, 3704.007. Similar to 3704.003.

Plan and elevations. Inscr. *3 November 1936, mjs* [Manuel J. Sandoval]. Pencil on tracing paper, 22¼ × 27¾ in. FLLWF, 3704.012. *Monograph,* 6: 53.

Plan and elevations. Pencil on tracing paper, 19¼ × 35½ in. FLLWF, 3704.018.

Plan and elevations. Inscr. *FLLW, and mjs.* Color pencil on blueprint, 22½ × 36 in. FLLWF, 3704.032. Shows changes in the proportions of cabinetry and the extension of the office.

Plan of private office, with elevation and details. Inscr. *31 December 1924. Benno Janssen, arch.* Photostat, 23½ × 18 in. FLLWF, unnumbered. Photostat of the office replaced by Wright's design.

Elevations. Pencil on tracing paper, 20 × 35¼ in. FLLWF, 3704.014. Shows desk and wall with storage cases; wall with louvers. *Monograph,* 6: 54.

Elevation. Pencil on tracing paper, 19¼ × 35 in. FLLWF, 3704.020. Shows desk and wall with storage cases.

Elevation. Pencil on tracing paper, 20 × 35¼ in. FLLWF, 3704.015. Shows desk and wall with entry door.

Elevation. Pencil on tracing paper, 17 × 36 in. FLLWF, 3704.025. Related to 3704.015.

Mural and desk: elevation. Pencil and color pencil on tracing paper, 20 × 29 in. FLLWF, 3704.002. *Monograph,* 6: 52. Cat. 33.

Mural elevation. Pencil on tracing paper, 22½ × 35½ in. FLLWF, 3704.013.

Mural elevation. Inscr. *FLLW, mjs.* Blueprint, 22½ × 36 in. FLLWF, 3704.031.

FURNISHINGS

Desk and cabinet: details. Pencil on tracing paper, 19¼ × 35 in. FLLWF, 3704.005.

Desk and cabinet: details. Pencil on tracing paper, 20½ × 36 in. FLLWF, 3704.006. Preliminary drawing for 3704.005; includes detail for light fixture.

Furniture: plans, sections, and elevations for hassock, food cart, and armchair. Pencil on tracing paper, 21½ × 36 in. FLLWF, 3704.008.

Furniture: plans, sections, and elevations for ottoman, food cart, and armchair. Pencil on tracing paper, 23½ × 35½ in. FLLWF, 3704.016.

Furniture: plans, sections, and elevations for hassock, food cart, and armchair. Pencil on tracing paper, 23¾ × 36 in. FLLWF, 3704.009. Preliminary drawing for 3704.008 and 3704.016.

Furniture: ottoman, food cart, and chair. Inscr. *FLLW, mjs.* Color pencil on blueprint, 22¾ × 36 in. FLLWF, 3704.030.

Curved-back chair: plan, elevations, and section. Inscr. *mjs.* Pencil on tracing paper, 23½ × 28½ in. FLLWF, 3704.011. *Monograph*, 6: 57. Cat. 34.

Curved-back chair. Blueprint, 23½ × 28¼ in. FLLWF, 3704.010. Print of 3704.011.

Chair. Inscr. *May 1937, FLLW.* Pencil on tracing paper, 19 × 26¾ in. FLLWF, 3704.017. *Monograph*, 6: 55.

Chair revisions: plan and elevations. 18¼ × 27 in. FLLWF, 3704.029.

Food cart. Inscr. *FLLW.* Pencil on tracing paper, 18½ × 26¾ in. FLLWF, 3704.019. *Monograph*, 6: 56.

Cushions. Pencil on tracing paper, 17¾ × 23¼ in. FLLWF, 3704.021.

Glass light fixture: elevation and section. Pencil on tracing paper, 20 × 30 in. FLLWF, 3704.028.

Glass light fixture: elevation and section. Pencil on tracing paper, 17¾ × 26¾ in. FLLWF, 3704.027. Preliminary drawing for 3704.028.

Life Magazine House (1938)

Note: The title plates transpose Kaufmann and Blackbourn (the family selected by Life *magazine) as the name of the client.*

Paving plan. Pencil on tracing paper, 32⅛ × 35 in. FLLWF, 3919.001. Heavily reworked.

Upper floor plan. Ink and pencil on tracing paper, 29⅛ × 35⅞ in. FLLWF, 3919.002. *Monograph*, 6: 336.

Kitchen and laundry: plan. Pencil on tracing paper, 21⅞ × 36 in. FLLWF, 3919.003.

Excavation and mat plan. Pencil on tracing paper, 33½ × 36 in. FLLWF, 3919.004, no. 1.

Main floor plan. Pencil on tracing paper, 29⅜ × 36 in. FLLWF, 3919.005, no. 2.

Upper floor plan and roof framing. Inscr. *Revised 25 November 1938.* Pencil on tracing paper, 30¼ × 36 in. FLLWF, 3919.006, no. 3. Specifies steel framing.

Elevations: street, garden, end, and sunken garden. Pencil on tracing paper, 29½ × 36 in. FLLWF, 3919.007, no. 4. *Monograph*, 6: 337.

Section. Pencil on tracing paper, 30¼ × 36 in. FLLWF, 3919.008, no. 5A. Specifies glass tubing for the clerestory windows.

Section. Pencil on tracing paper, 31⅛ × 36 in. FLLWF, 3919.009, no. 5B. *Monograph*, 6: 338.

Section. Inscr. *Beauty is the expression of the truth Art is the creation of beauty.* Pencil on tracing paper, 32 × 36 in. FLLWF, 3919.010. *Monograph*, 6: 339.

Pittsburgh Point (1947)

Scheme 1

PERSPECTIVE VIEWS

Bird's-eye view from Mount Washington. Ink, pencil, and color pencil on tracing paper, 33½ × 73¾ in. FLLWF, 4821.003. *Monograph*, 12: 152.

Bird's-eye view from Mount Washington. Inscr. *FLLW.* Sepia ink and pencil on tracing paper, 31½ × 35¾ in. FLLWF, 4821.004. *Monograph*, 7: 376. Cat. 35.

View from Mount Washington. Ink and pencil on tracing paper, folded, 30½ × 46½ in. FLLWF, 4821.025.

PLANS

Plan. Pencil and color pencil on tracing paper, 54½ × 100¾ in. FLLWF, 4821.001.

Plan at parking level. Inscr. *20 April 1947, FLLW.* Pencil and color pencil on tracing paper, 18 × 21½ in. FLLWF, 4821.040. Cat. 36.

Half plan (north) at parking level, datum 714 ft. Ink, pencil, and color pencil on tracing paper, 40 × 87½ in. FLLWF, 4821.035. Includes elaborate and fanciful rendering of animals in zoo and aquarium.

Half plan (north) at parking level. Pencil and color pencil on tracing paper, 42 × 95½ in. FLLWF, 4821.013. Preliminary drawing for 4821.035.

Half plan (north) at parking level, datum 714 ft. Ink, pencil, and color pencil on tracing paper, 39¾ × 87½ in. FLLWF, 4821.037. Preliminary drawing for 4821.035.

Half plan (south) at parking level, datum 714 ft. Ink, pencil, and color pencil on tracing paper, 38½ × 87 in. FLLWF, 4821.034.

Half plan (south) at parking level. Pencil and color pencil on tracing paper, 41¾ × 87½ in. FLLWF, 4821.011. Preliminary drawing for 4821.034.

Half plan (north) at convention hall level. Pencil and color pencil on tracing paper, 42 × 93 in. FLLWF, 4821.012. Preliminary study.

Half plan (south) at parkway level, datum 730 ft. Ink, pencil, and color pencil on tracing paper, 39 × 73 in. FLLWF, 4821.038.

Half plan (south) at opera house level. Pencil and color pencil on tracing paper, 42 × 102 in. FLLWF, 4821.014. Preliminary drawing for 4821.038.

Plan at opera house level, including aquarium building, datum 762 ft. Ink, pencil, and color pencil on tracing paper, 40 × 87 in. FLLWF, 4821.033. *Monograph*, 7: 378.

Half plan at opera house balcony level, datum 780 ft. Ink, pencil, and color pencil on tracing paper, 40½ × 87 in. FLLWF, 4821.032.

Plan at opera house balcony level. Pencil and color pencil on tracing paper, 37½ × 75 in. FLLWF, 4821.018. Preliminary drawing for 4821.032.

Half plan (south) at opera house balcony level. Pencil and color pencil on tracing paper, 42 × 74½ in. FLLWF, 4821.019. Preliminary drawing for 4821.032.

Half plan (south) at sports arena and winter garden level, datum 882 ft. Ink, pencil, and color pencil on tracing paper, 39¾ × 87¼ in. FLLWF, 4821.031.

Half plan (south) at sports arena and winter garden level. Pencil and color pencil on tracing paper, 37¼ × 76 in. FLLWF, 4821.016. Preliminary drawing for 4821.031.

Half plan (south) at sports arena entrance, datum 897 ft. Ink, pencil, and color pencil on tracing paper, 39¾ × 87½ in. FLLWF, 4821.030.

Half plan (south) at sports arena entrance. Pencil and color pencil on tracing paper, 36 × 77½ in. FLLWF, 4821.015. Preliminary drawing for 4821.030.

Half plan (south) at roof garden level, datum 922 ft. Ink, pencil, and color pencil on tracing paper, 39½ × 87 in. FLLWF, 4821.029.

Half plan (south) at roof garden level. Pencil and color pencil on tracing paper, 42 × 75½ in. FLLWF, 4821.017. Preliminary drawing for 4821.029.

ELEVATIONS AND SECTIONS

South elevation and section. Pencil and color pencil on tracing paper, 21¾ × 98½ in. FLLWF, 4821.002.

South elevation. Ink, pencil, and color pencil on tracing paper, 40 × 88 in. FLLWF, 4821.036. *Monograph*, 7: 377. Cat. 37.

South elevation. Pencil and color pencil on tracing paper, 24 × 92½ in. FLLWF, 4821.007. Preliminary drawing for 4821.036.

Bridge elevation. Pencil and color pencil on tracing paper, 21¼ × 84 in. FLLWF, 4821.006.

Longitudinal section. Pencil and color pencil on tracing paper, 21 × 58½ in. FLLWF, 4821.020.

Longitudinal section. Pencil on tracing paper, 21¼ × 59 in. FLLWF, 4821.022. Corresponds to 4821.020.

Longitudinal section through exhibition hall and arena. Ink, pencil, and color pencil on tracing paper, 31 × 81½ in. FLLWF, 4821.005. *Monograph*, 7: 379. Cat. 38.

Section through exhibition hall and arena. Pencil and color pencil on tracing paper, 45 × 83 in. FLLWF, 4821.008. Preliminary drawing for 4821.005.

Cross section of opera house and elevation of bridge. Pencil on tracing paper, 20 × 54½ in. FLLWF, 4821.023.

Section through opera house and bridge. Pencil and color pencil on tracing paper, 42 × 108 in. FLLWF, 4821.010. Preliminary drawing for 4821.023.

Elevation and section of opera house and bridge. Ink, pencil, and color pencil on tracing paper, 39¾ × 107½ in. FLLWF, 4821.028.

Elevation and section of office tower from east. Pencil and color pencil on tracing paper, 36 × 55 in. FLLWF, 4821.026. *Monograph*, 7: 381.

Elevation and section of office buildings from west. Ink, pencil, and color pencil on tracing paper, 45½ × 77 in. FLLWF, 4821.039.

Section through concert garden and zoo. Pencil and color pencil on tracing paper, 42 × 83½ in. FLLWF, 4821.009. Preliminary drawing for 4821.039.

Longitudinal section through aquarium. Pencil and color pencil on tracing paper, 32 × 58½ in. FLLWF, 4821.021. Cat. 39. Annotations describe structure; at top is a roof detail.

Section through aquarium. Pencil on tracing paper, 16¾ × 40¾ in. FLLWF, 4821.024. Includes plan and detail.

Section through aquarium. Ink, pencil, and color pencil on tracing paper, 39½ × 56½ in. FLLWF, 4821.027. *Monograph*, 7: 380.

Scheme 2

PRELIMINARY SCHEME, WITH OFFICE TOWER AND CANTILEVERED BRIDGES

Elevation, looking northeast. Pencil and color pencil on tracing paper, 16¾ × 24½ in. FLLWF, 4836.026. Corresponds to 4836.027; transitional scheme.

Elevation, looking northwest. Pencil and color pencil on tracing paper, 16¾ × 24½ in. FLLWF, 4836.027. Corresponds to 4836.026; transitional scheme.

Office building elevations. Pencil on tracing paper, 36 × 41 in. FLLWF, 4836.023. A note calls for marble at the base.

Bridge elevation. Pencil and color pencil on tracing paper, 19¾ × 50½ in. FLLWF, 4836.033. Transforms bridge to cable-stayed design.

Longitudinal section and elevation. Pencil on tracing paper, 26 × 51 in. FLLWF, 4836.024. Development of elevations 4836.026 and 4836.027.

Cross section through site, with west elevation of office tower. Pencil and color pencil on tracing paper, 36 × 50½ in. FLLWF, 4836.018.

FINAL SCHEME, WITH CABLE-STAYED BRIDGES

PERSPECTIVE VIEWS

View from the east. Inscr. *FLLW*. Ink, gouache, pencil, and color pencil on tracing paper, 29 × 44 in. FLLWF, 4836.004. *Monograph*, 12: 148. Cat. 41.

View from the east. Pencil on tracing paper, 33¾ × 42½ in. FLLWF, 4636.034.

View from the east. Pencil on tracing paper, 29½ × 42 in. FLLWF, 4836.037. Preliminary drawing for 4636.034.

Bird's-eye view from the east. Pencil and color pencil on tracing paper, 34½ × 43½ in. FLLWF, 4836.025. *Monograph*, 7: 382.

View from the Ohio River. Pencil and color pencil on tracing paper, 19½ × 48¼ in. FLLWF, 4836.049.

Night view from the Ohio River, perspective. Paint on posterboard, 25 × 38 in. Del. Allen Davison. FLLWF, 4836.009. *Monograph*, 12: 149. Cat. 43.

PLANS

Plan. Ink, pencil, and color pencil on tracing paper, 18 × 21½ in. FLLWF, 4836.022. *Monograph*, 7: 384. Drawing for Scheme 1 has been overdrawn in blue pencil for Scheme 2.

Plan. Ink, pencil, and color pencil on tracing paper, 39½ × 56½ in. FLLWF, 4836.021. *Monograph*, 7: 383.

Site plan studies. Pencil and color pencil on blueprint, 30 × 42 in. FLLWF, 4836.035. Drawn on plan of the Point prepared by the Pittsburgh Regional Planning Association in November 1945.

Plan at lower parking level, datum 714 ft. Pencil and color pencil on tracing paper, 18 × 25½ in. FLLWF, 4836.030. Same scale and format as 4821.040, with revisions transforming Scheme 1 to Scheme 2.

Plan at city street level, datum 730 ft. Inscr. *20 October 1947, FLLW*. Ink, pencil, and color pencil on tracing paper, 35¼ × 55 in. FLLWF, 4836.002.

Plan at city street level, datum 730 ft. Pencil and color pencil on tracing paper, 36¼ × 52¼ in. FLLWF, 4836.017. *Monograph*, 7: 386. Preliminary drawing for 4836.002.

Plan at city street level, datum 730 ft. Pencil and color pencil on tracing paper, 18 × 25½ in. FLLWF, 4836.029.

Plan at parkway level, datum 741 ft. Inscr. *20 October 1947, FLLW*. Ink, pencil, and color pencil on tracing paper, 35¾ × 55½ in. FLLWF, 4836.001.

Plan at parkway level, datum 741 ft. Pencil and color pencil on tracing paper, 36¼ × 53¼ in. FLLWF, 4836.016. Preliminary drawing for 4836.001.

Plan at park foyer level, datum 752 ft. Inscr. *20 October 1947, FLLW*. Ink, pencil, and color pencil on tracing paper, 36¼ × 46½ in. FLLWF, 4836.038.

Plan at park foyer level, datum 752 ft. Pencil and color pencil on tracing paper, 36¼ × 30 in. FLLWF, 4836.015. Preliminary drawing for 4836.038.

Plan at promenade level, datum 763 ft. Inscr. *20 October 1947, FLLW*. Ink, pencil, and color pencil on tracing paper, 36 × 56½ in. FLLWF, 4836.040. *Monograph*, 7: 385.

Plan at promenade level, datum 763 ft. Pencil and color pencil on tracing paper, 36 × 28 in. FLLWF, 4836.014. Preliminary drawing for 4836.040.

Plan at upper bridge level. Pencil and color pencil on tracing paper, 18 × 25½ in. FLLWF, 4836.028. Corresponds to 4821.040.

Plan at skyway level, datum 770 ft. Pencil and color pencil on tracing paper, 36¼ × 51½ in. FLLWF, 4836.032.

Plan at truck level, datum 794 ft. Pencil and color pencil on tracing paper, 36¼ × 28½ in. FLLWF, 4836.020.

Plan at garden top level, datum 851 ft. Inscr. [date illegible], *FLLW*. Ink, pencil, and color pencil on tracing paper, 30¾ × 46 in. FLLWF, 4836.006.

Plan at garden top level, datum 851 ft. Pencil and color pencil on tracing paper, 36¼ × 25½ in. FLLWF, 4836.011. Preliminary drawing for 4836.006.

TRAFFIC CIRCULATION PLANS

Regional traffic studies. Ink, pencil, and color pencil on tracing paper, 32¼ × 26¾ in. FLLWF, 4836.043. Three studies comparing Wright's scheme to that of the Pittsburgh Regional Planning Association.

Traffic circulation plan. Ink, pencil, and color pencil on tracing paper, 33 × 60 in. FLLWF, 4836.041. Preliminary study.

Traffic circulation plan, showing bridge exits. Pencil and color pencil on tracing paper, 18¼ × 25¾ in. FLLWF, 4836.044. Preliminary drawing for 4836.041.

Traffic circulation plan, showing city street level approach ramps. Pencil and color pencil on tracing paper, 25½ × 36¼ in. FLLWF, 4836.046. Preliminary drawing for 4836.041.

Traffic circulation plan, showing elevated approach ramps. Pencil and color pencil on tracing paper, 14¾ × 20 in. FLLWF, 4836.045. Preliminary drawing for 4836.041.

Traffic circulation at passenger auto level. Ink, pencil, and color pencil on tracing paper, 32¼ × 25¾ in. FLLWF, 4836.008. Corresponds to 4836.047.

Traffic circulation at passenger auto level. Pencil and color pencil on tracing paper, 36¼ × 25½ in. FLLWF, 4836.047. Corresponds to 4836.008.

Traffic circulation plan at truck level. Ink, pencil, and color pencil on tracing paper, 32½ × 26¾ in. FLLWF, 4836.042. Preliminary study.

ELEVATIONS

South elevation. Inscr. *20 October 1947, FLLW*. Ink, pencil, and color pencil on tracing paper, 36 × 55½ in. FLLWF, 4836.039.

South elevation. Pencil and color pencil on tracing paper, 36 × 51½ in. FLLWF, 4836.013. Preliminary drawing for 4836.039.

West elevation. Inscr. *20 October 1947, FLLW*. Color pencil on tracing paper, 28⅜ × 56¼ in. Carnegie Museum of Art, Pittsburgh, 86.24; FLLWF, 4836.003. *Monograph*, 7: 387. Cat. 40.

West elevation. Pencil on tracing paper, 34¼ × 55 in. FLLWF, 4836.019. Preliminary drawing for 4836.003.

West elevation. Pencil on tracing paper, 21½ × 60 in. FLLWF, 4836.048. Transforms the office tower into the "Bastion."

SECTIONS

Longitudinal section. Inscr. *20 October 1947, FLLW*. Ink, pencil, and color pencil on tracing paper, 29¾ × 59 in. FLLWF, 4836.005.

Longitudinal section. Pencil and color pencil on tracing paper, 36¼ × 47¼ in. FLLWF, 4836.012. Preliminary drawing for 4836.005.

Longitudinal and cross sections through Monongahela River bridge. Inscr. *20 October 1947, FLLW*. Ink, pencil, and color pencil on tracing paper, 32 × 57 in. FLLWF, 4836.007. Cat. 42.

Sections through bridge. Pencil and color pencil on tracing paper, 35 × 15¾ in. FLLWF, 4836.054.

Section through bridge and approach ramps. Pencil and color pencil on tracing paper, 33¼ × 48¾ in. FLLWF, 4836.050. Preliminary drawing for 4836.007.

Bridge: sections. Pencil and color pencil on tracing paper, 35 × 16¼ in. FLLWF, 4836.053. *Monograph*, 7: 388. Same as 4836.052; preliminary drawing for 4836.007.

Bridge: sections. Pencil and color pencil on tracing paper, 33½ × 15¾ in. FLLWF, 4836.052.

Bridge: sections. Pencil on tracing paper, 13¾ × 18 in. FLLWF, 4836.051.

Sections through park bowl and bridge. Pencil and color pencil on tracing paper, 15½ × 29 in. FLLWF, 4836.036.

Bridge: cross section. Inscr. *23 September 1947*. Pencil and color pencil on tracing paper, 16¾ × 34¾ in. FLLWF, 4836.031.

Parking Garage (1949)

DATED DRAWINGS AND RELATED PRELIMINARY LAYOUTS

Perspective view of Cherry Way entrance. Inscr. *20 September 1949, FLLW*. Ink, pencil, and color pencil on tracing paper, 34 × 46½ in. FLLWF, 4923.052. *Monograph*, 7: 541.

Perspective view of Cherry Way entrance. Pencil on tracing paper, 18 × 28 in. FLLWF, 4923.037. Preliminary drawing for 4923.052.

Perspective view of Cherry Way entrance. Pencil on tracing paper, 17¼ × 36 in. FLLWF, 4923.038. Preliminary drawing for 4923.052, with slightly different vantage point than 4923.037.

Perspective view from Smithfield Street and Fourth Avenue. Inscr. *20 September 1949*. Ink, pencil, and color pencil on tracing paper, 35½ × 46¾ in. FLLWF, 4923.053. *Monograph*, 7: 540, 12: 158. Cat. 44.

Perspective view from Smithfield Street. Pencil on tracing paper, 23 × 36 in. FLLWF, 4923.036. Preliminary drawing for 4923.053.

Tunnel level: plan. Inscr. *20 September 1949, FLLW*. Ink, pencil, and color pencil on tracing paper, 35½ × 47 in. FLLWF, 4923.042.

Store mezzanine level: plan. Inscr. *20 September 1949, FLLW*. Ink, pencil, and color pencil on tracing paper, 36 × 47 in. FLLWF, 4923.044.

Smithfield Street level: plan. Inscr. *20 September 1949, FLLW*. Ink, pencil, and color pencil on tracing paper, 35¾ × 48 in. FLLWF, 4923.043.

Cherry Way level: plan. Inscr. *20 September 1949, FLLW*. Ink, pencil, and color pencil on tracing paper, 36 × 47 in. FLLWF, 4923.039. *Monograph*, 7: 539.

Cherry Way level: plan. Pencil and color pencil on tracing paper, 36 × 40 in. FLLWF, 4923.021. Preliminary drawing for 4923.039.

Typical level: plan. Inscr. *20 September 1949, FLLW*. Ink, pencil, and color pencil on tracing paper, 35½ × 46¾ in. FLLWF, 4923.040.

Typical level: plan. Ink, pencil, and color pencil on tracing paper, 22¾ × 20 in. FLLWF, 4923.041. Variant scheme ordered by different unit system than 4923.040.

Roof level: plan. Inscr. *20 September 1949, FLLW*. Ink, pencil, and color pencil on tracing paper, 36 × 47 in. FLLWF, 4923.045. *Monograph*, 7: 538.

Diamond Street elevation. Ink, pencil, and color pencil on tracing paper, 35½ × 46¾ in. FLLWF, 4923.049. Corresponds to drawings dated 20 September 1949.

Smithfield Street elevation. Inscr. *20 September 1949, FLLW*. Ink, pencil, and color pencil on tracing paper, 35¾ × 48 in. FLLWF, 4923.050. Similar but not identical to 4923.034.

Cherry Way elevation. Inscr. *20 September 1949, FLLW*. Ink, pencil, and color pencil on tracing paper, 36 × 47 in. FLLWF, 4923.051. *Monograph*, 7: 542.

Section. Ink, pencil, and color pencil on tracing paper, 35⅝ × 46⅝ in. FLLWF, 4923.047. *Monograph*, 7: 543. Corresponds to drawings dated 20 September 1949.

Section. Inscr. *20 September 1949, FLLW*. Ink, pencil, and color pencil on tracing paper, 36 × 46¾ in. FLLWF, 4923.048. Cat. 45.

Detail of cable suspension system. Inscr. *20 September 1949, FLLW*. Ink, pencil, and color pencil on tracing paper, 36¼ × 47 in. FLLWF, 4923.046.

View from Smithfield Street. Ink and pencil on tracing paper, 23¼ × 36 in. FLLWF, 4923.035. Preliminary study.

View from Smithfield Street. Pencil and color pencil on tracing paper, 36 × 46⅝ in. FLLWF, 4923.054. Shows variant scheme, without corner buttresses.

View from Smithfield Street and Diamond Street. Ink and pencil on tracing paper, 22 × 36 in. FLLWF, unnumbered.

PLANS

Plan. Pencil and color pencil on blue line print, 42 × 44 in. FLLWF, 4923.001. Drawn on property plan.

Tunnel level. Pencil and color pencil on tracing paper, 36¼ × 40½ in. FLLWF, 4923.013. Part of set consisting of 4923.013–16.

Tunnel level. Pencil on tracing paper, 33¾ × 42 in. FLLWF, 4923.019. Preliminary layout.

Store level. Pencil and color pencil on tracing paper, 36 × 42¾ in. FLLWF, 4923.014. Part of set consisting of 4923.013–16.

Store level. Ink, pencil, and color pencil on tracing paper, 36¼ × 41½ in. FLLWF, 4923.016. Preliminary drawing for 4923.014; part of set consisting of 4923.013–16.

Store level. Pencil on tracing paper, 33¾ × 42 in. FLLWF, 4923.018. Preliminary layout.

Smithfield Street level. Pencil and color pencil on tracing paper, 36¼ × 42¼ in. FLLWF, 4923.015. Includes chart listing square-footage allocations for the retail area and other elements; part of set consisting of 4923.013–16.

Cherry Way level. Pencil on tracing paper, 36¼ × 41¾ in. FLLWF, 4923.002.

Cherry Way level. Pencil on tracing paper, 44 × 36 in. FLLWF, 4923.004. Differs from 4923.002 in arrangement of corner piers.

Plan. Pencil on tracing paper, 36¼ × 39 in. FLLWF, 4923.009. Corresponds to 4923.004; estimates parking capacity.

Typical parking level. Pencil and color pencil on tracing paper, 39 × 36 in. FLLWF, 4923.022. Drawn to calculate parking capacity and to study traffic circulation.

Quarter plan of typical parking level. Pencil and color pencil on tracing paper, 19¼ × 20 in. FLLWF, unnumbered. Includes annotations calculating parking capacity.

Quarter plan of typical parking level. Pencil and color pencil on tracing paper, 28 × 15 in. FLLWF, unnumbered. Includes annotations calculating parking capacity.

Quarter plan of typical parking level. Pencil on tracing paper, 27 × 26 in. FLLWF, unnumbered. Lightly drawn plan with many calculations and notes on recto and verso.

Half plan of typical parking level. Pencil and color pencil on tracing paper, 28 × 15 in. FLLWF, unnumbered. Includes annotations calculating parking capacity.

Upper parking levels. Pencil on tracing paper, 34½ × 41¾ in. FLLWF, 4923.003.

Roof level. Pencil and color pencil on tracing paper, 37 × 46 in. FLLWF, 4923.020. Indicates concrete canopies and cables.

ELEVATIONS

Diamond Street elevation. Pencil and color pencil on tracing paper, 36 × 42 in. FLLWF, 4923.005. Preliminary scheme.

Diamond Street elevation. Pencil on tracing paper, 36 × 39½ in. FLLWF, 4923.006. Preliminary scheme.

Diamond Street elevation. Pencil on tracing paper, 21½ × 42 in. FLLWF, 4923.017. Indicates tensile structure.

Diamond Street elevation. Pencil and color pencil on tracing paper, 21¼ × 36 in. FLLWF, 4923.031.

Fourth Avenue elevation. Pencil and color pencil on tracing paper, 21½ × 42 in. FLLWF, 4923.027.

Fourth Avenue elevation. Pencil and color pencil on tracing paper, 21¼ × 36 in. FLLWF, 4923.023. Preliminary drawing for 4923.027.

Smithfield Street elevation. Pencil and color pencil on tracing paper, 21 × 42 in. FLLWF, 4923.029.

Smithfield Street elevation. Ink, pencil, and color pencil on tracing paper, 36 × 47 in. FLLWF, 4923.034.

Cherry Way elevation. Pencil and color pencil on tracing paper, 23 × 42 in. FLLWF, 4923.030.

Cherry Way elevation. Ink, pencil, and color pencil on tracing paper, 36 × 47 in. FLLWF, 4923.033. Marked with revisions.

SECTIONS

Section. Pencil and color pencil on tracing paper, 24 × 39¼ in. FLLWF, 4923.007. Preliminary development of tensile structure.

Section. Pencil and color pencil on tracing paper, 21½ × 36 in. FLLWF, 4923.008. No indication of the structural cables.

Section. Pencil and color pencil on tracing paper, 21 × 42 in. FLLWF, 4923.028.

Section. Pencil and color pencil on tracing paper, 20 × 36 in. FLLWF, 4923.024. Preliminary drawing for 4923.028.

Section. Pencil and color pencil on tracing paper, 22¾ × 42 in. FLLWF, 4923.025.

Section. Pencil and color pencil on tracing paper, 22½ × 42 in. FLLWF, 4923.026. This scheme shows the atrium as a cone that is narrow at the bottom and wide at the top, similar to the Guggenheim Museum.

Section. Pencil and color pencil on tracing paper, 22½ × 36 in. FLLWF, 4923.032.

STRUCTURAL DETAILS

Structural details of cable system. Pencil on tracing paper, 36 × 44¾ in. FLLWF, 4923.010. Preliminary drawing for 4923.046.

Structural details of cable system. Pencil on tracing paper, 36½ × 44½ in. FLLWF, 4923.011.

Structural details of cable system. Pencil on tracing paper, 36¼ × 46 in. FLLWF, 4923.012.

Structural diagrams. Ink and pencil on tracing paper, 36 × 10¾ in. FLLWF, unnumbered.

Point View Residences (1951–53)

Scheme 1A

DRAWINGS DATED 8 JUNE 1952

> *Note: All of these drawings are inscribed 1927–52, which links the scheme to the unrealized Elizabeth Noble apartment building planned for Los Angeles.*

Street level: plan. Inscr. *8 June 1952, FLLW.* Ink, pencil, and color pencil on tracing paper, 34½ × 30½ in. FLLWF, 5222.004. *Monograph,* 8: 118. Cat. 47.

Apartments at lower levels: plan. Inscr. *8 June 1952, FLLW.* Ink, pencil, and color pencil on tracing paper, 34¼ × 30¾ in. FLLWF, 5222.002. *Monograph,* 8: 115. Includes overdrawing indicating modifications of room dimensions and furniture layout.

Street level: plan. Pencil and color pencil on tracing paper, 36¼ × 30½ in. FLLWF, 5222.029. Preliminary drawing for 5222.002.

Apartments at garage level: plan. Inscr. *8 June 1952, FLLW.* Ink, pencil, and color pencil on tracing paper, 36 × 30 in. FLLWF, 5222.003. *Monograph,* 8: 117. Includes overdrawing with alternative furniture layouts and marginal drawings of air conditioning ducts.

Main living floor of upper-level apartments: plan. Inscr. *8 June 1952, FLLW.* Ink, pencil, and color pencil on tracing paper, 34½ × 31 in. FLLWF, 5222.005. *Monograph,* 8: 116.

Main living floor of upper-level apartments: plan. Pencil and color pencil on tracing paper, 20½ × 18 in. FLLWF, 5222.013. Preliminary drawing for 5222.005.

Bedroom floor of upper-level apartments: plan. Inscr. *8 June 1952, FLLW.* Ink, pencil, and color pencil on tracing paper, 34¼ × 30¾ in. FLLWF, 5222.006.

Bedroom floor of upper-level apartments: plan. Pencil and color pencil on tracing paper, 33 × 21½ in. FLLWF, 5222.015. Preliminary drawing for 5222.006.

Penthouse plan. Inscr. *8 June 1952, FLLW.* Ink, pencil, and color pencil on tracing paper, 34¼ × 30¾ in. FLLWF, 5222.007. Includes overdrawing indicating revisions and marginal drawings of bathroom layouts.

South elevation. Inscr. *8 June 1952, FLLW.* Ink, pencil, and color pencil on tracing paper, 34¼ × 30¾ in. FLLWF, 5222.008.

East elevation. Inscr. *8 June 1952, FLLW.* Ink, pencil, and color pencil on tracing paper, 14½ × 31 in. FLLWF, 5222.009. Fragment of larger sheet.

West elevation. Inscr. *8 June 1952, FLLW.* Ink, pencil, and color pencil on tracing paper, 15¼ × 30¾ in. FLLWF, 5222.010. Fragment of larger sheet.

Cross section. Inscr. *8 June 1952, FLLW.* Ink, pencil, and color pencil on tracing paper, 13½ × 30¾ in. FLLWF, 5222.011. Fragment of larger sheet.

UNDATED DRAWINGS

Parking garage: plan. Pencil and color pencil on tracing paper, 36 × 38 in. FLLWF, 5222.016.

Main living floors: plans. Pencil and color pencil on tracing paper, 27¼ × 22¾ in. FLLWF, 5222.026. Corresponds to 5222.025.

Apartment plans for upper floors. Pencil and color pencil on tracing paper, 7½ × 22½ in. FLLWF, 5222.030. Early scheme; fragment cut from a larger drawing.

Penthouse plan. Pencil and color pencil on tracing paper, 28¼ × 14¾ in. FLLWF, 5222.012.

Penthouse plan. Pencil and color pencil on tracing paper, 14 × 36 in. FLLWF, 5222.014.

Penthouse: plan of bedroom level. Ink and pencil on tracing paper, 36¼ × 30¼ in. FLLWF, 5222.023. Drawn freehand on a grid.

North and south elevations. Pencil and color pencil on tracing paper, 28¼ × 36 in. FLLWF, 5222.019.

South elevation. Pencil and color pencil on tracing paper, 36 × 30½ in. FLLWF, 5222.022. Details of massing and fenestration differ from 5222.019.

West elevation. Pencil and color pencil on tracing paper, 26½ × 36 in. FLLWF, 5222.024. Corresponds to 5222.021.

East elevation. Pencil and color pencil on tracing paper, 26¼ × 36 in. FLLWF, 5222.021. Corresponds to 5222.024.

Cross section. Pencil and color pencil on tracing paper, 27¾ × 36 in. FLLWF, 5222.025. Corresponds to 5222.026.

Longitudinal section. Pencil and color pencil on tracing paper, 27 × 36 in. FLLWF, 5222.018. Preliminary study.

Longitudinal section. Pencil and color pencil on tracing paper, 28¼ × 36 in. FLLWF, 5222.020.

Scheme 1B

Note: This scheme differs from Scheme 1A in its angled position on the site and in details of massing and fenestration.

PERSPECTIVE VIEWS

View from northeast. Inscr. *June '53*. Ink, pencil, and color pencil on tracing paper, 35 × 30 in. FLLWF, 5222.001. *Monograph*, 8: 119. Cat. 46.

View from east. Pencil on tracing paper, 36¼ × 30½ in. FLLWF, 5222.070. Preliminary drawing for 5222.001.

View from east. Pencil on tracing paper, 36 × 40¾ in. FLLWF, 5222.069. Preliminary study.

ELEVATION AND SECTIONS

West elevation. Ink and pencil on tracing paper, 36¼ × 30½ in. FLLWF, 5222.071. Incomplete; only guidelines drawn.

Section, viewed from street. Ink and pencil on tracing paper, 36¼ × 30½ in. FLLWF, 5222.072. Incomplete; only guidelines drawn.

Longitudinal section. Ink and pencil on tracing paper, 36¼ × 30½ in. FLLWF, 5222.073. Incomplete; only guidelines drawn.

WORKING DRAWINGS SET

Basement level: plan. Ink, pencil, and color pencil on tracing paper, 36½ × 29¾ in. FLLWF, 5222.031. Set includes list of drawings, no. 2.

Servants' rooms and caretaker's apartment: plan. Ink, pencil, and color pencil on tracing paper, 36 × 30 in. FLLWF, 5222.032, no. 3.

Typical apartments: plan. Ink, pencil, and color pencil on tracing paper, 34¼ × 30 in. FLLWF, 5222.033, no. 4.

Street level: plan. Ink, pencil, and color pencil on tracing paper, 36 × 30 in. FLLWF, 5222.034, no. 5.

Apartments at mezzanine level: plan. Ink, pencil, and color pencil on tracing paper, 34½ × 30 in. FLLWF, 5222.035, no. 6.

Apartments at living room level: plan. Ink, pencil, and color pencil on tracing paper, 34¼ × 30 in. FLLWF, 5222.036, no. 7.

Penthouse: plans of main, bedroom, and terrace levels. Ink, pencil, and color pencil on tracing paper, 36 × 30 in. FLLWF, 5222.037, no. 8.

Penthouse: plans of main, bedroom, and terrace levels. Ink, pencil, and color pencil on tracing paper, 36¼ × 30 in. FLLWF, 5222.017. Preliminary drawing for 5222.037.

South elevation. Ink, pencil, and color pencil on tracing paper, 36 × 30½ in. FLLWF, 5222.038, no. 9.

East elevation. Ink, pencil, and color pencil on tracing paper, 36½ × 30 in. FLLWF, 5222.039, no. 10. *Monograph*, 8: 120.

North elevation. Ink, pencil, and color pencil on tracing paper, 36¼ × 30 in. FLLWF, 5222.040, no. 11. *Monograph*, 8: 121.

West elevation. Ink, pencil, and color pencil on tracing paper, 36¼ × 30 in. FLLWF, 5222.041, no. 12.

Cross section. Ink, pencil, and color pencil on tracing paper, 36¼ × 31½ in. FLLWF, 5222.042, no. 13. *Monograph*, 8: 122.

Longitudinal section. Ink, pencil, and color pencil on tracing paper, 36¼ × 30½ in. FLLWF, 5222.043, no. 14. *Monograph*, 8: 123.

Cross section of apartment layout. Ink, pencil, and color pencil on tracing paper, 36¼ × 30 in. FLLWF, 5222.044, no. 15.

Elevation: details. Ink, pencil, and color pencil on tracing paper, 36¼ × 30¾ in. FLLWF, 5222.045, no. 16. Preliminary study.

Sash: details. Ink, pencil, and color pencil on tracing paper, 36¼ × 30½ in. FLLWF, 5222.046, no. 17. Preliminary study.

Window schedule. Ink, pencil, and color pencil on tracing paper, 36¼ × 31¼ in. FLLWF, 5222.047, no. 18.

Kitchen layouts. Ink, pencil, and color pencil on tracing paper, 36¼ × 30½ in. FLLWF, 5222.048, no. 19.

Bathroom layouts. Ink, pencil, and color pencil on tracing paper, 36¼ × 30 in. FLLWF, 5222.049, no. 20.

Bathroom layouts. Ink, pencil, and color pencil on tracing paper, 36¼ × 30¼ in. FLLWF, 5222.050, no. 21.

Structural plan. Ink, pencil, and color pencil on tracing paper, 36¼ × 30 in. FLLWF, 5222.051, no. S-1.

Structural plan for basement level. Ink, pencil, and color pencil on tracing paper, 36¼ × 29¾ in. FLLWF, 5222.052, no. S-2.

Structural plan for basement level. Ink, pencil, and color pencil on tracing paper, 36 × 30 in. FLLWF, 5222.053, no. S-3.

Structural plan, datum 1,110 ft. Ink, pencil, and color pencil on tracing paper, 36¼ × 30 in. FLLWF, 5222.054, no. S-4.

Structural plan of garage, datum 1,101 ft. Ink, pencil, and color pencil on tracing paper, 36¼ × 30 in. FLLWF, 5222.055, no. S-4G.

Structural plan, datum 1,122 ft. Ink, pencil, and color pencil on tracing paper, 36¼ × 30 in. FLLWF, 5222.056, no. S-5.

Structural plan of garage, datum 1,119 ft. Ink, pencil, and color pencil on tracing paper, 36¼ × 29¾ in. FLLWF, 5222.057, no. S-5G.

Structural plan, datum 1,137 ft. Ink, pencil, and color pencil on tracing paper, 36¼ × 30 in. FLLWF, 5222.058, no. S-6.

Structural plan and sections, datum 1,128 ft. Ink, pencil, and color pencil on tracing paper, 36¼ × 30¼ in. FLLWF, 5222.059, no. S-7.

Structural sections, datum 1,137 ft., and steel schedule. Ink, pencil, and color pencil on tracing paper, 36¼ × 30 in. FLLWF, 5222.060.

Structural plan, datum 1,174 ft. Ink, pencil, and color pencil on tracing paper, 36¼ × 29¾ in. FLLWF, 5222.061, no. S-8.

Structural plan, datum 1,185 ft. Ink, pencil, and color pencil on tracing paper, 36¼ × 30 in. FLLWF, 5222.062, no. S-9.

Air conditioning plan. Ink, pencil, and color pencil on tracing paper, 36¼ × 29½ in. FLLWF, 5222.063, no. AC-1. Incomplete; only guidelines drawn.

Air conditioning plan for penthouse. Ink, pencil, and color pencil on tracing paper, 36¼ × 30 in. FLLWF, 5222.064, no. AC-3. Incomplete; only guidelines drawn.

Electrical wiring and plumbing plan for apartments. Ink, pencil, and color pencil on tracing paper, 36¼ × 30 in. FLLWF, 5222.065, no. WP-1. Incomplete; only guidelines drawn.

Electrical wiring and plumbing plan for street level. Ink, pencil, and color pencil on tracing paper, 36¼ × 30 in. FLLWF, 5222.066, no. WP-2. Incomplete; only guidelines drawn.

Electrical wiring and plumbing plan for penthouse. Ink, pencil, and color pencil on tracing paper, 36¼ × 30 in. FLLWF, 5222.067, no. WP-3. Incomplete; only guidelines drawn.

Elevator diagram. Ink, pencil, and color pencil on tracing paper, 36¼ × 29¼ in. FLLWF, 5222.068.

13 drawings, Inscr. *23 August* [19]*52*. Ink and color pencil on tracing paper, 36¼ × 31½ in. or smaller. Acc. nos. NYDA.1000.004.00106–119 (includes wrapper).

Scheme 2 (1953)

Perspective view from northwest. Inscr. *11 April 1953, FLLW*. Ink, pencil, and color pencil on tracing paper, 34½ × 29 in. FLLWF, 5310.001. *Monograph*, 8: 196, 12: 170. Cat. 48.

Servants' rooms level: plan. Ink, pencil, and color pencil on tracing paper, 32¼ × 30 in. FLLWF, 5310.006. Corresponds to 5310.007.

Street level: plan. Ink, pencil, and color pencil on tracing paper, 32¾ × 29½ in. FLLWF, 5310.007. Corresponds to 5310.006.

Penthouse, living room level: plan. Ink, pencil, and color pencil on tracing paper, 33¾ × 29¾ in. FLLWF, 5310.046. Corresponds to 5310.006.

Penthouse mezzanine: plan. Ink, pencil, and color pencil on tracing paper, 32¾ × 30 in. FLLWF, 5310.046. Corresponds to 5310.006.

Northeast elevation. Inscr. *void*. Ink, pencil, and color pencil on tracing paper, 33 × 30 in. FLLWF, 5222.028. Corresponds to 5222.027.

South elevation. Inscr. *void*. Ink, pencil, and color pencil on tracing paper, 30½ × 30 in. FLLWF, 5222.027. Study establishing heights; corresponds to 5222.028.

Study for air conditioning ducts. Pencil on tracing paper, 21 × 36 in. FLLWF, 5310.008. Drawn freehand; annotated.

SCHEME 2A

Note: This scheme is similar to Scheme 2B except that it is set farther out on the slope of Mount Washington.

Site plan. Ink, pencil, and color pencil on tracing paper, 33 × 36 in. FLLWF, 5310.003. Drawn on sheet for Scheme 1.

Driveway plan. Pencil and color pencil on tracing paper, 33½ × 36 in. FLLWF, 5310.005. Drawn on sheet with title block for Scheme 1 plumbing and electrical details.

East elevation. Pencil on tracing paper, 31¾ × 36 in. FLLWF, 5310.004. Partially drawn.

INCOMPLETE WORKING DRAWINGS SET

Site plan. Inscr. *4 July 1953, FLLW*. Ink, pencil, and color pencil on tracing paper, 33 × 36 in. FLLWF, 5310.009, no. 1. *Monograph*, 8: 197. Includes index of sheets in set.

Garage plan. Ink, pencil, and color pencil on tracing paper, 33½ × 36 in. FLLWF, 5310.058, no. 2A.

Street level: plan. Inscr. *4 July 1953, rev. 1 August 1953, FLLW*. Ink, pencil, and color pencil on tracing paper, 34 × 36 in. FLLWF, 5310.012, no. 3.

Street level: plan. Inscr. *4 July 1953, FLLW.* Ink, pencil, and color pencil on tracing paper, 32 × 36 in. FLLWF, 5310.013, no. 4.

Street level: plan. Ink, pencil, and color pencil on tracing paper, 33 × 36 in. FLLWF, 5310.049, no. 4.

Penthouse, living room level: plan. Inscr. *4 July 1953, FLLW.* Ink, pencil, and color pencil on tracing paper, 34 × 36 in. FLLWF, 5310.011.

Penthouse, upper floor: plan. Pencil and color pencil on tracing paper, 32¾ × 36 in. FLLWF, 5310.050, no. 7.

Sheet metal soffit and fascia for penthouse. Inscr. *4 July 1953, FLLW.* Ink, pencil, and color pencil on tracing paper, 34½ × 36 in. FLLWF, 5310.010. Incomplete; only a few baselines have been drawn.

SCHEME 2B

Note: This scheme is similar to Scheme 2A except that it is set closer to the street line to reduce the dimensions of retaining walls and foundations.

Site plan. Ink, pencil, and color pencil on tracing paper, 35 × 32½ in. FLLWF, 5310.002. Cat. 49. Includes superimposed street-level plans of Scheme 1B and Scheme 2B.

WORKING DRAWINGS SET

Site and basement plan. Inscr. *4 July 1953, FLLW.* Ink, pencil, and color pencil on tracing paper, 33¼ × 36 in. FLLWF, 5310.014, no. 1. Includes index of drawings in set.

Servants' rooms: plan. Inscr. *4 July 1953, FLLW.* Ink, pencil, and color pencil on tracing paper, 33 × 36 in. FLLWF, 5310.015, no. 2. *Monograph,* 8: 198.

Garage level: plan. Inscr. *4 July 1953, rev. 1 December 1953, FLLW.* Ink, pencil, and color pencil on tracing paper, 33¼ × 36 in. FLLWF, 5310.016, no. 3.

Street level: plan. Inscr. *4 July 1953, rev. 1 December 1953, FLLW.* Ink, pencil, and color pencil on tracing paper, 33¼ × 36 in. FLLWF, 5310.017, no. 4.

Typical residences: plan. Inscr. *4 July 1953, rev. 1 August 1953, FLLW.* Ink, pencil, and color pencil on tracing paper, 33¼ × 36 in. FLLWF, 5310.018, no. 5.

Penthouse, living room level: plan. Inscr. *4 July 1953, FLLW.* Ink, pencil, and color pencil on tracing paper, 33 × 36 in. FLLWF, 5310.019, no. 6.

Penthouse, upper floor: plan. Inscr. *4 July 1953, FLLW.* Ink, pencil, and color pencil on tracing paper, 33 × 36 in. FLLWF, 5310.020, no. 7.

Penthouse: plans. Ink, pencil, and color pencil on tracing paper, 34 × 36 in. FLLWF, 5310.057. Preliminary drawing for 5310.020.

West elevation and section through garage. Inscr. *4 July 1953, rev. 1 December 1953, FLLW.* Ink, pencil, and color pencil on tracing paper, 33 × 36 in. FLLWF, 5310.021, no. 8.

East elevation and section through garage. Inscr. *4 July 1953, FLLW.* Ink, pencil, and color pencil on tracing paper, 33¼ × 36 in. FLLWF, 5310.022, no. 9. *Monograph,* 8: 199.

South elevation. Inscr. *4 July 1953, FLLW.* Ink, pencil, and color pencil on tracing paper, 33 × 36 in. FLLWF, 5310.023, no. 10. *Monograph,* 8: 200.

Section. Inscr. *4 July 1953, FLLW.* Ink, pencil, and color pencil on tracing paper, 33 × 36 in. FLLWF, 5310.024, no. 11.

Details for elevations, penthouse roof, walls, glazing, interior partitions, and stone grill. Inscr. *4 July 1953, FLLW.* Ink, pencil, and color pencil on tracing paper, 33 × 36 in. FLLWF, 5310.025, no. 12. Drawing specifies brick exterior facing with metal soffit and fascia.

Fireplace details, door schedule, and stairway details. Inscr. *4 July 1953, FLLW.* Ink, pencil, and color pencil on tracing paper, 34 × 36¼ in. FLLWF, 5310.026, no. 13.

Kitchen: details. Inscr. *4 July 1953, FLLW.* Ink, pencil, and color pencil on tracing paper, 34 × 36¼ in. FLLWF, 5310.027, no. 14.

Structural details. Inscr. *4 July 1953, FLLW.* Ink, pencil, and color pencil on tracing paper, 34 × 36¼ in. FLLWF, 5310.028, no. S-1. Specifies concrete reinforced with corrugated metal mesh; includes schedule of wall types and footings.

Structural plans and details. Inscr. *4 July 1953, FLLW.* Ink, pencil, and color pencil on tracing paper, 34 × 36 in. FLLWF, 5310.029, no. S-2.

Structural plans and details. Pencil and color pencil on tracing paper, 35½ × 36 in. FLLWF, 5310.051. Preliminary drawing for 5310.029.

Garage: structural plans and details. Inscr. *4 July 1953, FLLW.* Ink, pencil, and color pencil on tracing paper, 33¼ × 36 in. FLLWF, 5310.030, no. S-3.

Garage: structural plans and details. Pencil and color pencil on tracing paper, 33¼ × 36 in. FLLWF, 5310.059. Preliminary drawing for 5310.030.

Street level: structural plans and details. Inscr. *4 July 1953, FLLW.* Ink, pencil, and color pencil on tracing paper, 35 × 36 in. FLLWF, 5310.031, no. S-4.

Typical residence: structural plans and details. Inscr. 4 July 1953, FLLW. Ink, pencil, and color pencil on tracing paper, 34 × 36 in. FLLWF, 5310.032, no. S-5.

Typical residence: structural plans and details. Pencil and color pencil on tracing paper, 34 × 36 in. FLLWF, 5310.055. Preliminary drawing for 5310.032.

Penthouse: structural plans and details. Inscr. *4 July 1953, FLLW.* Ink, pencil, and color pencil on tracing paper, 33½ × 36 in. FLLWF, 5310.033, no. S-6.

Penthouse: structural plans and details. *Inscr. 4 July 1953, FLLW.* Ink, pencil, and color pencil on tracing paper, 33¼ × 36 in. FLLWF, 5310.034, no. S-7.

Basement: plumbing and air conditioning plan. Inscr. *4 July 1953, FLLW.* Ink, pencil, and color pencil on tracing paper, 33¼ × 36 in. FLLWF, 5310.035, no. A-1.

Servants' level: plumbing and air conditioning plan. Inscr. *4 July 1953, FLLW.* Ink, pencil, and color pencil on tracing paper, 33 × 36 in. FLLWF, 5310.036, no. A-2.

Street level: plumbing and air conditioning plan. Inscr. *4 July 1953, FLLW.* Ink, pencil, and color pencil on tracing paper, 32 × 36 in. FLLWF, 5310.037, no. A-3.

Typical residence: plumbing and air conditioning plan. Inscr. *4 July 1953, FLLW.* Ink, pencil, and color pencil on tracing paper, 33 × 36 in. FLLWF, 5310.038, no. A-4.

Typical residence: plumbing and air conditioning plan. Ink, pencil, and color pencil on tracing paper, 33 × 36 in. FLLWF, 5310.044, no. 4-A. Incomplete; includes base plan only.

Penthouse, main living floor: plumbing and air conditioning plan. Inscr. *4 July 1953, FLLW.* Ink, pencil, and color pencil on tracing paper, 33¼ × 36 in. FLLWF, 5310.039, no. A-5.

Penthouse, main living floor: plumbing and air conditioning plan. Ink, pencil, and color pencil on tracing paper, 33¾ × 36 in. FLLWF, 5310.045, no. 5-A. Incomplete; includes base plan only.

Penthouse, upper floor: plumbing and air conditioning plan. Inscr. *4 July 1953, FLLW.* Ink, pencil, and color pencil on tracing paper, 33¾ × 36 in. FLLWF, 5310.040, no. A-6.

Electrical plans for basement, servants' rooms, and garage. Inscr. *4 July 1953, FLLW.* Ink, pencil, and color pencil on tracing paper, 34¼ × 36 in. FLLWF, 5310.041, no. E-1.

Electrical plans for typical residence, penthouse, and entrance court. Inscr. *4 July 1953, FLLW.* Ink, pencil, and color pencil on tracing paper, 33 × 36 in. FLLWF, 5310.042, no. E-2.

Elevator diagram. Inscr. *4 July 1953, FLLW.* Ink, pencil, and color pencil on tracing paper, 33 × 36 in. FLLWF, 5310.043, no. E-3.

MISCELLANEOUS PLANS

Typical residence. Pencil and color pencil on tracing paper, 16 × 25 in. FLLWF, 5310.056.

Penthouse: structural plan. Pencil and color pencil on tracing paper, 17 × 31 in. FLLWF, 5310.048. Cut from a larger drawing.

Terraces: structural plans, datum 1,185 ft. and datum 1,194 ft. Pencil and color pencil on tracing paper, 18 × 17 in. FLLWF, 5310.052. Preliminary study.

Penthouse: structural plans. Pencil and color pencil on tracing paper, 21 × 25 in. FLLWF, 5310.053. Preliminary study.

Penthouse roof: structural plan. Pencil and color pencil on tracing paper, folded, 15¼ × 16½ in. FLLWF, 5310.054. Preliminary study.

Structural steel layout. Blueprints, 24 × 36 in. FLLWF, unnumbered. Prints prepared by engineers at the American Bridge Co. accompany a letter containing cost estimate and dated 10 September 1953, from F. K. McDaniel, president, to Edgar Kaufmann. Kaufmann had asked McDaniel's company to prepare an alternative to Wright's reinforced-concrete structure.

AVERY LIBRARY HOLDINGS

31 black line prints on paper, 4 blue line prints on paper, 2 blue line prints with blue crayon on paper, 1 blue line print with ink and watercolor wash on paper, 35⅜ × 38¾ in. or smaller. Acc. nos. NYDA.1000.004.00068–99.

Further Reading

GENERAL STUDIES OF FRANK LLOYD WRIGHT

Levine, Neil. *The Architecture of Frank Lloyd Wright.* Princeton, N.J.: Princeton University Press, 1996.

McCarter, Robert. *Frank Lloyd Wright.* London: Phaidon, 1997.

Pfeiffer, Bruce Brooks, and Yukio Futagawa, eds. *Frank Lloyd Wright.* Vols. 1–8, *Monograph;* vols. 9–11, *Preliminary Studies;* vol. 12, *Renderings.* Tokyo: A.D.A. Edita, 1984–88.

Secrest, Meryle. *Frank Lloyd Wright.* New York: Knopf, 1992.

Wright, Frank Lloyd. *An Autobiography.* 1932; rev. ed. 1943. Reprint, New York: Barnes & Noble, 1998.

THE KAUFMANNS AND THEIR PATRONAGE OF ART
AND ARCHITECTURE

Christ-Janer, Albert. *Boardman Robinson.* Chicago: University of Chicago Press, 1946.

Cleary, Richard. "Edgar J. Kaufmann, Frank Lloyd Wright and the Pittsburgh Point Park Coney Island in Automobile Scale," in *Journal of the Society of Architectural Historians* 52 (June 1993): 139–58.

Harris, Leon. *Merchant Princes: An Intimate History of Jewish Families Who Built Great Department Stores.* New York: Harper & Row, 1979.

Hoffmann, Donald. *Frank Lloyd Wright's Fallingwater: The House and Its History.* 2d rev. ed. New York: Dover, 1993.

Kaufmann, Edgar jr. *Fallingwater: A Frank Lloyd Wright Country House.* New York: Abbeville, 1986.

Lorant, Stefan. *Pittsburgh: The Story of an American City.* New York: Doubleday, 1964.

Lubove, Roy. *Twentieth-Century Pittsburgh: Government, Business, and Environmental Change,* vol. 1. 1969. Reprint, Pittsburgh: University of Pittsburgh Press, 1995.

McCarter, Robert. *Fallingwater: Frank Lloyd Wright.* London: Phaidon, 1994.

Trapp, Frank Anderson. *Peter Blume.* New York: Rizzoli, 1987.

Waggoner, Lynda S. *Fallingwater: Frank Lloyd Wright's Romance with Nature.* New York: Universe Books for the Western Pennsylvania Conservancy, 1996.

Wilk, Christopher. *Frank Lloyd Wright: The Kaufmann Office.* London: Victoria & Albert Museum, 1993.

GOOD DESIGN AND MERCHANDISING

Davies, Karen. *At Home in Manhattan: Modern Decorative Arts, 1925 to the Depression.* Exh. cat. New Haven, Conn.: Yale University Art Gallery, 1983.

Edelberg, Martin, ed. *Design 1935–1965: What Modern Was, Selections from the Liliane and David M. Stewart Collection.* Montreal and New York: Musée des Arts Décoratifs de Montréal and Abrams, 1991.

Kaufmann, Edgar jr. *What Is Modern Design?* Introductory Series to the Modern Arts, no. 3. New York: Museum of Modern Art, 1950.

Kaufmann, Edgar jr. *What Is Modern Interior Design?* Introductory Series to the Modern Arts, no. 4. New York: Museum of Modern Art, 1953.

Leach, William. *Land of Desire: Merchants, Power, and the Rise of a New American Culture.* New York: Pantheon, 1993.

Meikle, Jeffrey L. *Twentieth Century Limited: Industrial Design in America, 1925–1939.* Philadelphia: Temple University Press, 1979.

Miller, R. Craig. *Modern Design in the Metropolitan Museum of Art 1890–1990.* New York: Metropolitan Museum of Art and Abrams, 1990.

Riley, Terence, and Edward Eigen, "Between the Museum and the Market-place: Selling Good Design," in *The Museum of Modern Art at Mid-Century: At Home and Abroad, Studies in Modern Art* 4 (1994): 150–79.

Index

Carnegie Museum of Art Board

MARQETRY WALL

RADIATOR ENCLOSUR
⅞" PLYWOOD

3'-6"   1'-8"

PLYWOOD

ESK   SEAT

⅞" PLYWOOD

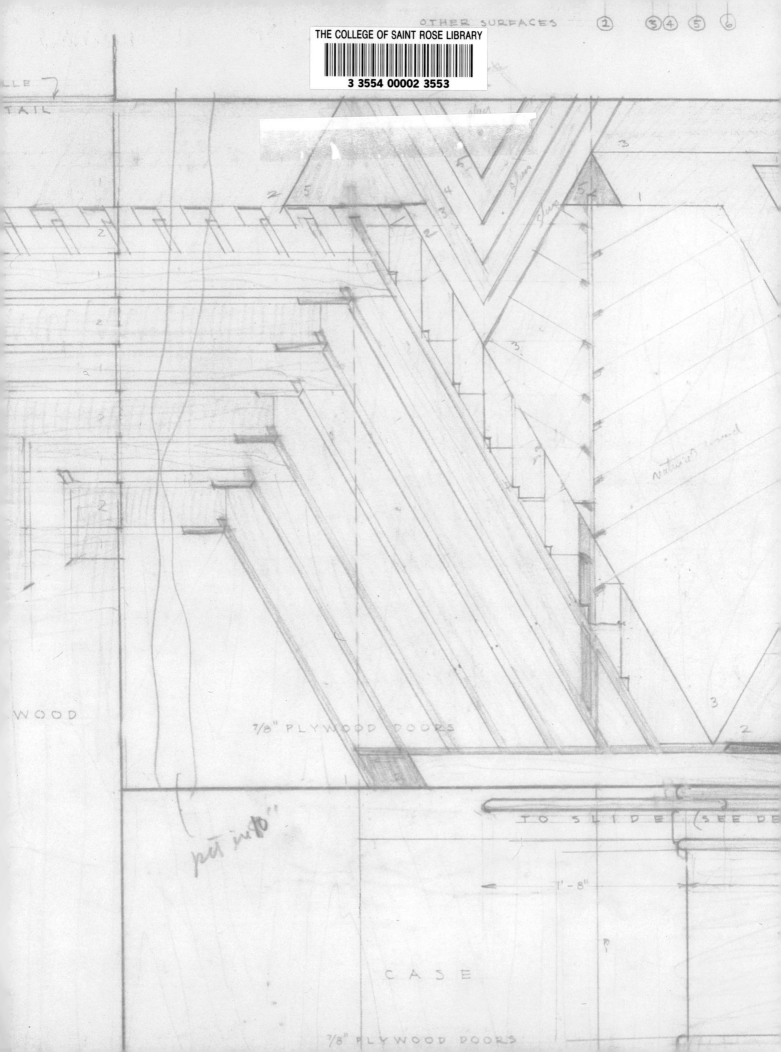

7/8" PLYWOOD DOORS

WOOD

CASE

7/8" PLYWOOD DOORS